D0123859

CRONE ™

Written by
DENNIS CULVER

Art, Cover, and Chapter Break Art by
JUSTIN GREENWOOD

Color Art by
BRAD SIMPSON

Letters by
PAT BROSSEAU

CRONE CREATED BY DENNIS CULVER
AND JUSTIN GREENWOOD

DARK HORSE BOOKS

President and Publisher MIKE RICHARDSON
Editor BRETT ISRAEL
Digital Art Technician JOSIE CHRISTENSEN
Collection Designer JEN EDWARDS

NEIL HANKERSON *Executive Vice President* TOM WEDDLE *Chief Financial Officer* RANDY STRADLEY *Vice President of Publishing* NICK McWHORTER *Chief Business Development Officer* DALE LaFOUNTAIN *Chief Information Officer* MATT PARKINSON *Vice President of Marketing* VANESSA TODD-HOLMES *Vice President of Production and Scheduling* MARK BERNARDI *Vice President of Book Trade and Digital Sales* KEN LIZZI *General Counsel* DAVE MARSHALL *Editor in Chief* DAVEY ESTRADA *Editorial Director* CHRIS WARNER *Senior Books Editor* CARY GRAZZINI *Director of Specialty Projects* LIA RIBACCHI *Art Director* MATT DRYER *Director of Digital Art and Prepress* MICHAEL GOMBOS *Senior Director of Licensed Publications* KARI YADRO *Director of Custom Programs* KARI TORSON *Director of International Licensing* SEAN BRICE *Director of Trade Sales*

CRONE

Crone™ © 2020 Dennis Culver and Justin Greenwood. All rights reserved. No portion of this publication may be reproduced or transmitted, in any form or by any means, without the express written permission of Dark Horse Comics LLC. Names, characters, places, and incidents featured in this publication either are the product of the author's imagination or are used fictitiously. Any resemblance to actual persons (living or dead), events, institutions, or locales, without satiric intent, is coincidental. Dark Horse Comics® and the Dark Horse logo are trademarks of Dark Horse Comics LLC., registered in various categories and countries.

This volume collects and reprints the comic book series Crone #1–#5.

Library of Congress Cataloging-in-Publication Data

Names: Culver, Dennis, writer. | Greenwood, Justin (Comic book artist),
    artist. | Simpson, Brad (Bradley Darwin), 1975- colourist. | Brosseau,
    Pat, letterer.
Title: Crone /written by Dennis Culver ; art, cover, and chapter break art
    by Justin Greenwood ; color art by Brad Simpson ; letters by Pat
    Brosseau.
Description: First edition. | Milwaukie, OR : Dark Horse Books, 2020. |
    "Crone created by Dennis Culver and Justin Greenwood." | Summary: "The
    Sword Saviour and Champion of Men once known as BLOODY BLISS is now
    nothing more than a reclusive old CRONE. When an old enemy returns it's
    up to Bliss to once more defend the Three Kingdoms. Does she have the
    strength to answer the call for one last adventure? Only Dennis Culver
    (Burnouts, E is for Extinction) and Justin Greenwood (Stumptown, The
    Last Siege) know for sure in this story that is equal parts Unforgiven
    and Xena Warrior Princess"-- Provided by publisher.
Identifiers: LCCN 2019058634 | ISBN 9781506716367 (trade paperback) | ISBN
    9781506716374 (epub)
Subjects: LCSH: Comic books, strips, etc.
Classification: LCC PN6728.C73 C85 2020 | DDC 741.5/973--dc23
LC record available at https://lccn.loc.gov/2019058634

Comic Shop Locator Service: comicshoplocator.com

Published by Dark Horse Books
A division of Dark Horse Comics LLC
10956 SE Main Street
Milwaukie, OR 97222

First edition: November 2020
Ebook ISBN: 978-1-50671-637-4
Trade Paperback ISBN: 978-1-50671-636-7

10 9 8 7 6 5 4 3 2 1
Printed in China

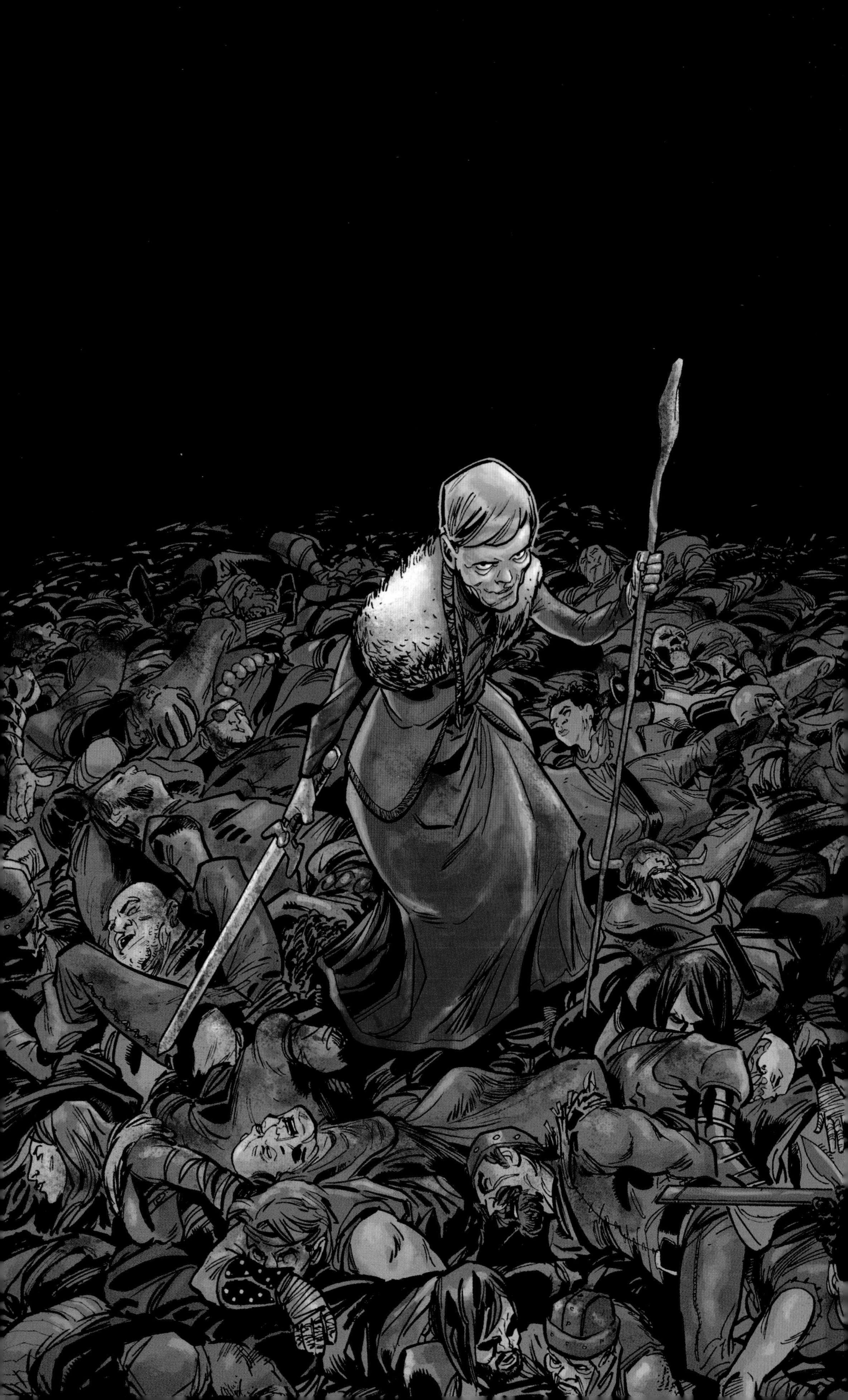

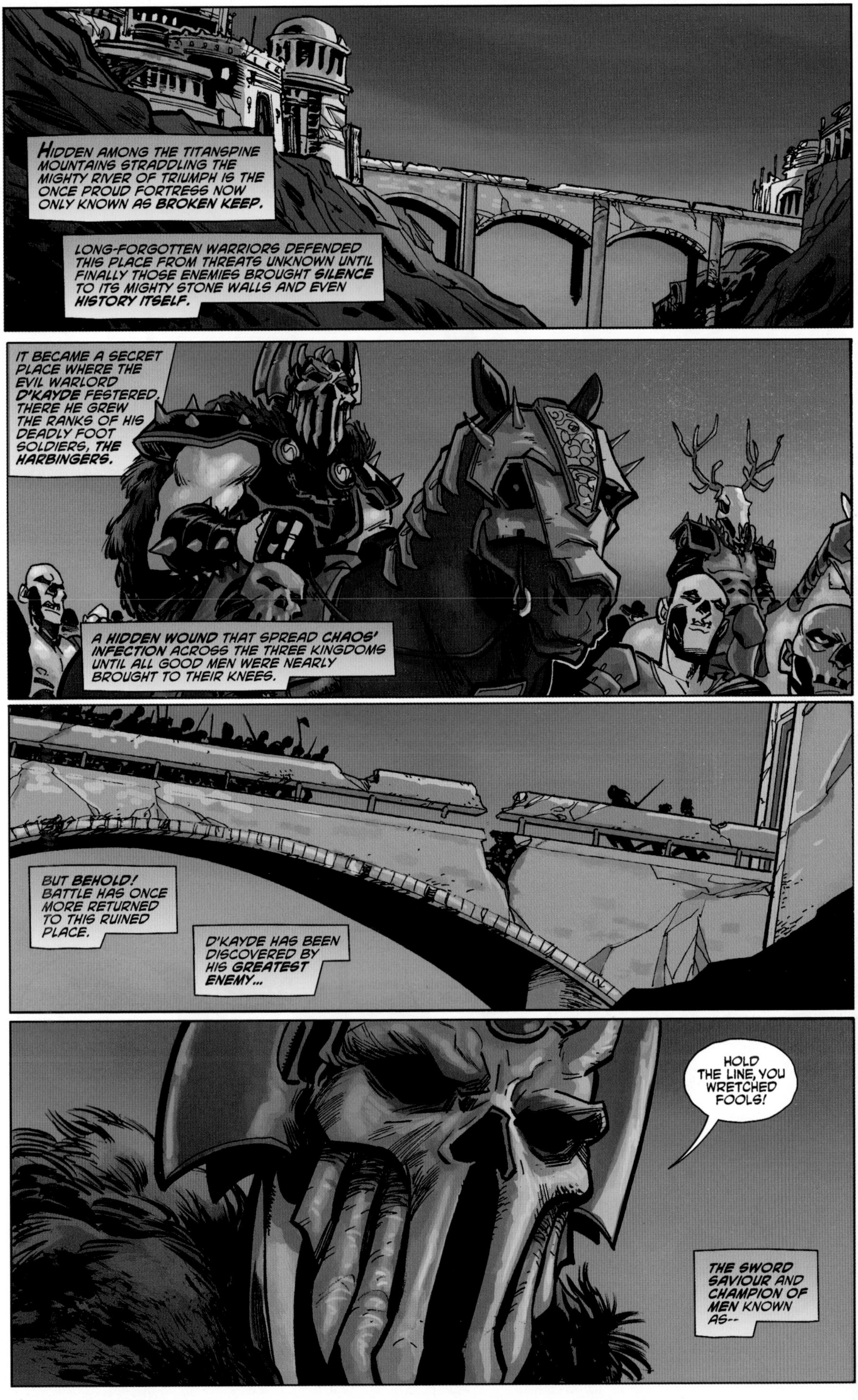
HIDDEN AMONG THE TITANSPINE MOUNTAINS STRADDLING THE MIGHTY RIVER OF TRIUMPH IS THE ONCE PROUD FORTRESS NOW ONLY KNOWN AS BROKEN KEEP.
LONG-FORGOTTEN WARRIORS DEFENDED THIS PLACE FROM THREATS UNKNOWN UNTIL FINALLY THOSE ENEMIES BROUGHT SILENCE TO ITS MIGHTY STONE WALLS AND EVEN HISTORY ITSELF.
IT BECAME A SECRET PLACE WHERE THE EVIL WARLORD D'KAYDE FESTERED. THERE HE GREW THE RANKS OF HIS DEADLY FOOT SOLDIERS, THE HARBINGERS.
A HIDDEN WOUND THAT SPREAD CHAOS' INFECTION ACROSS THE THREE KINGDOMS UNTIL ALL GOOD MEN WERE NEARLY BROUGHT TO THEIR KNEES.
BUT BEHOLD! BATTLE HAS ONCE MORE RETURNED TO THIS RUINED PLACE.
D'KAYDE HAS BEEN DISCOVERED BY HIS GREATEST ENEMY...
HOLD THE LINE, YOU WRETCHED FOOLS!
THE SWORD SAVIOUR AND CHAMPION OF MEN KNOWN AS--

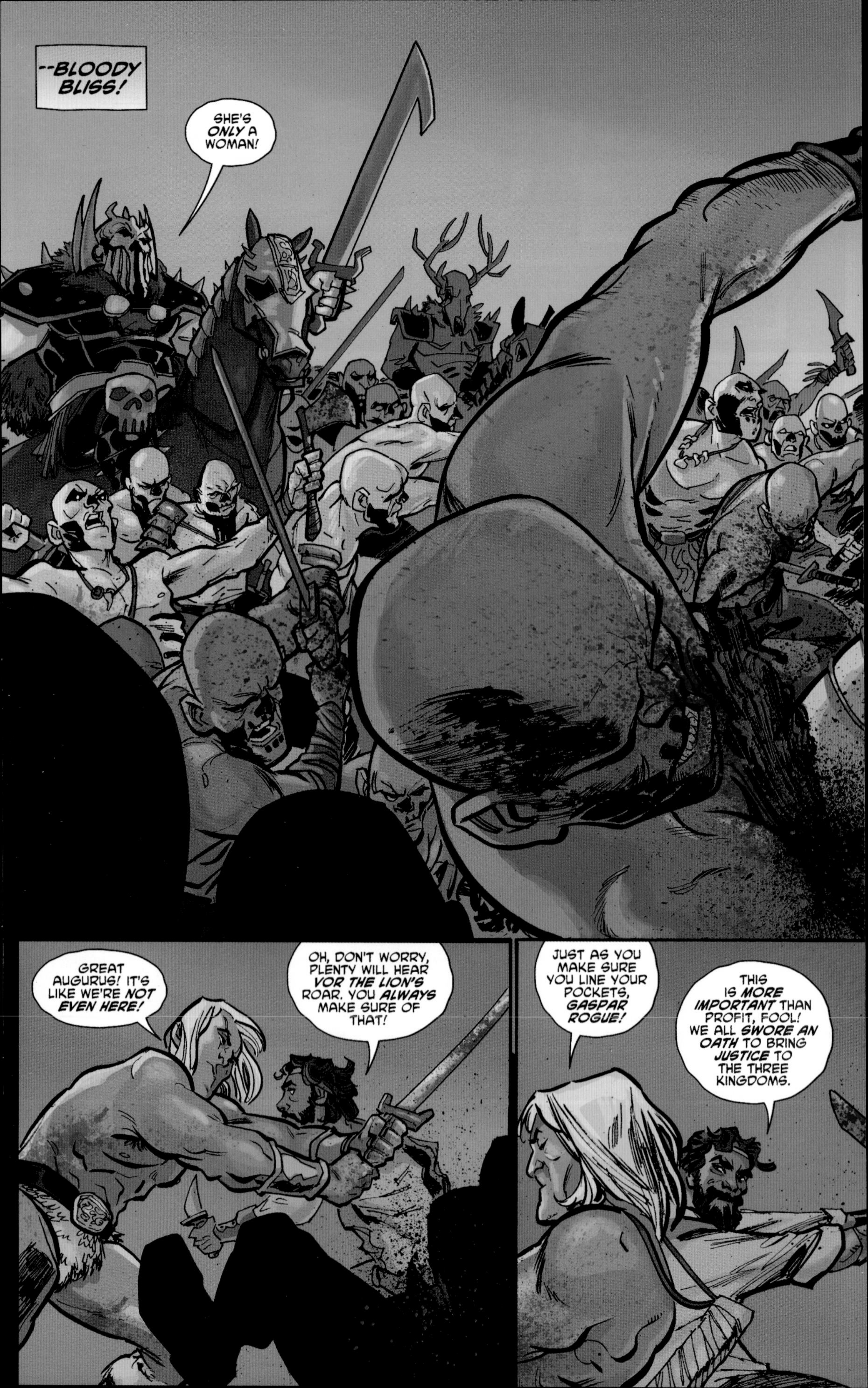
--BLOODY BLISS!
SHE'S ONLY A WOMAN!
GREAT AUGURUS! IT'S LIKE WE'RE NOT EVEN HERE!
OH, DON'T WORRY, PLENTY WILL HEAR VOR THE LION'S ROAR. YOU ALWAYS MAKE SURE OF THAT!
JUST AS YOU MAKE SURE YOU LINE YOUR POCKETS, GASPAR ROGUE!
THIS IS MORE IMPORTANT THAN PROFIT, FOOL! WE ALL SWORE AN OATH TO BRING JUSTICE TO THE THREE KINGDOMS.

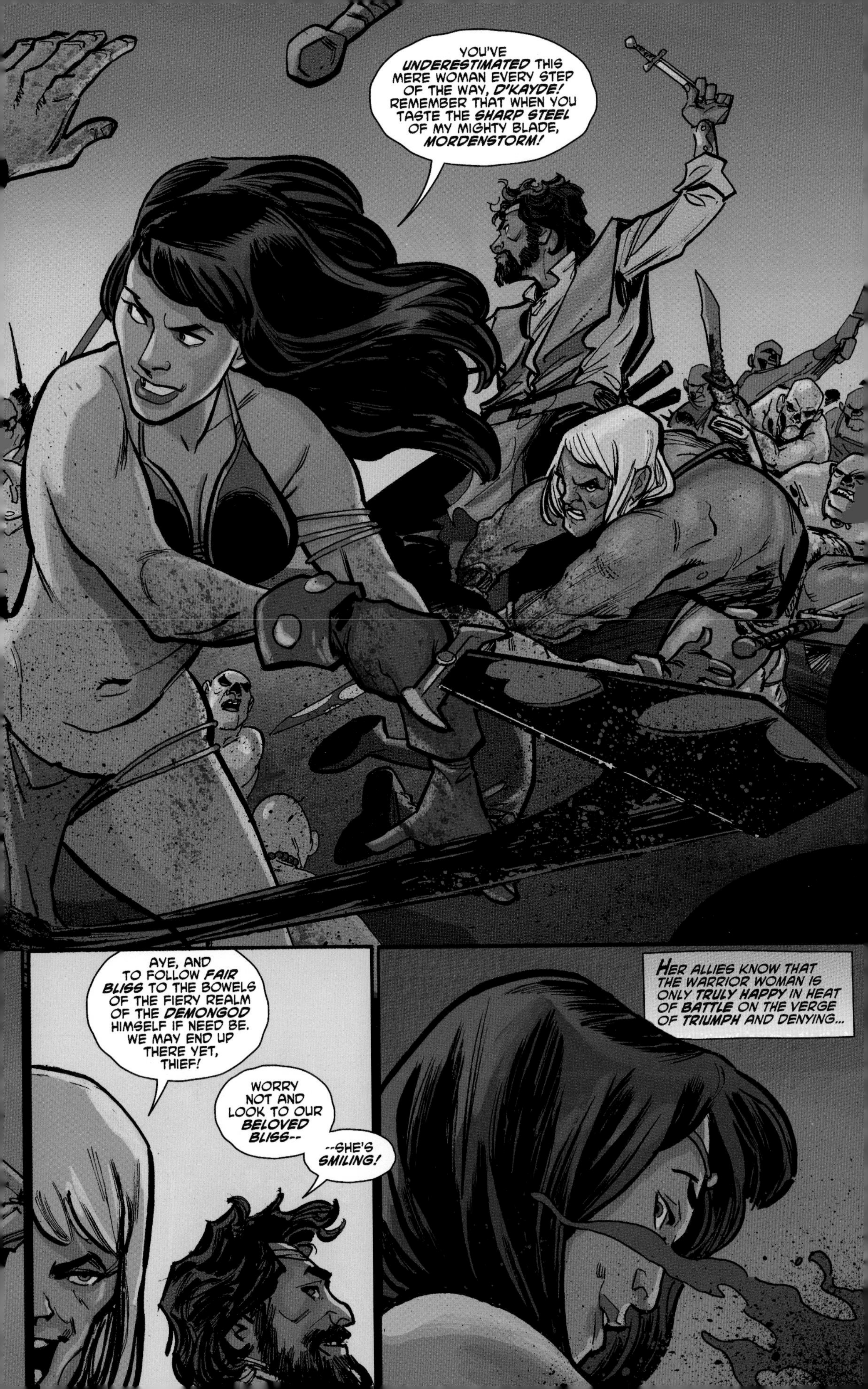
YOU'VE UNDERESTIMATED THIS MERE WOMAN EVERY STEP OF THE WAY, D'KAYDE! REMEMBER THAT WHEN YOU TASTE THE SHARP STEEL OF MY MIGHTY BLADE, MORDENSTORM!
AYE, AND TO FOLLOW FAIR BLISS TO THE BOWELS OF THE FIERY REALM OF THE DEMONGOD HIMSELF IF NEED BE. WE MAY END UP THERE YET, THIEF!
WORRY NOT AND LOOK TO OUR BELOVED BLISS--
--SHE'S SMILING!
HER ALLIES KNOW THAT THE WARRIOR WOMAN IS ONLY TRULY HAPPY IN HEAT OF BATTLE ON THE VERGE OF TRIUMPH AND DENYING...

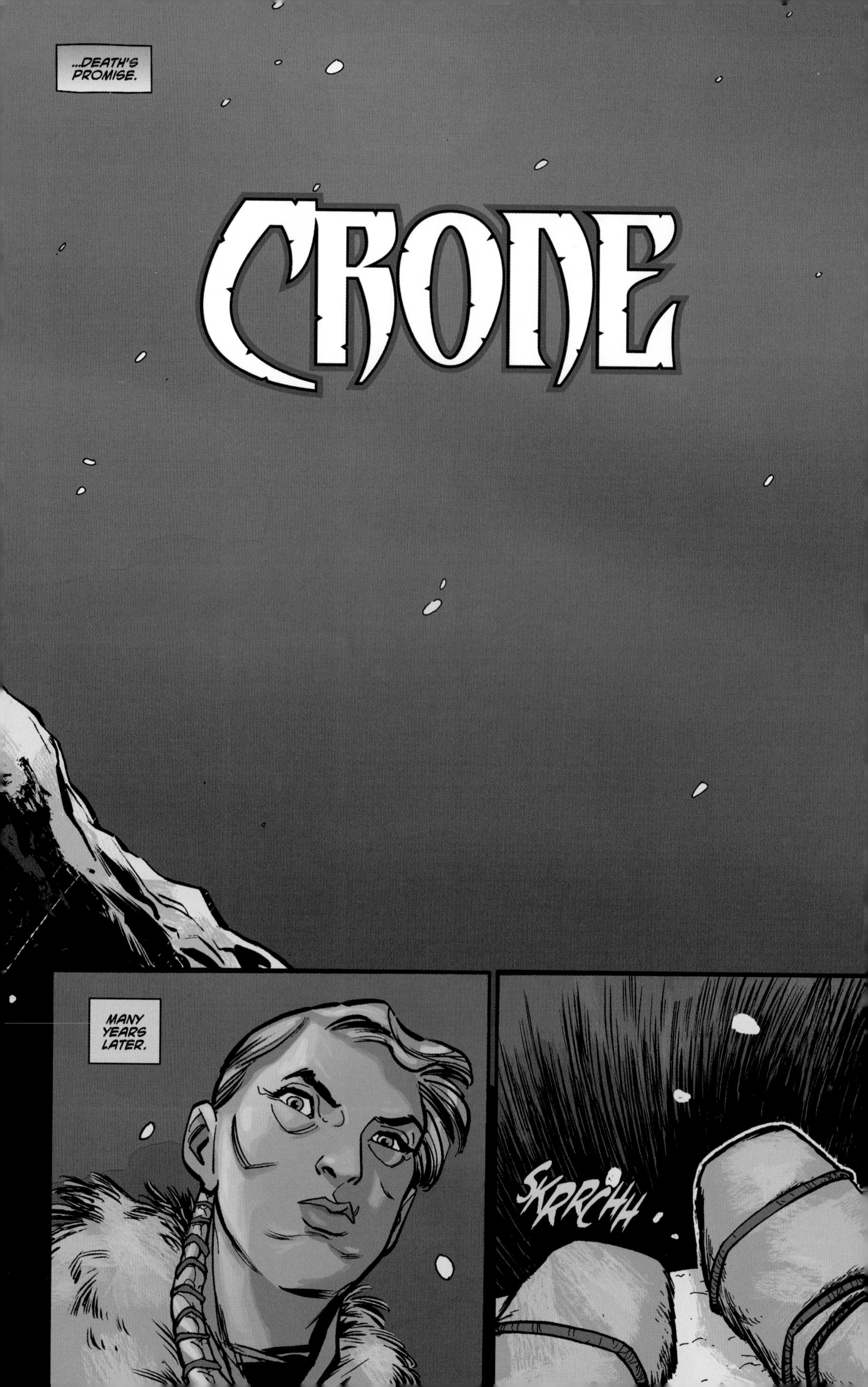
...DEATH'S PROMISE.
CRONE
MANY YEARS LATER.
SKRCHH

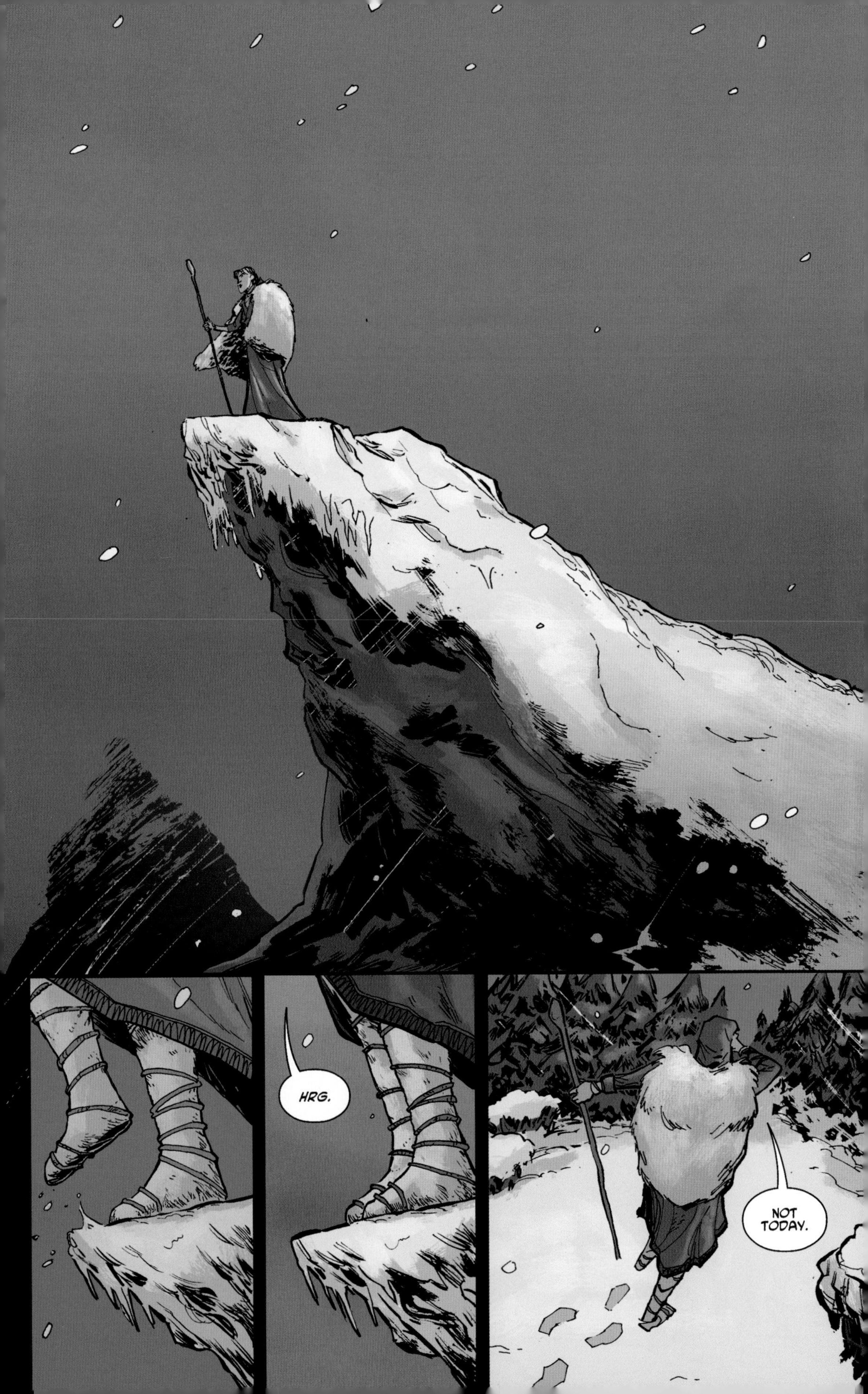
HRG.
NOT TODAY.

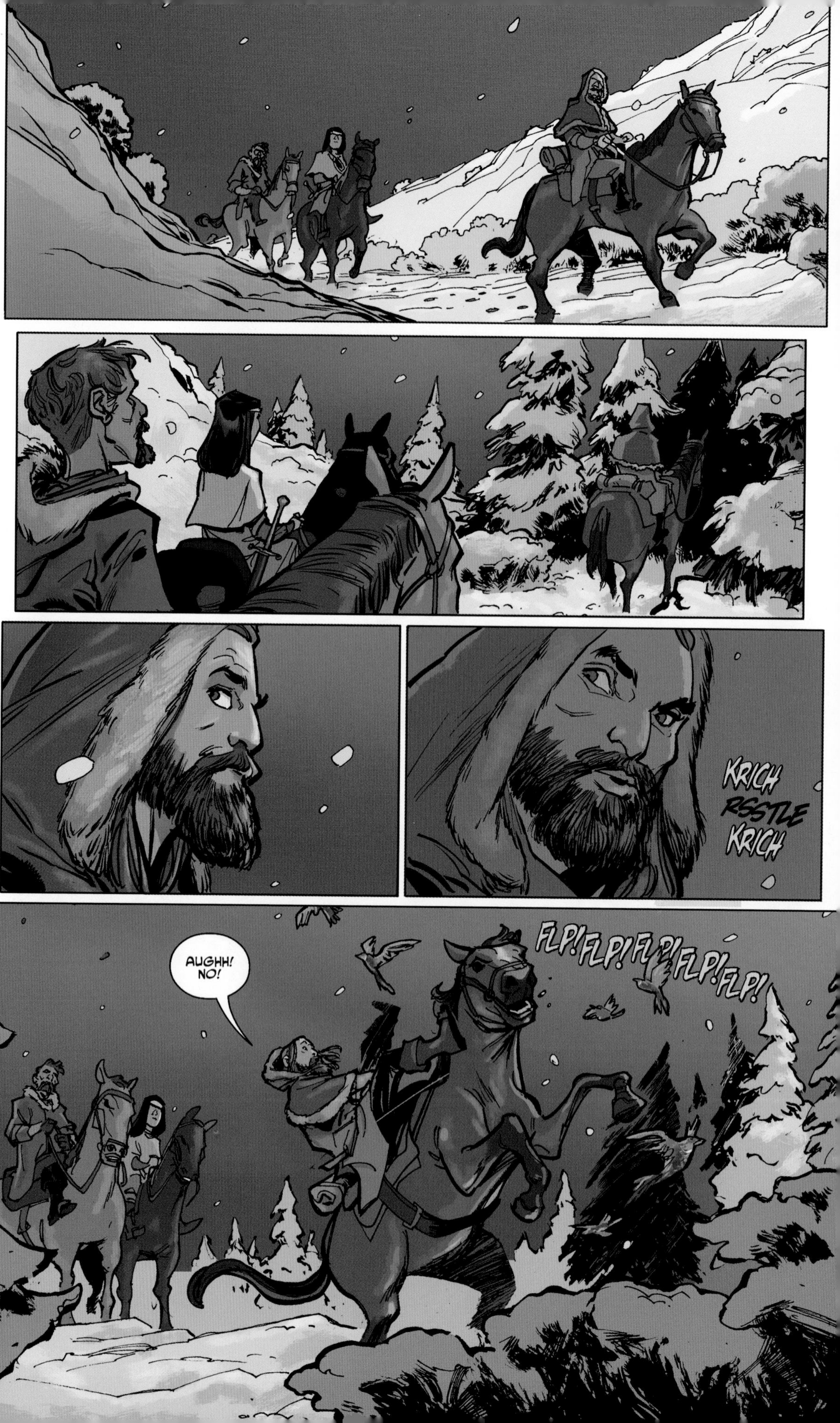
KRICH
RSSTLE
KRICH
AUGHH! NO!
FLP! FLP! FLP! FLP! FLP!

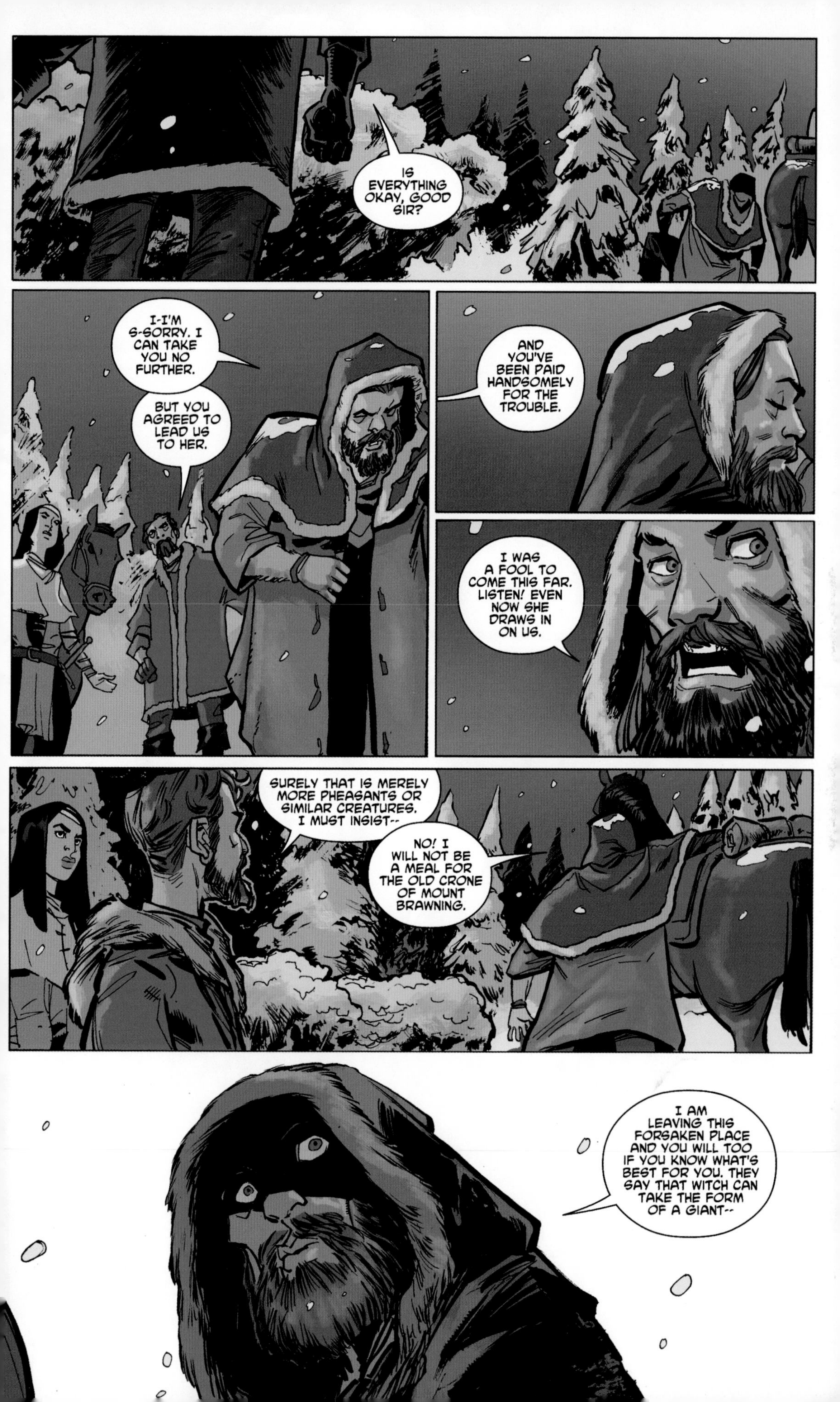
IS EVERYTHING OKAY, GOOD SIR?
I-I'M S-SORRY. I CAN TAKE YOU NO FURTHER.
BUT YOU AGREED TO LEAD US TO HER.
AND YOU'VE BEEN PAID HANDSOMELY FOR THE TROUBLE.
I WAS A FOOL TO COME THIS FAR. LISTEN! EVEN NOW SHE DRAWS IN ON US.
SURELY THAT IS MERELY MORE PHEASANTS OR SIMILAR CREATURES. I MUST INSIST--
NO! I WILL NOT BE A MEAL FOR THE OLD CRONE OF MOUNT BRAWNING.
I AM LEAVING THIS FORSAKEN PLACE AND YOU WILL TOO IF YOU KNOW WHAT'S BEST FOR YOU. THEY SAY THAT WITCH CAN TAKE THE FORM OF A GIANT--

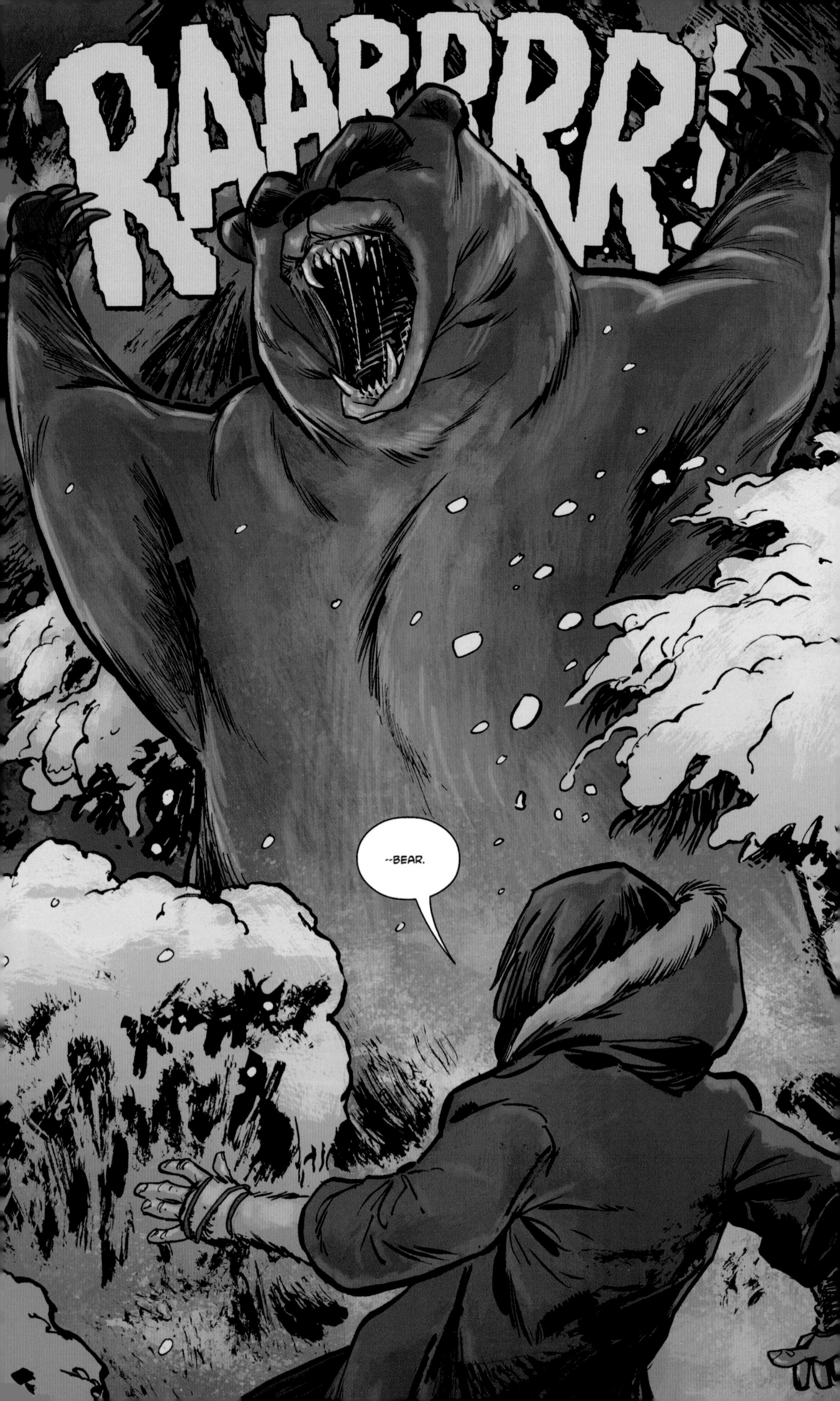
RAARRRR!
--BEAR.

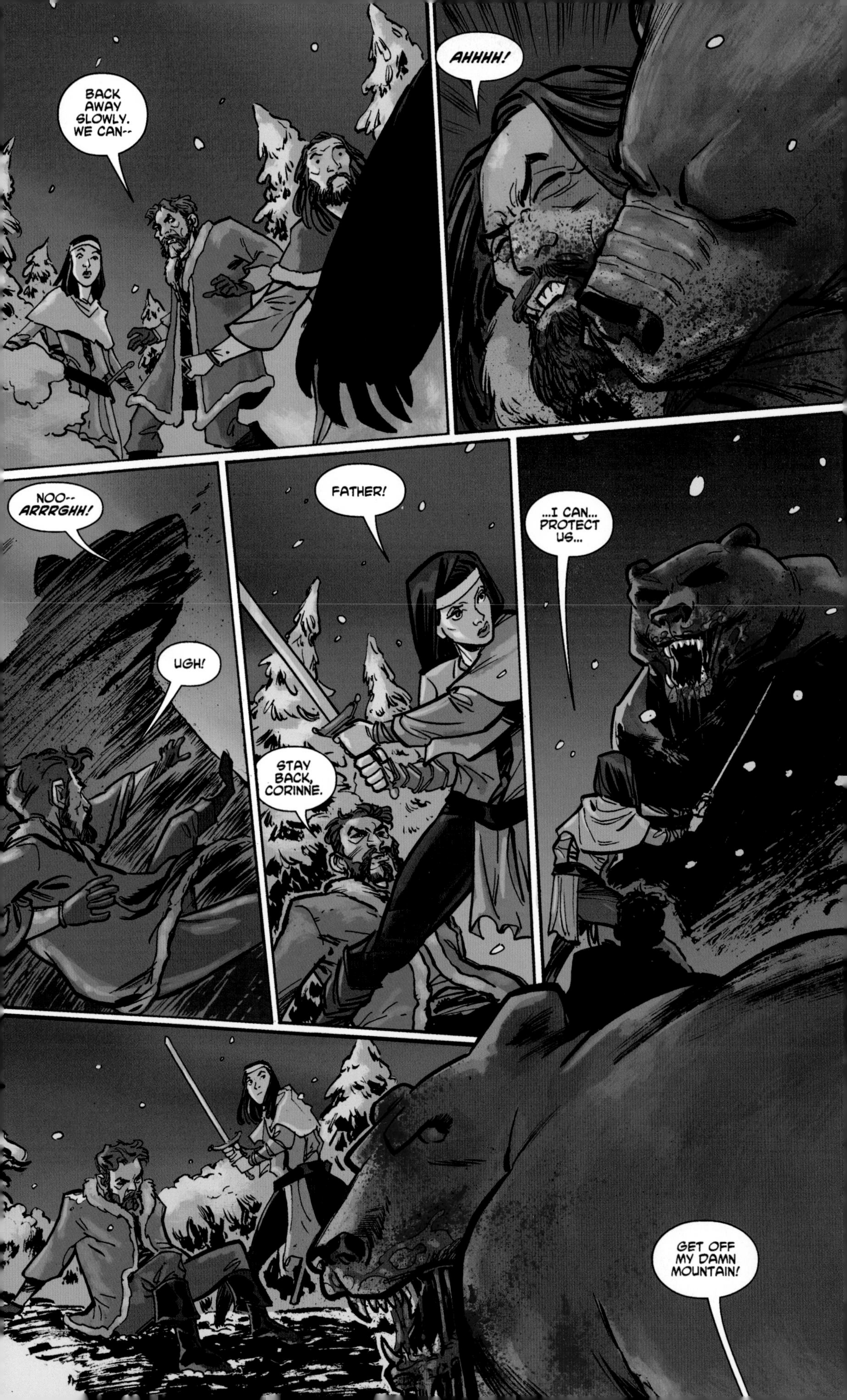

BACK AWAY SLOWLY. WE CAN--
AHHHH!
NOO-- ARRRGHH!
UGH!
FATHER!
STAY BACK, CORINNE.
...I CAN... PROTECT US...
GET OFF MY DAMN MOUNTAIN!

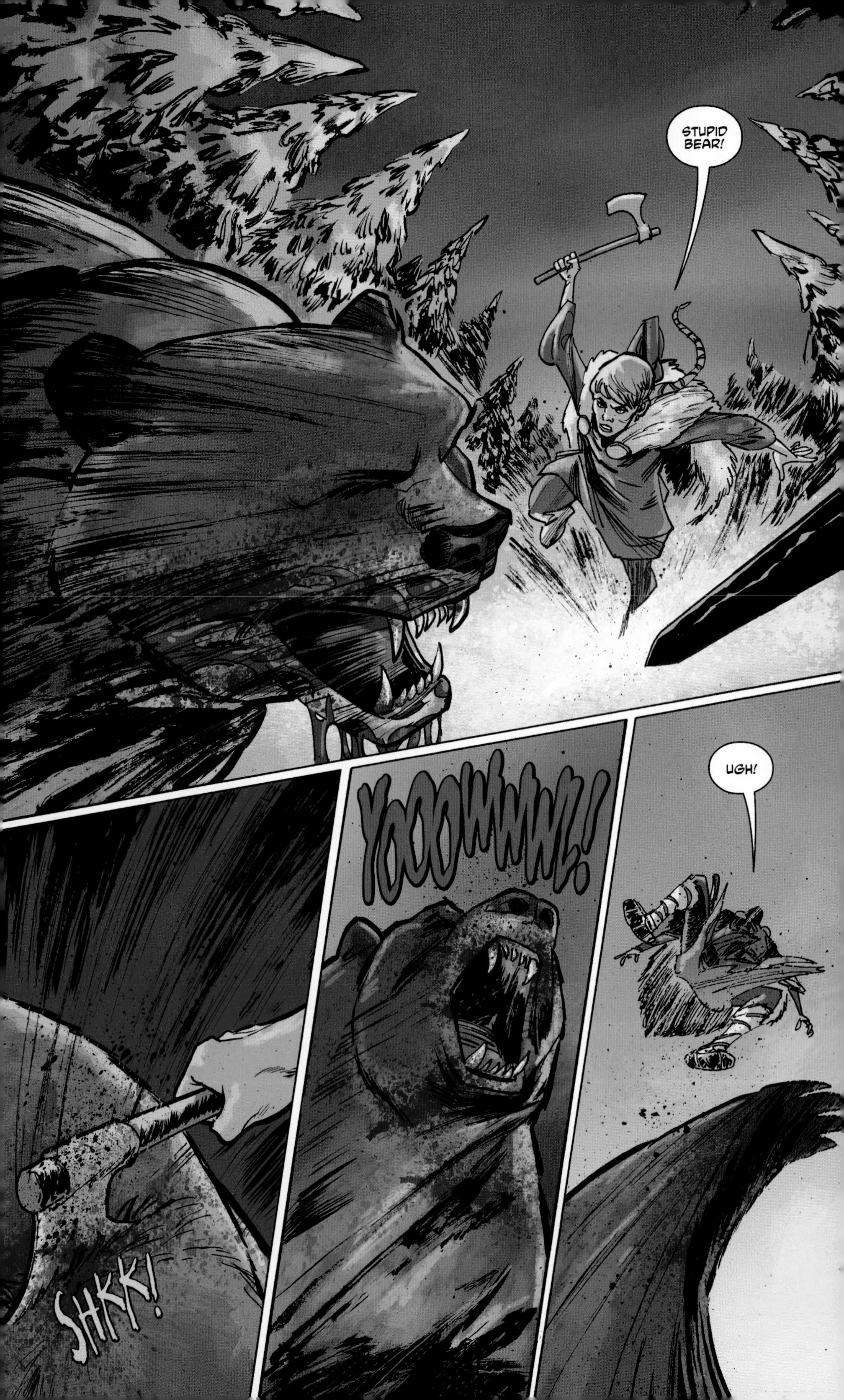
STUPID BEAR!
YOOOWWWZ!
UGH!
SHKK!

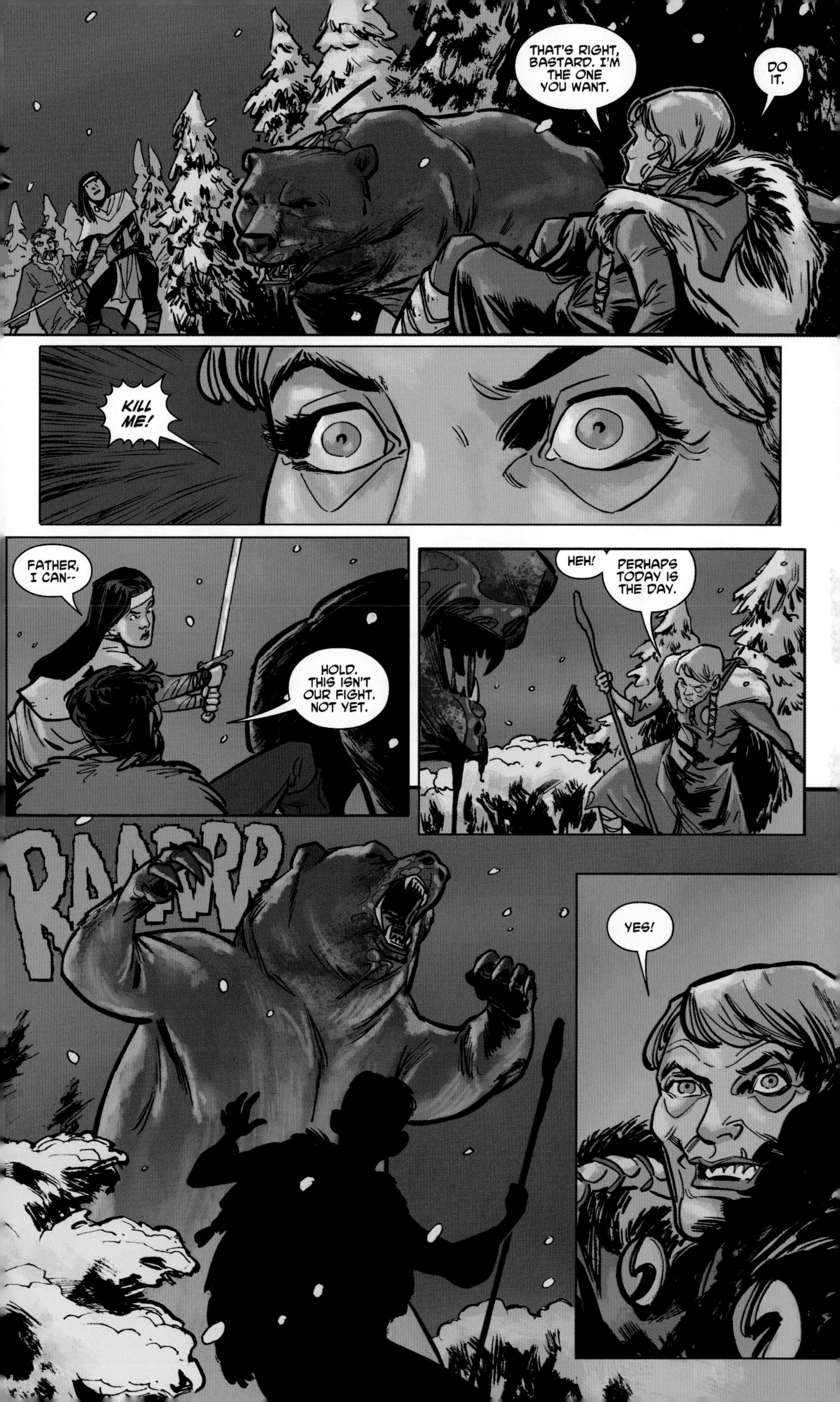
THAT'S RIGHT, BASTARD. I'M THE ONE YOU WANT.
DO IT.
KILL ME!
FATHER, I CAN--
HOLD. THIS ISN'T OUR FIGHT. NOT YET.
HEH!
PERHAPS TODAY IS THE DAY.
RAAWRR
YES!

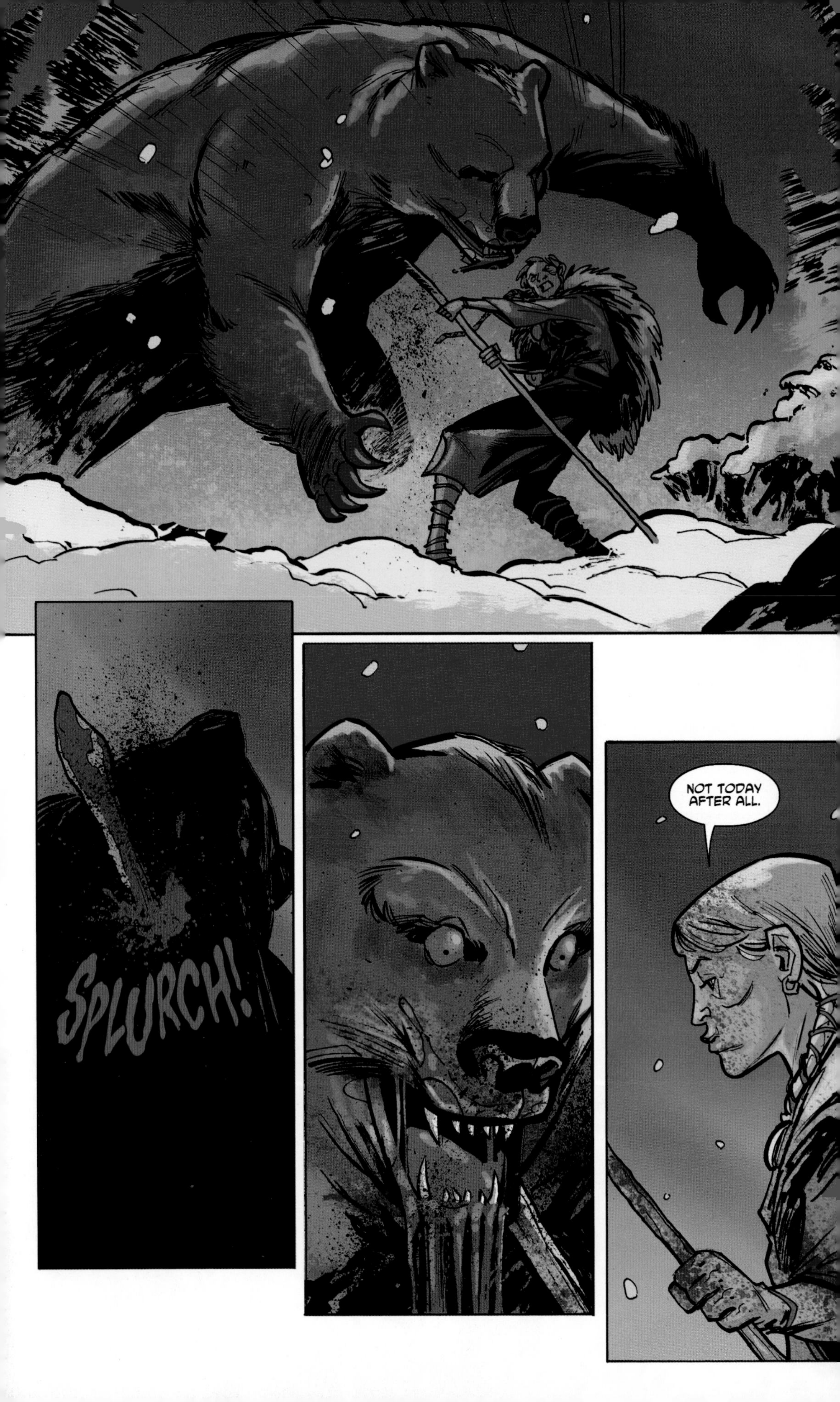
SPLURCH!
NOT TODAY AFTER ALL.

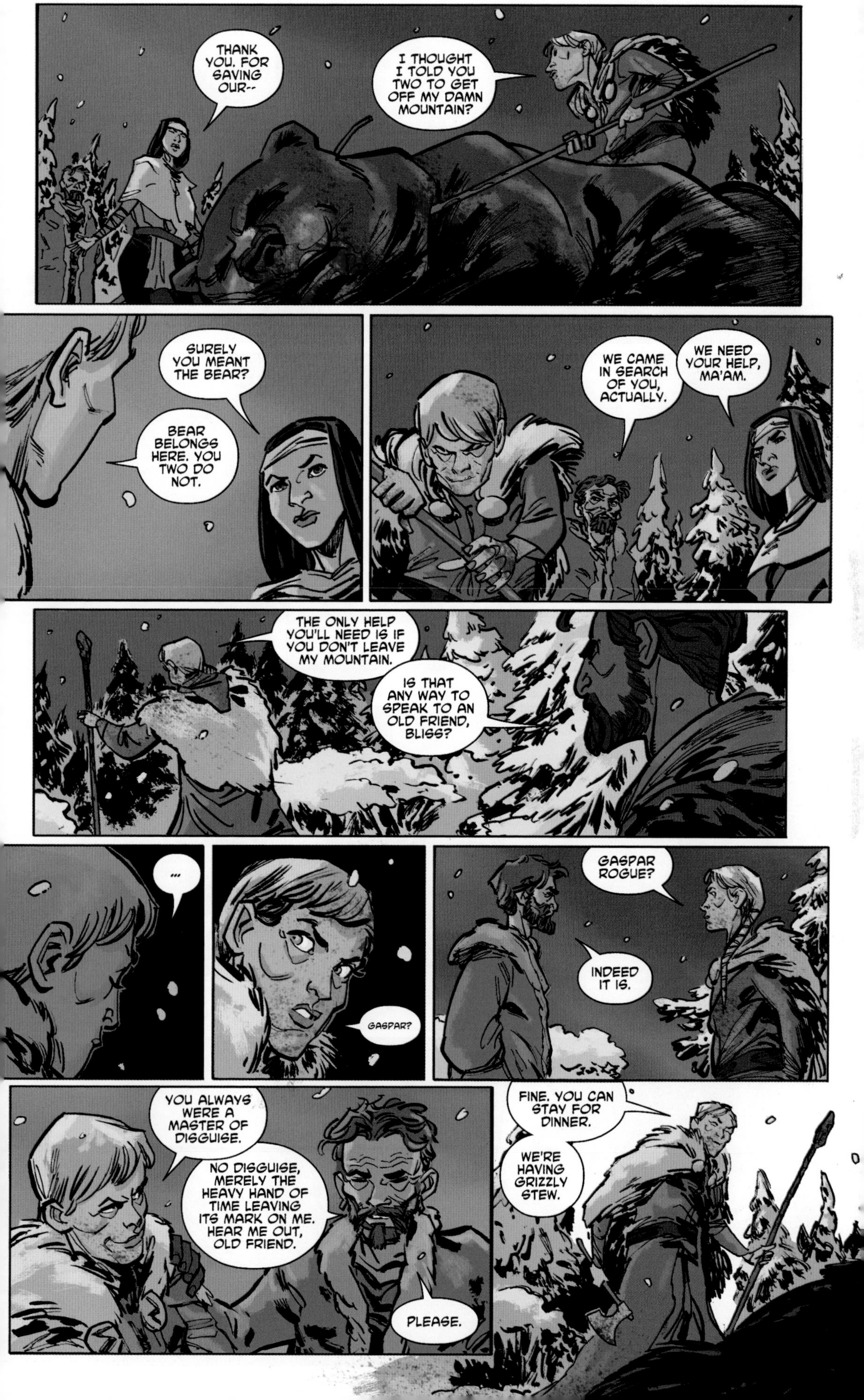
THANK YOU. FOR SAVING OUR--
I THOUGHT I TOLD YOU TWO TO GET OFF MY DAMN MOUNTAIN?
SURELY YOU MEANT THE BEAR?
BEAR BELONGS HERE. YOU TWO DO NOT.
WE NEED YOUR HELP, MA'AM.
WE CAME IN SEARCH OF YOU, ACTUALLY.
THE ONLY HELP YOU'LL NEED IS IF YOU DON'T LEAVE MY MOUNTAIN.
IS THAT ANY WAY TO SPEAK TO AN OLD FRIEND, BLISS?
...
GASPAR?
GASPAR ROGUE?
INDEED IT IS.
YOU ALWAYS WERE A MASTER OF DISGUISE.
NO DISGUISE, MERELY THE HEAVY HAND OF TIME LEAVING ITS MARK ON ME. HEAR ME OUT, OLD FRIEND.
PLEASE.
FINE. YOU CAN STAY FOR DINNER.
WE'RE HAVING GRIZZLY STEW.

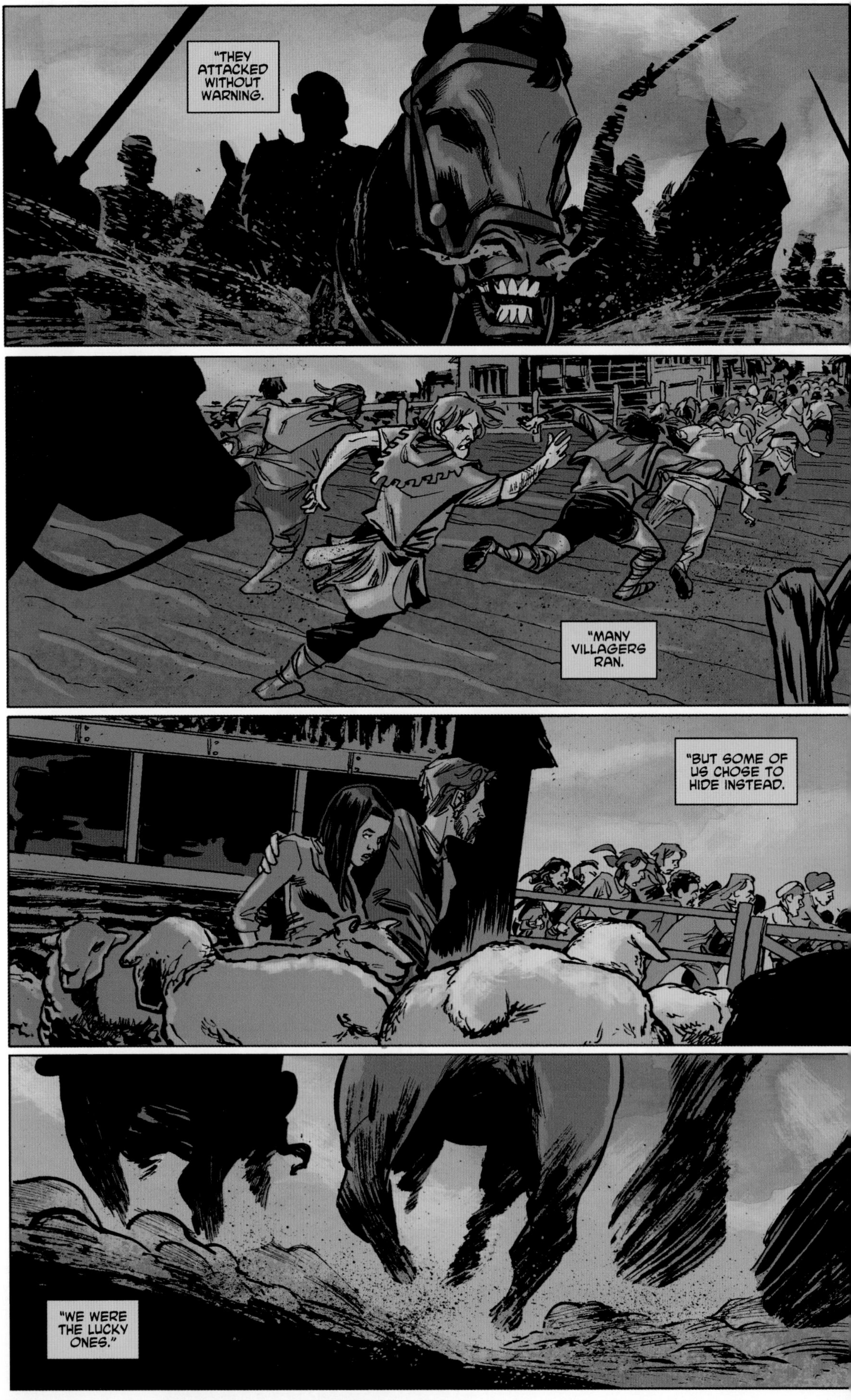
"THEY ATTACKED WITHOUT WARNING.
"MANY VILLAGERS RAN.
"BUT SOME OF US CHOSE TO HIDE INSTEAD.
"WE WERE THE LUCKY ONES."

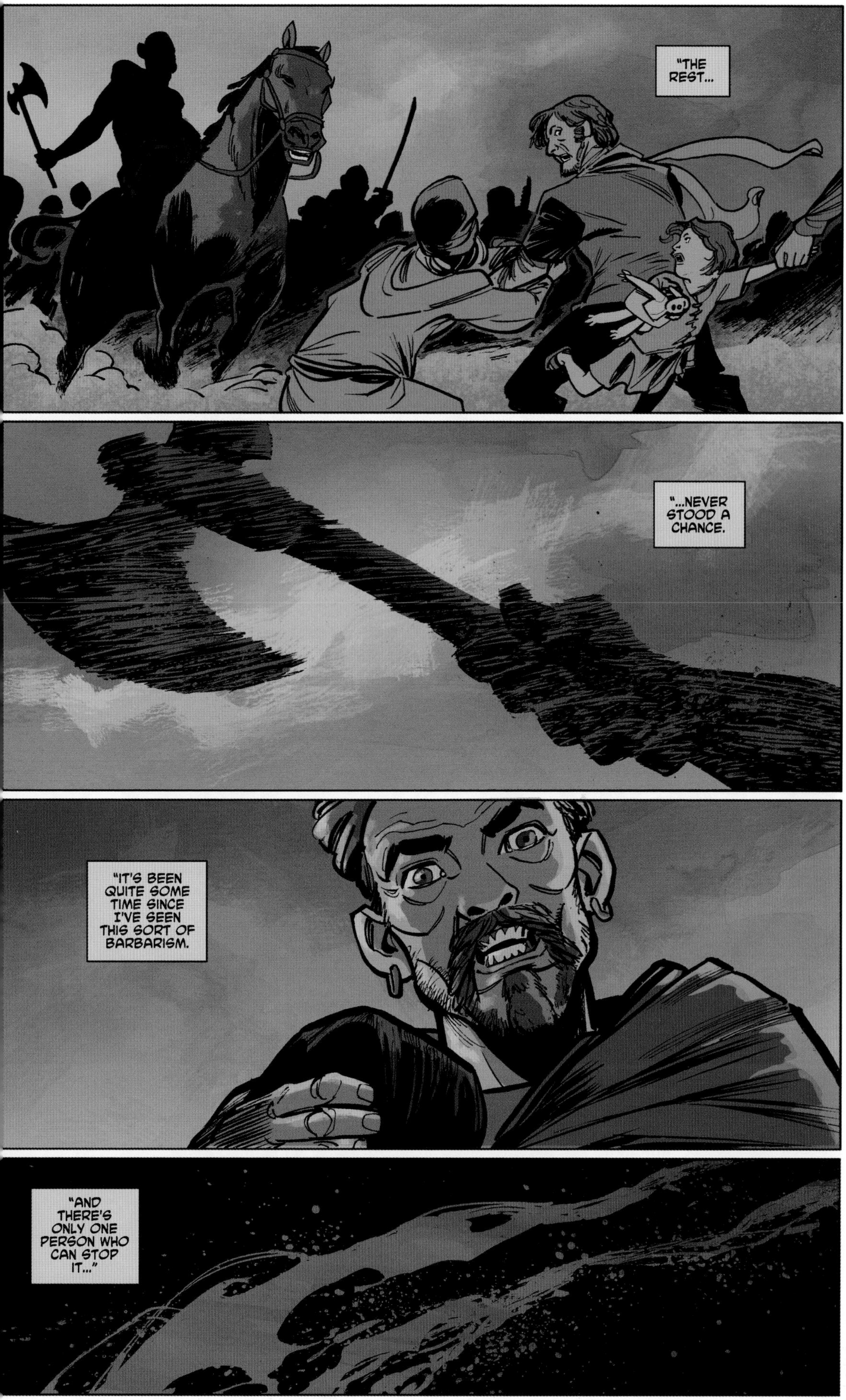
"THE REST...
"...NEVER STOOD A CHANCE.
"IT'S BEEN QUITE SOME TIME SINCE I'VE SEEN THIS SORT OF BARBARISM.
"AND THERE'S ONLY ONE PERSON WHO CAN STOP IT..."

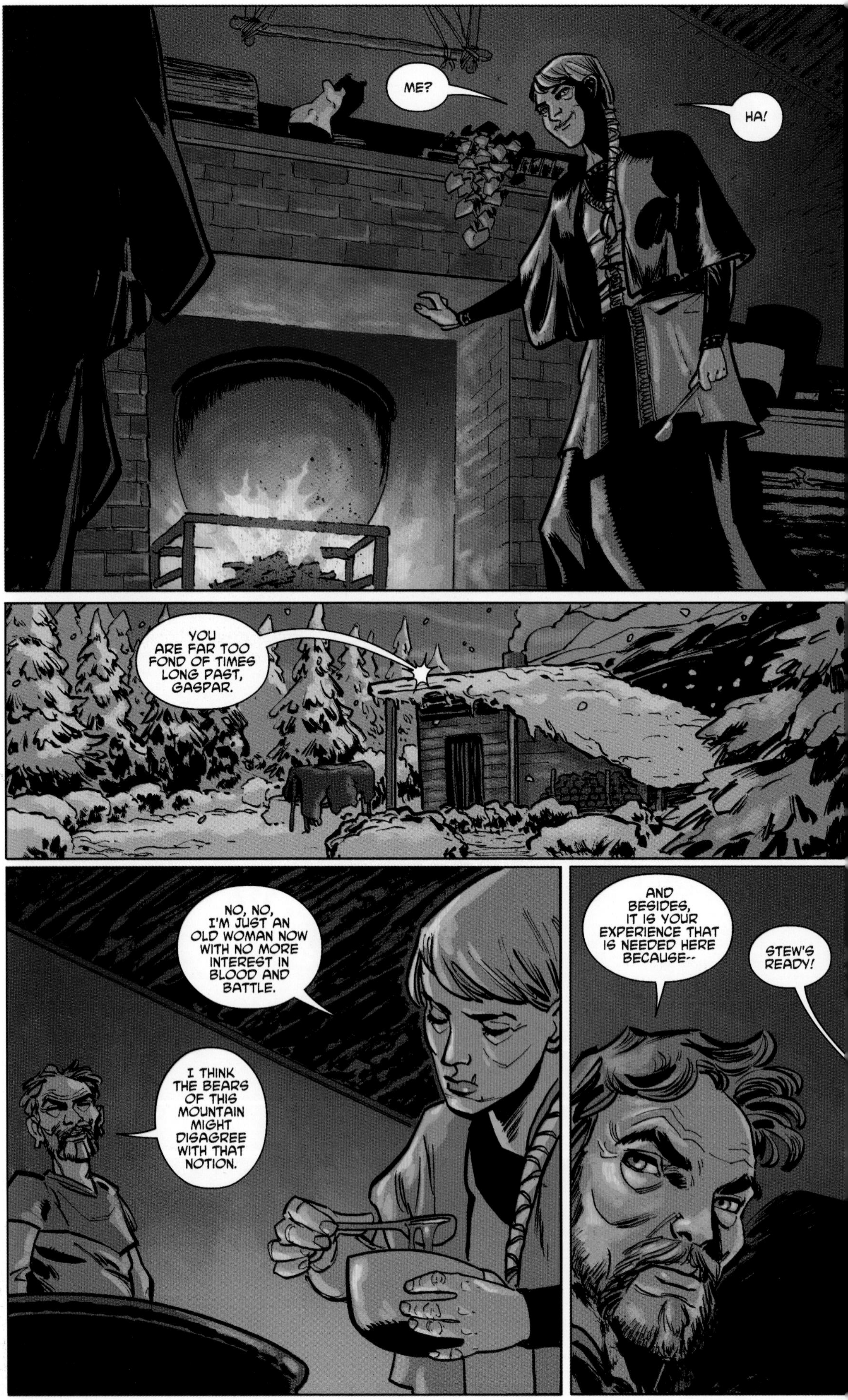

ME?
HA!
YOU ARE FAR TOO FOND OF TIMES LONG PAST, GASPAR.
NO, NO, I'M JUST AN OLD WOMAN NOW WITH NO MORE INTEREST IN BLOOD AND BATTLE.
I THINK THE BEARS OF THIS MOUNTAIN MIGHT DISAGREE WITH THAT NOTION.
AND BESIDES, IT IS YOUR EXPERIENCE THAT IS NEEDED HERE BECAUSE--
STEW'S READY!

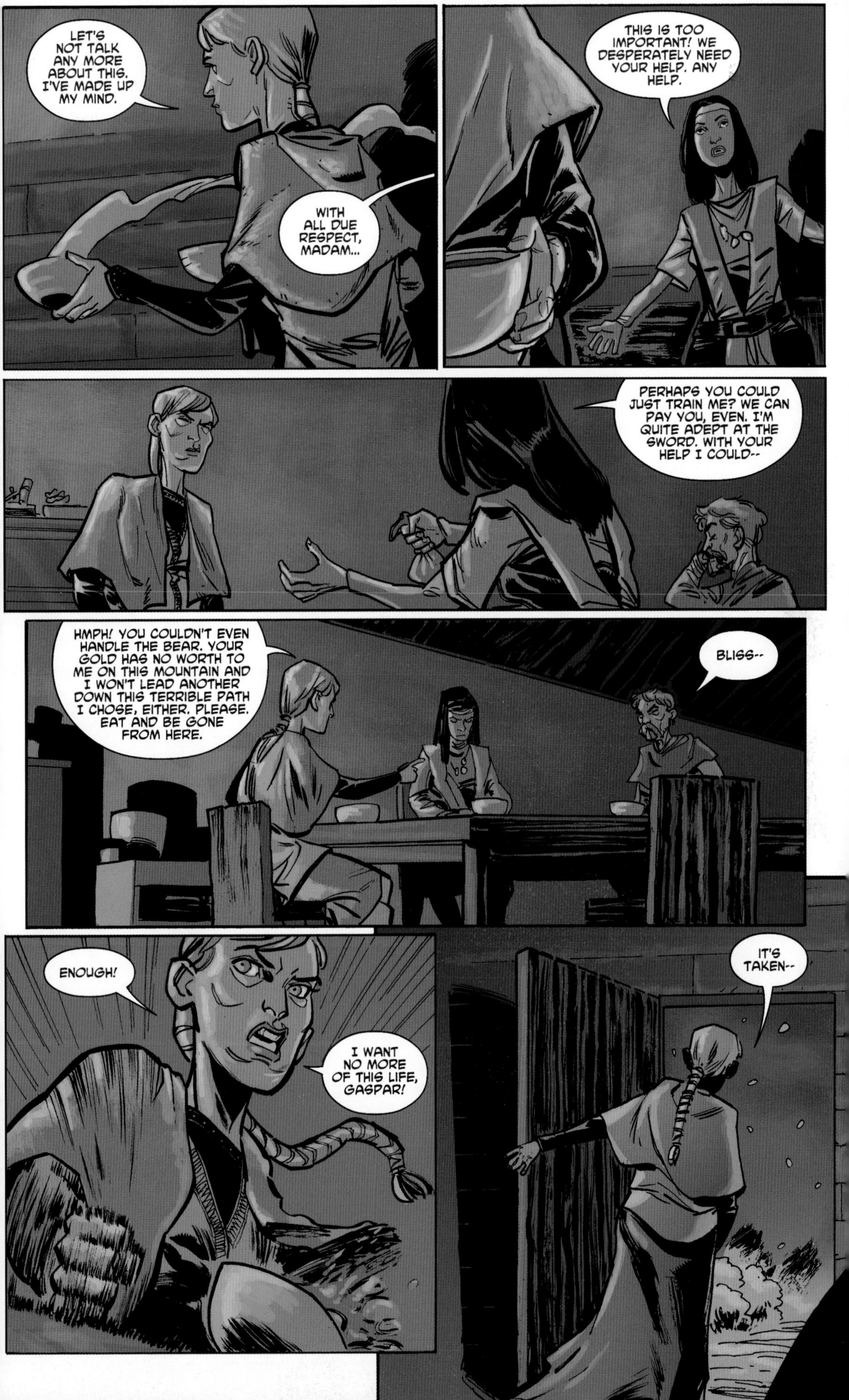
LET'S NOT TALK ANY MORE ABOUT THIS. I'VE MADE UP MY MIND.
WITH ALL DUE RESPECT, MADAM...
THIS IS TOO IMPORTANT! WE DESPERATELY NEED YOUR HELP. ANY HELP.
PERHAPS YOU COULD JUST TRAIN ME? WE CAN PAY YOU, EVEN. I'M QUITE ADEPT AT THE SWORD. WITH YOUR HELP I COULD--
HMPH! YOU COULDN'T EVEN HANDLE THE BEAR. YOUR GOLD HAS NO WORTH TO ME ON THIS MOUNTAIN AND I WON'T LEAD ANOTHER DOWN THIS TERRIBLE PATH I CHOSE, EITHER. PLEASE. EAT AND BE GONE FROM HERE.
BLISS--
ENOUGH!
I WANT NO MORE OF THIS LIFE, GASPAR!
IT'S TAKEN--

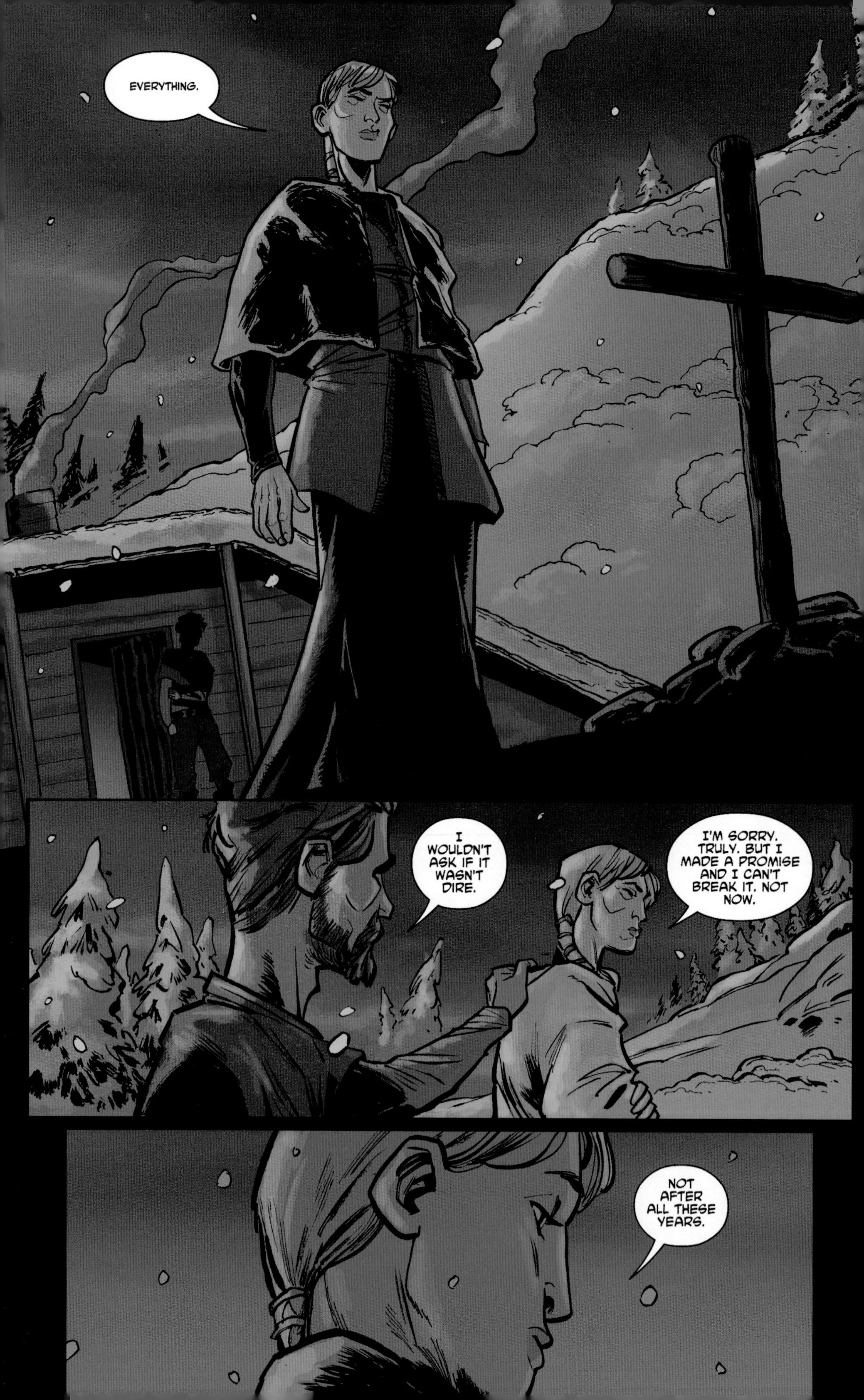
EVERYTHING.
I WOULDN'T ASK IF IT WASN'T DIRE.
I'M SORRY. TRULY. BUT I MADE A PROMISE AND I CAN'T BREAK IT. NOT NOW.
NOT AFTER ALL THESE YEARS.

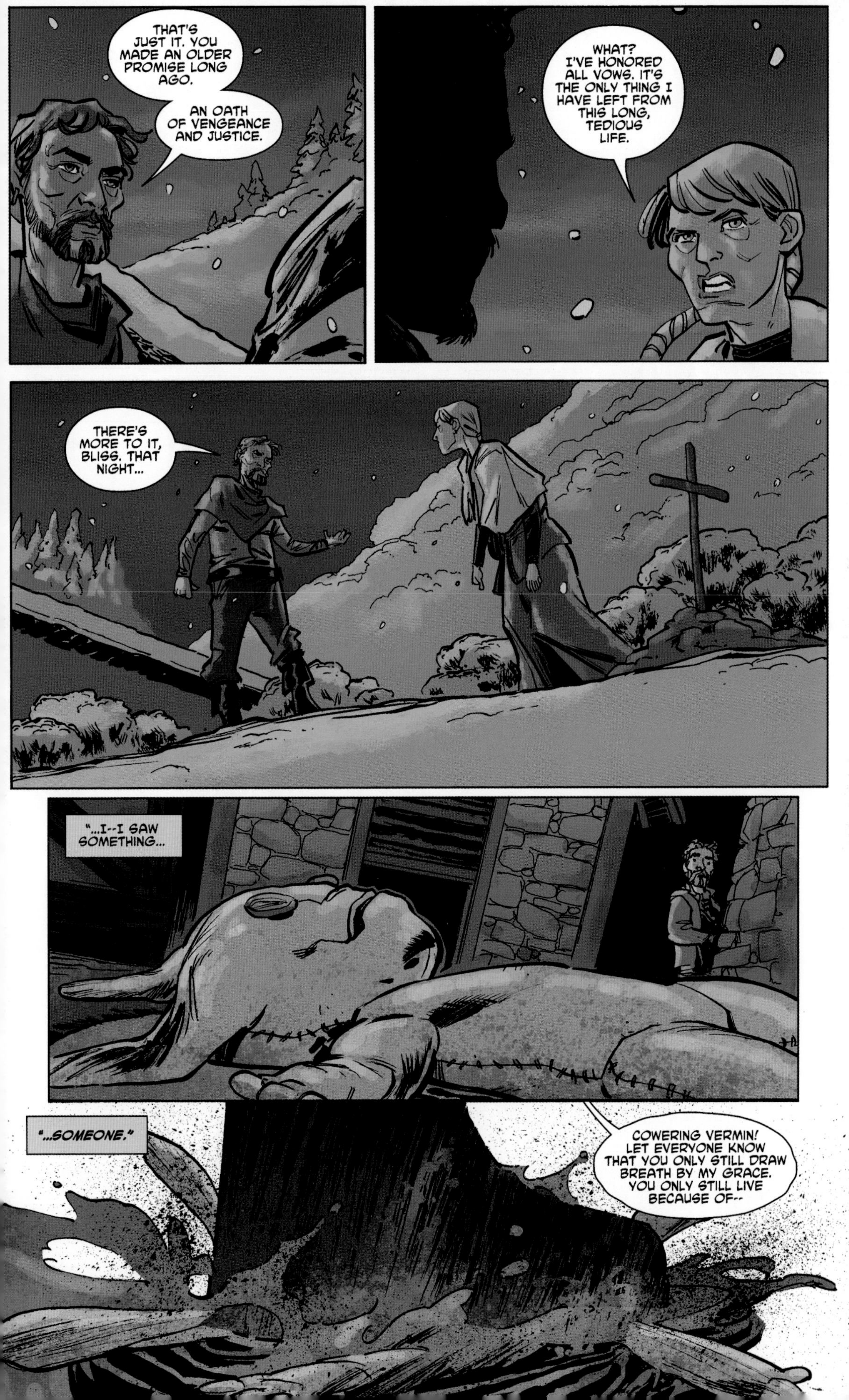
THAT'S JUST IT. YOU MADE AN OLDER PROMISE LONG AGO.
AN OATH OF VENGEANCE AND JUSTICE.
WHAT? I'VE HONORED ALL VOWS. IT'S THE ONLY THING I HAVE LEFT FROM THIS LONG, TEDIOUS LIFE.
THERE'S MORE TO IT, BLISS. THAT NIGHT...
"...I--I SAW SOMETHING...
"...SOMEONE."
COWERING VERMIN! LET EVERYONE KNOW THAT YOU ONLY STILL DRAW BREATH BY MY GRACE. YOU ONLY STILL LIVE BECAUSE OF--

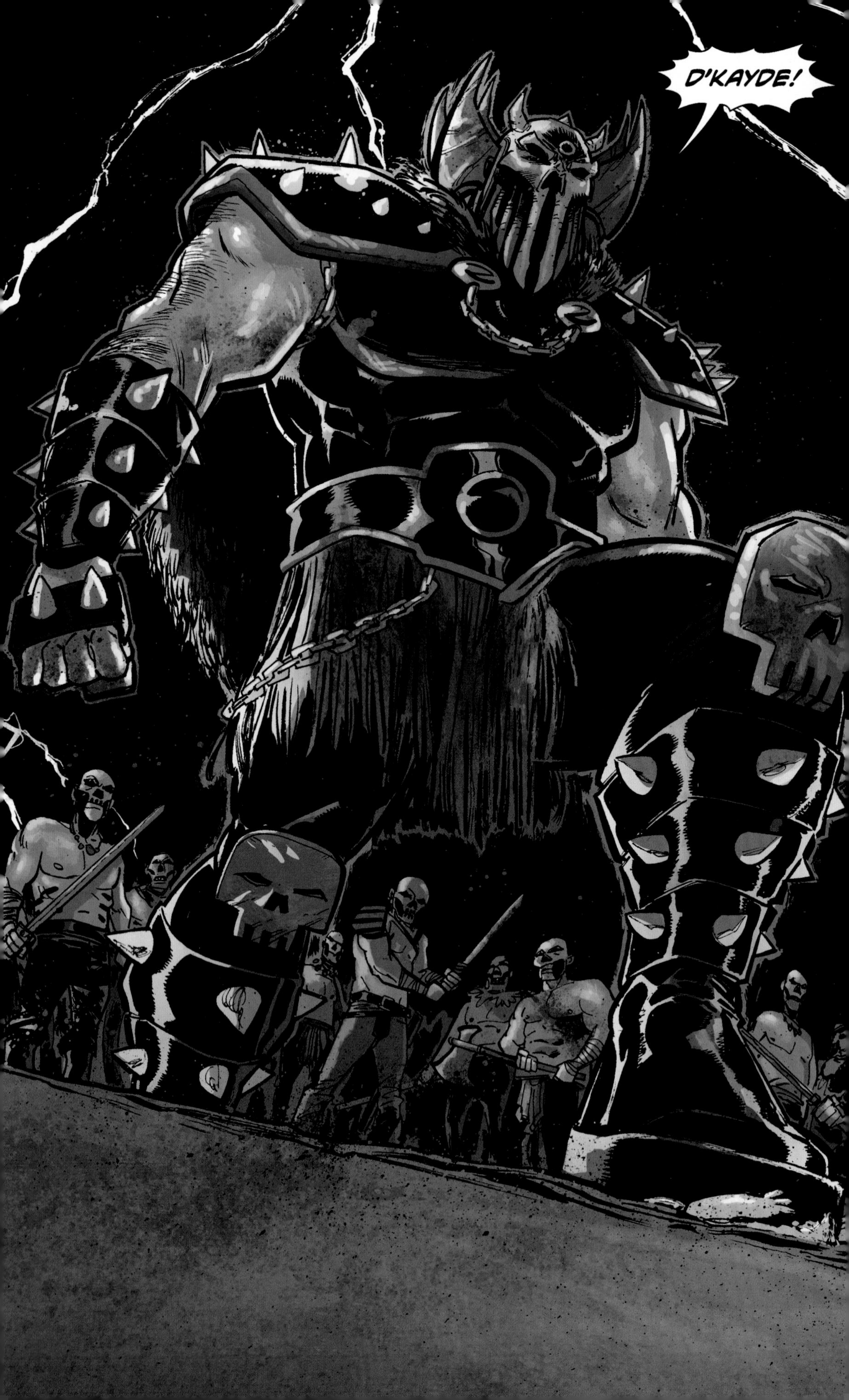
D'KAYDE!

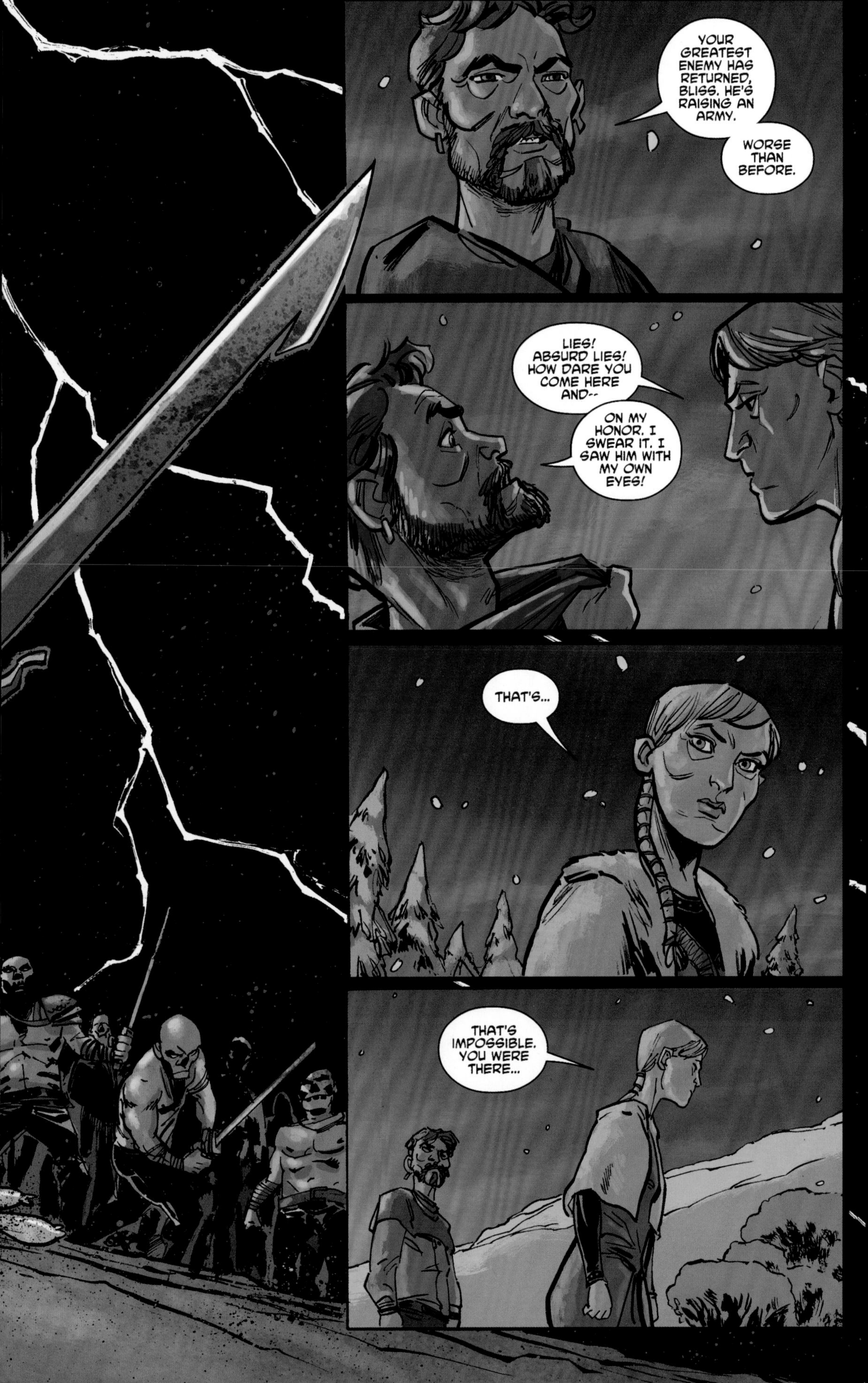
YOUR GREATEST ENEMY HAS RETURNED, BLISS. HE'S RAISING AN ARMY.
WORSE THAN BEFORE.
LIES! ABSURD LIES! HOW DARE YOU COME HERE AND--
ON MY HONOR. I SWEAR IT. I SAW HIM WITH MY OWN EYES!
THAT'S...
THAT'S IMPOSSIBLE. YOU WERE THERE...

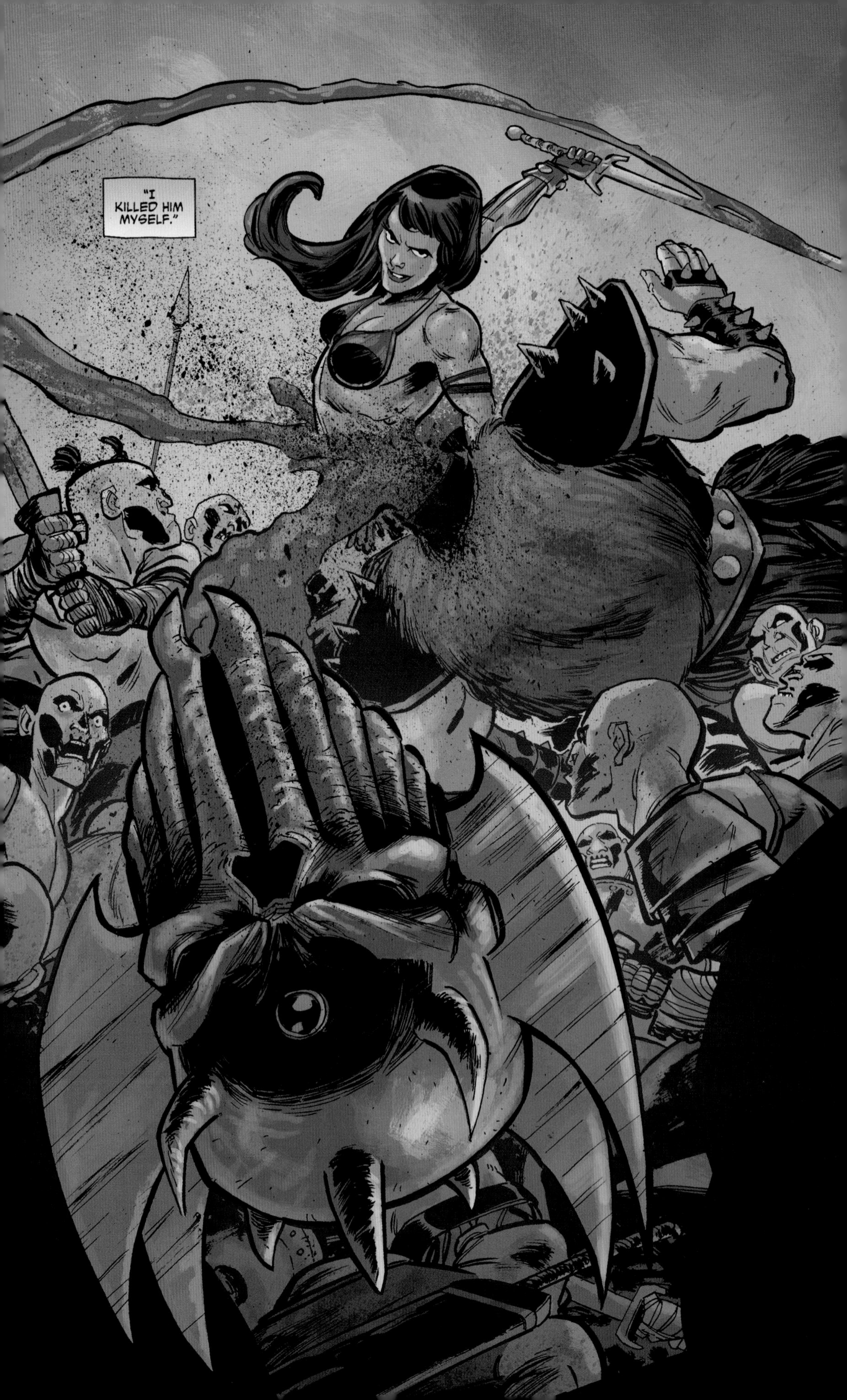
"I KILLED HIM MYSELF."

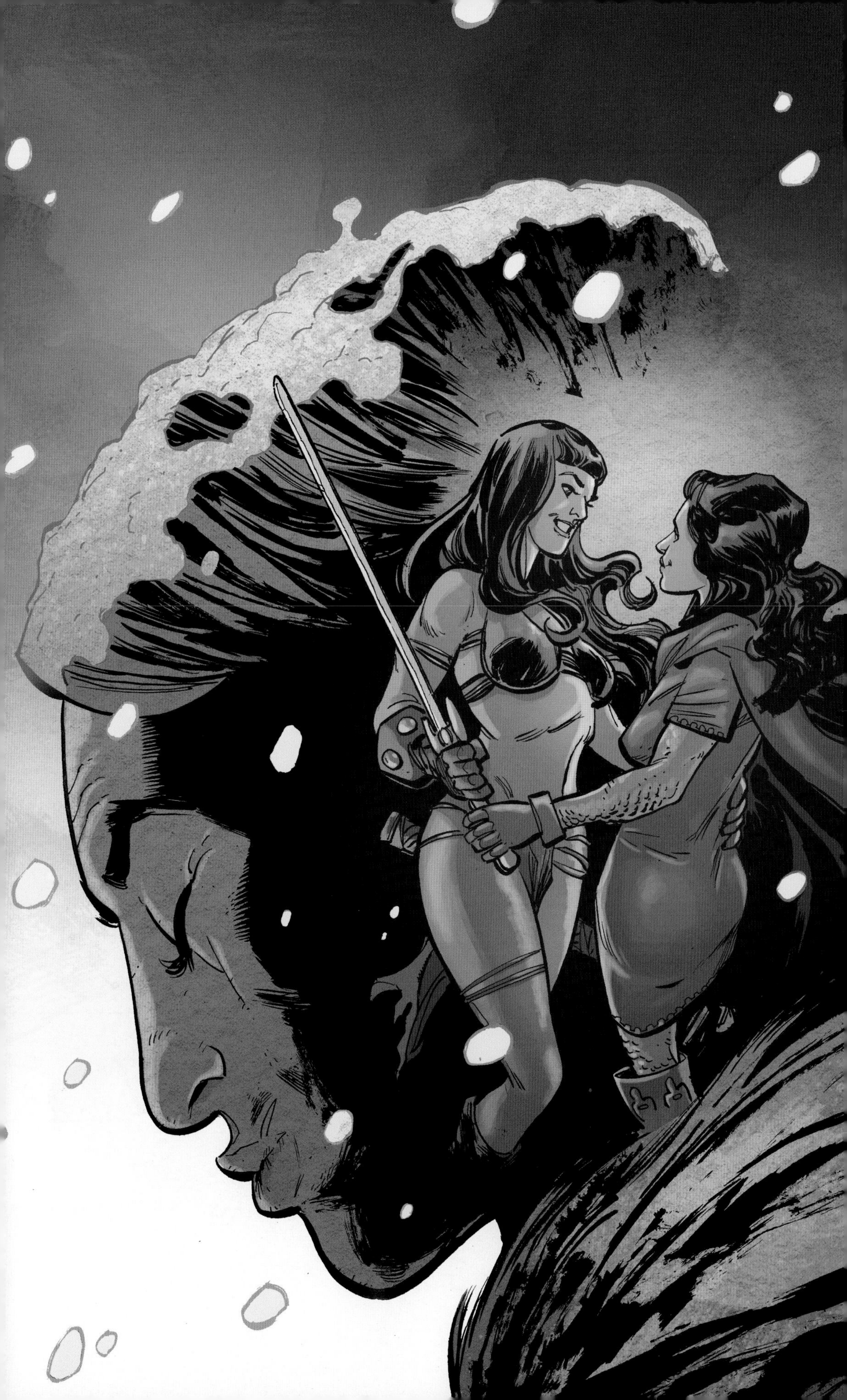

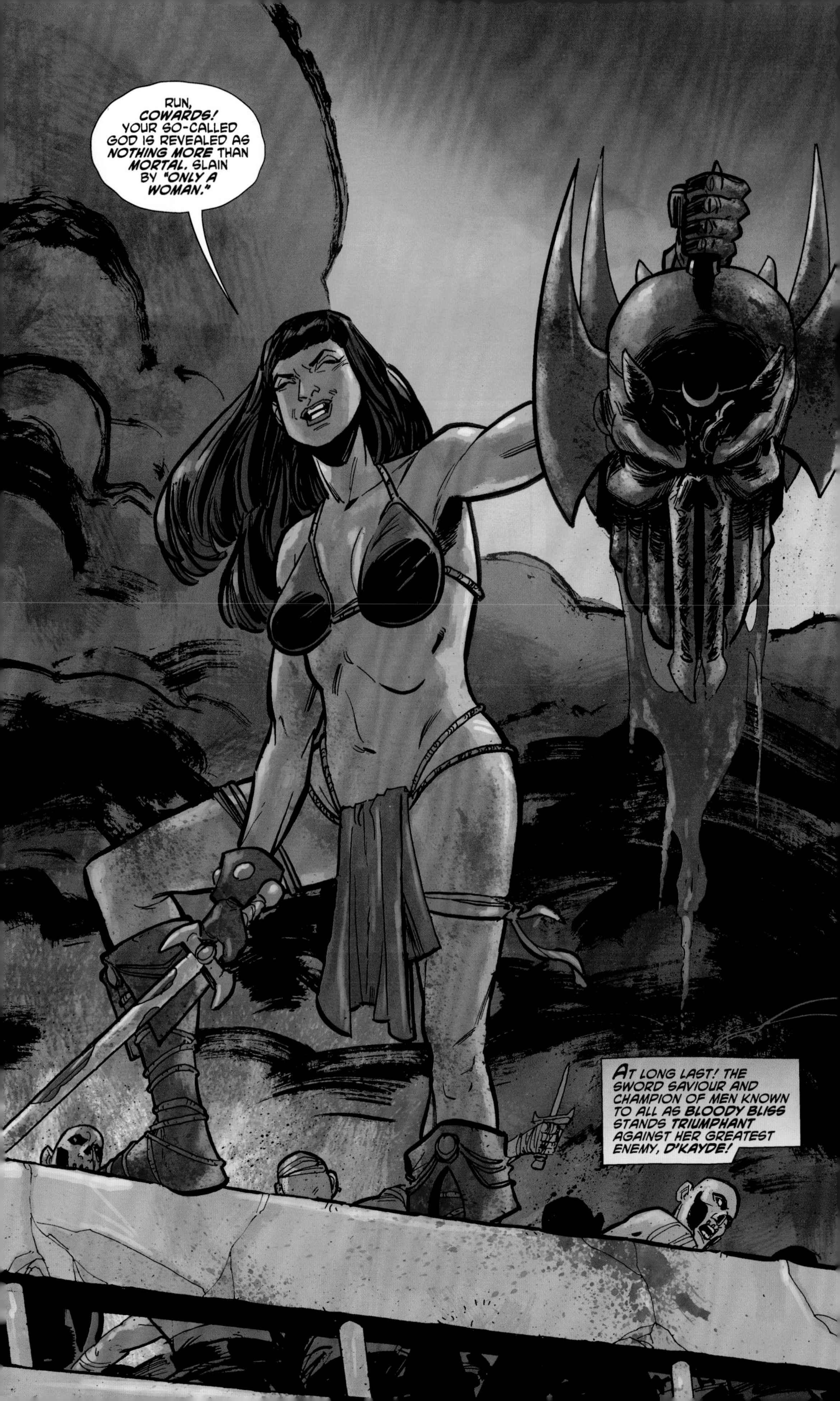
RUN, COWARDS! YOUR SO-CALLED GOD IS REVEALED AS NOTHING MORE THAN MORTAL. SLAIN BY "ONLY A WOMAN."
AT LONG LAST! THE SWORD SAVIOUR AND CHAMPION OF MEN KNOWN TO ALL AS BLOODY BLISS STANDS TRIUMPHANT AGAINST HER GREATEST ENEMY, D'KAYDE!

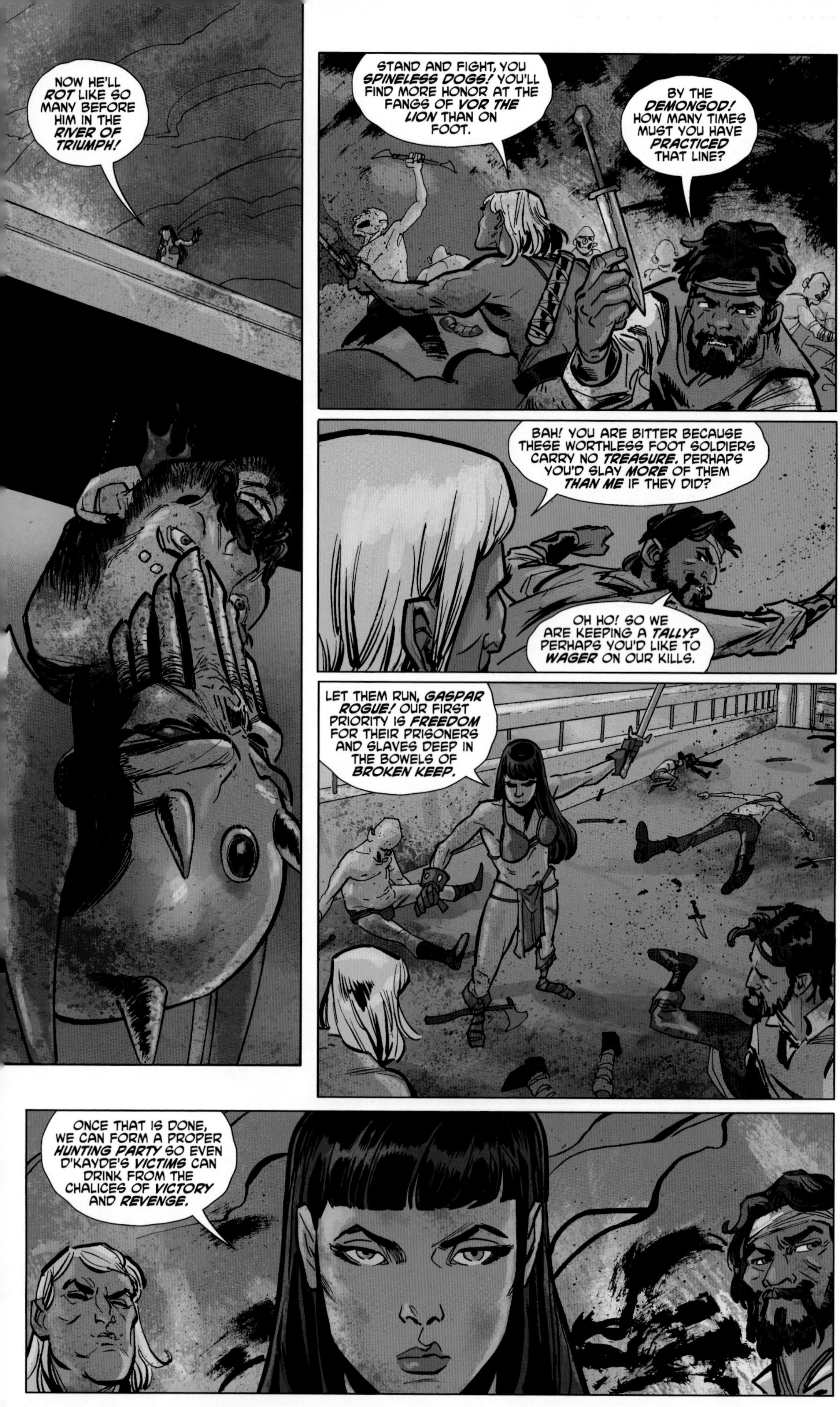
NOW HE'LL ROT LIKE SO MANY BEFORE HIM IN THE RIVER OF TRIUMPH!
STAND AND FIGHT, YOU SPINELESS DOGS! YOU'LL FIND MORE HONOR AT THE FANGS OF VOR THE LION THAN ON FOOT.
BY THE DEMONGOD! HOW MANY TIMES MUST YOU HAVE PRACTICED THAT LINE?
BAH! YOU ARE BITTER BECAUSE THESE WORTHLESS FOOT SOLDIERS CARRY NO TREASURE. PERHAPS YOU'D SLAY MORE OF THEM THAN ME IF THEY DID?
OH HO! SO WE ARE KEEPING A TALLY? PERHAPS YOU'D LIKE TO WAGER ON OUR KILLS.
LET THEM RUN, GASPAR ROGUE! OUR FIRST PRIORITY IS FREEDOM FOR THEIR PRISONERS AND SLAVES DEEP IN THE BOWELS OF BROKEN KEEP.
ONCE THAT IS DONE, WE CAN FORM A PROPER HUNTING PARTY SO EVEN D'KAYDE'S VICTIMS CAN DRINK FROM THE CHALICES OF VICTORY AND REVENGE.

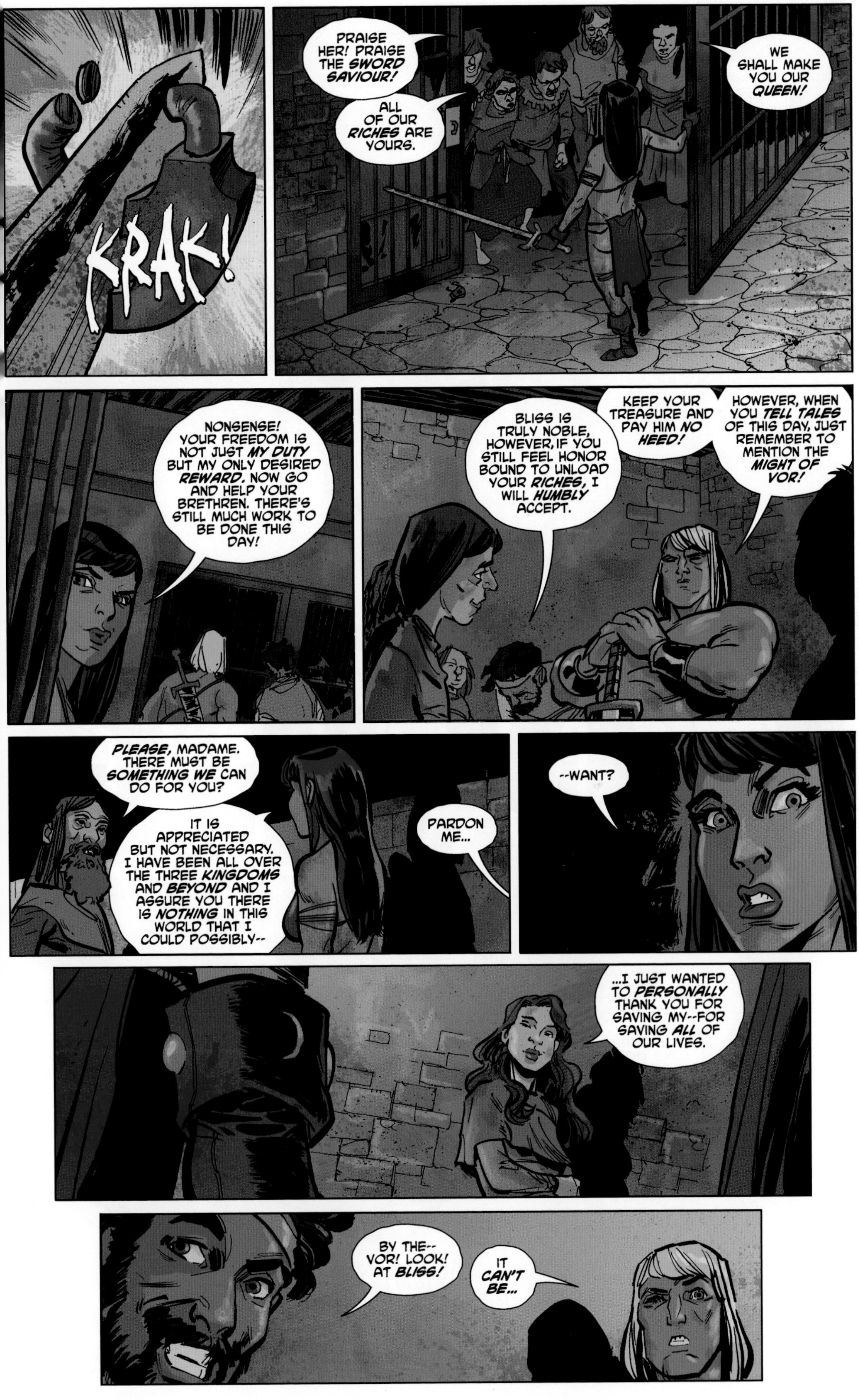
KRAK!
PRAISE HER! PRAISE THE SWORD SAVIOUR!
ALL OF OUR RICHES ARE YOURS.
WE SHALL MAKE YOU OUR QUEEN!
NONSENSE! YOUR FREEDOM IS NOT JUST MY DUTY BUT MY ONLY DESIRED REWARD. NOW GO AND HELP YOUR BRETHREN. THERE'S STILL MUCH WORK TO BE DONE THIS DAY!
BLISS IS TRULY NOBLE, HOWEVER, IF YOU STILL FEEL HONOR BOUND TO UNLOAD YOUR RICHES, I WILL HUMBLY ACCEPT.
KEEP YOUR TREASURE AND PAY HIM NO HEED!
HOWEVER, WHEN YOU TELL TALES OF THIS DAY, JUST REMEMBER TO MENTION THE MIGHT OF VOR!
PLEASE, MADAME. THERE MUST BE SOMETHING WE CAN DO FOR YOU?
IT IS APPRECIATED BUT NOT NECESSARY. I HAVE BEEN ALL OVER THE THREE KINGDOMS AND BEYOND AND I ASSURE YOU THERE IS NOTHING IN THIS WORLD THAT I COULD POSSIBLY--
PARDON ME...
--WANT?
...I JUST WANTED TO PERSONALLY THANK YOU FOR SAVING MY--FOR SAVING ALL OF OUR LIVES.
BY THE-- VOR! LOOK! AT BLISS!
IT CAN'T BE...

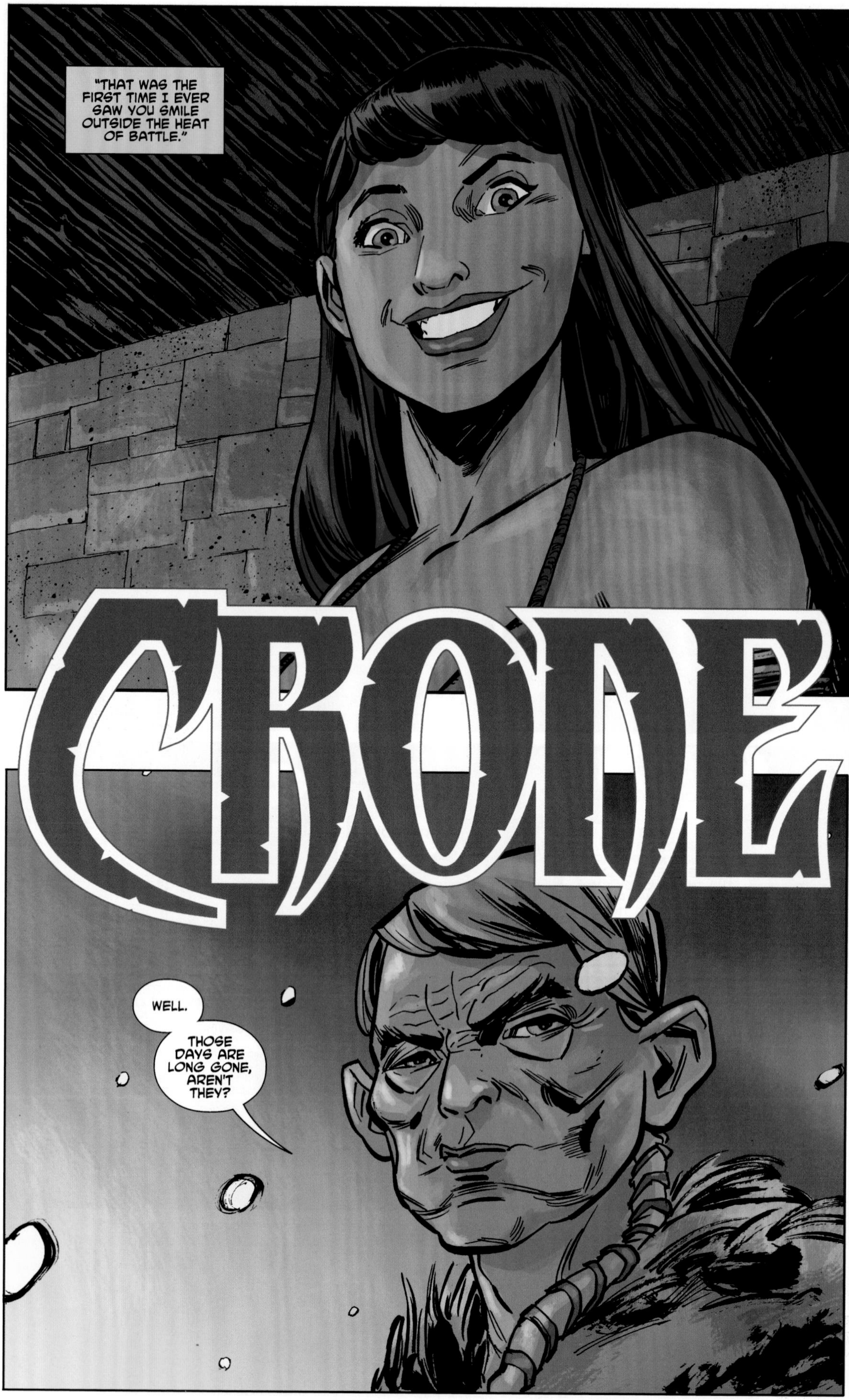
"THAT WAS THE FIRST TIME I EVER SAW YOU SMILE OUTSIDE THE HEAT OF BATTLE."
CRONE
WELL.
THOSE DAYS ARE LONG GONE, AREN'T THEY?

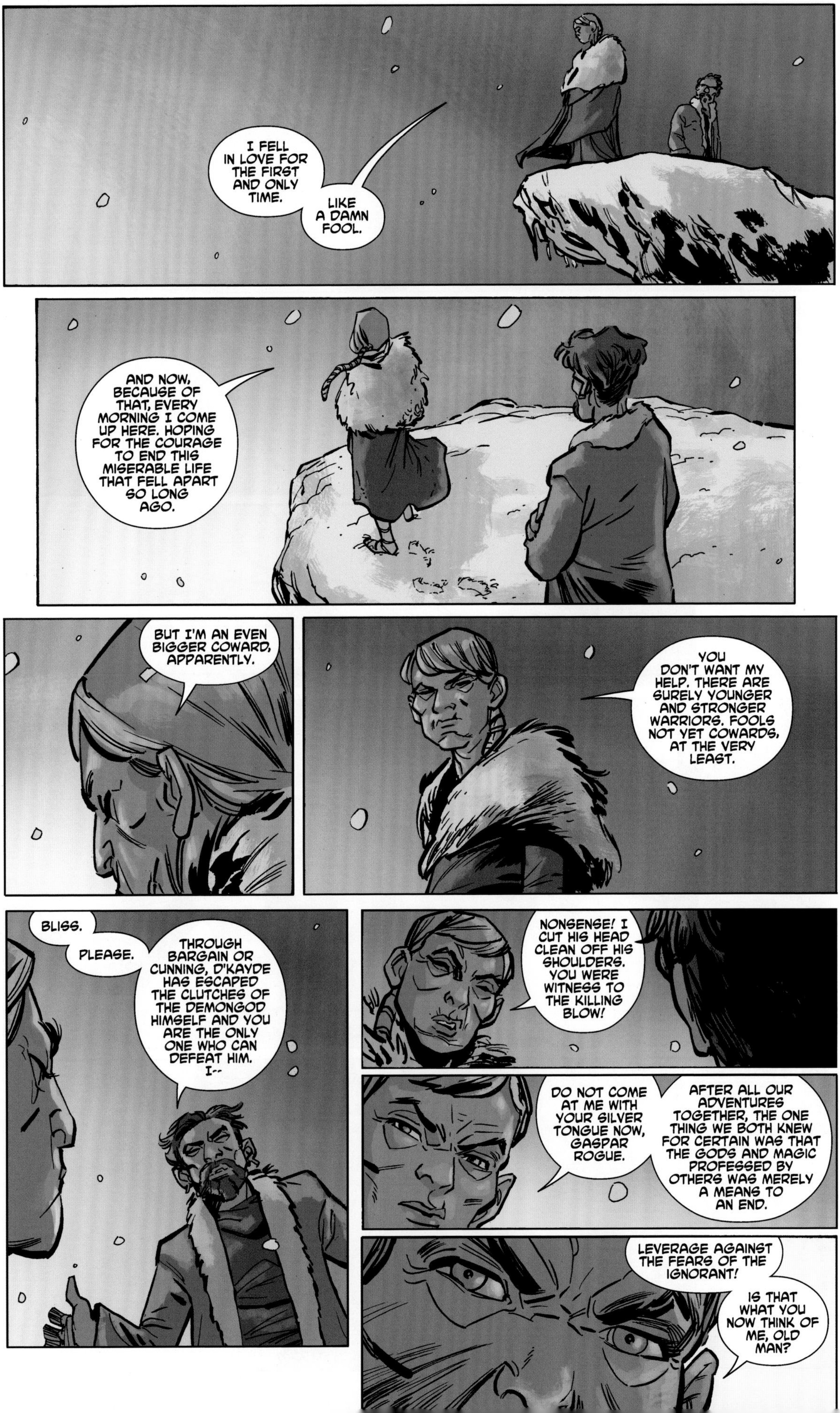
I FELL IN LOVE FOR THE FIRST AND ONLY TIME.
LIKE A DAMN FOOL.
AND NOW, BECAUSE OF THAT, EVERY MORNING I COME UP HERE. HOPING FOR THE COURAGE TO END THIS MISERABLE LIFE THAT FELL APART SO LONG AGO.
BUT I'M AN EVEN BIGGER COWARD, APPARENTLY.
YOU DON'T WANT MY HELP. THERE ARE SURELY YOUNGER AND STRONGER WARRIORS. FOOLS NOT YET COWARDS, AT THE VERY LEAST.
BLISS.
PLEASE.
THROUGH BARGAIN OR CUNNING, D'KAYDE HAS ESCAPED THE CLUTCHES OF THE DEMONGOD HIMSELF AND YOU ARE THE ONLY ONE WHO CAN DEFEAT HIM. I--
NONSENSE! I CUT HIS HEAD CLEAN OFF HIS SHOULDERS. YOU WERE WITNESS TO THE KILLING BLOW!
DO NOT COME AT ME WITH YOUR SILVER TONGUE NOW, GASPAR ROGUE.
AFTER ALL OUR ADVENTURES TOGETHER, THE ONE THING WE BOTH KNEW FOR CERTAIN WAS THAT THE GODS AND MAGIC PROFESSED BY OTHERS WAS MERELY A MEANS TO AN END.
LEVERAGE AGAINST THE FEARS OF THE IGNORANT!
IS THAT WHAT YOU NOW THINK OF ME, OLD MAN?

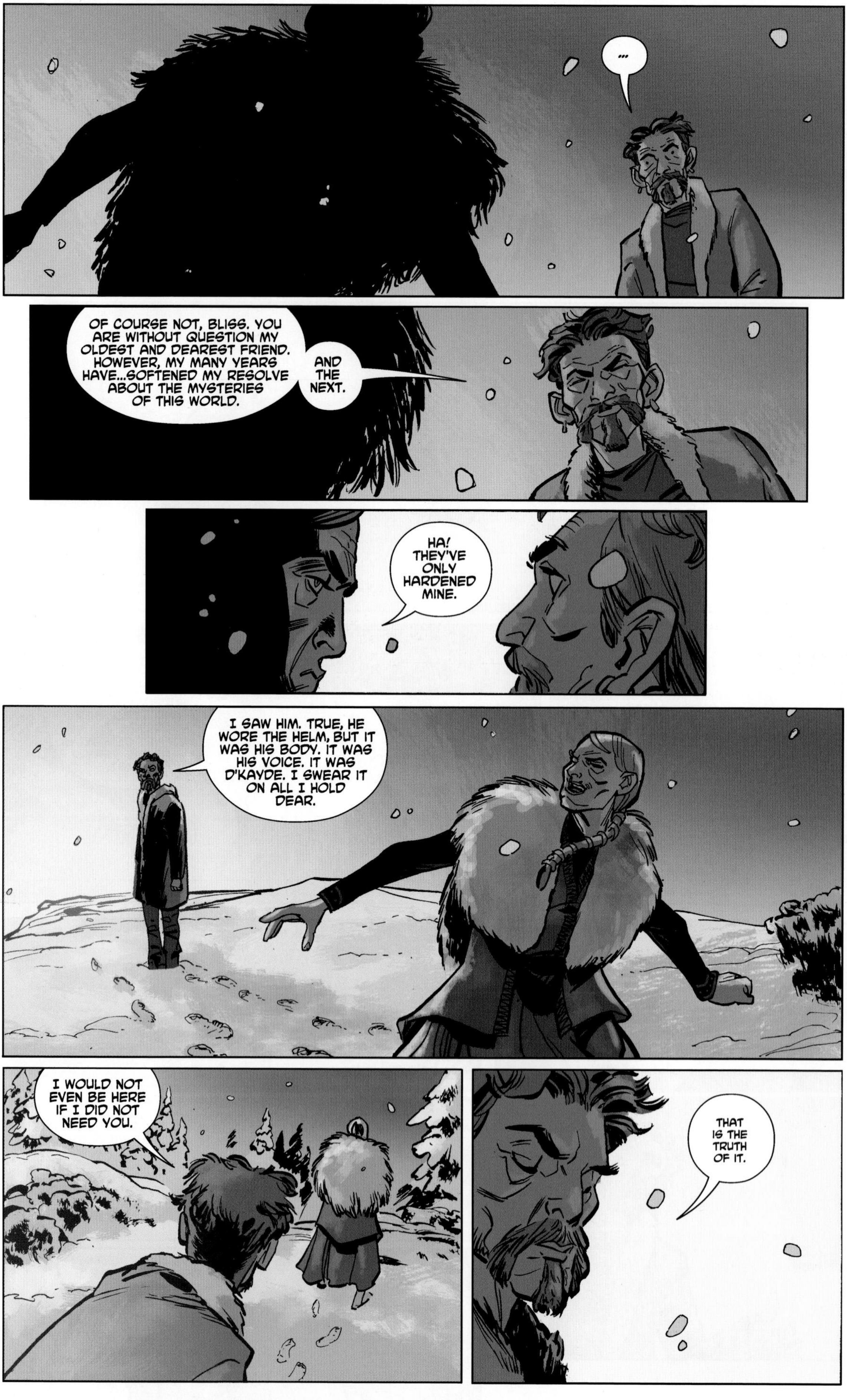
...
OF COURSE NOT, BLISS. YOU ARE WITHOUT QUESTION MY OLDEST AND DEAREST FRIEND. HOWEVER, MY MANY YEARS HAVE...SOFTENED MY RESOLVE ABOUT THE MYSTERIES OF THIS WORLD.
AND THE NEXT.
HA! THEY'VE ONLY HARDENED MINE.
I SAW HIM. TRUE, HE WORE THE HELM, BUT IT WAS HIS BODY. IT WAS HIS VOICE. IT WAS D'KAYDE. I SWEAR IT ON ALL I HOLD DEAR.
I WOULD NOT EVEN BE HERE IF I DID NOT NEED YOU.
THAT IS THE TRUTH OF IT.

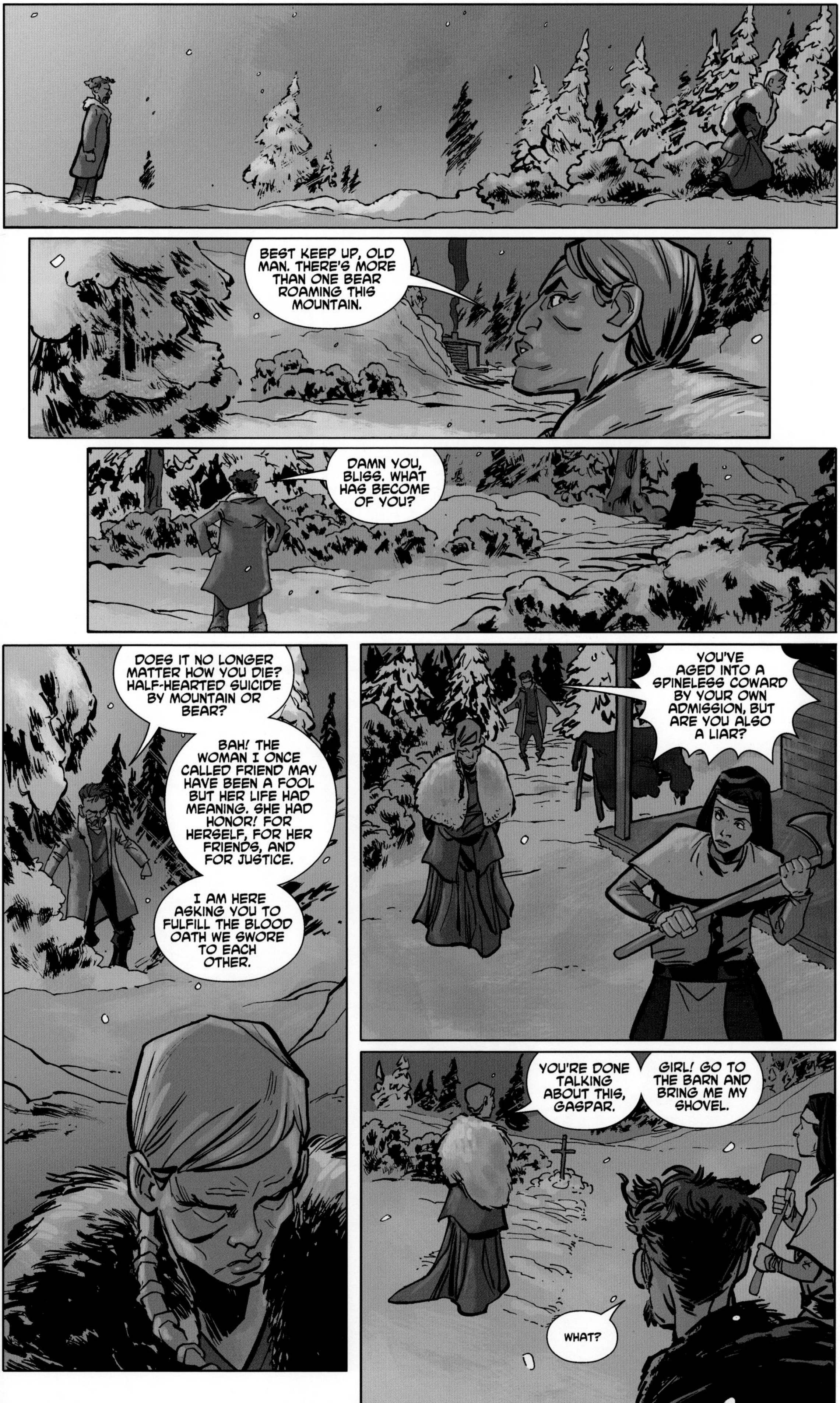
BEST KEEP UP, OLD MAN. THERE'S MORE THAN ONE BEAR ROAMING THIS MOUNTAIN.
DAMN YOU, BLISS. WHAT HAS BECOME OF YOU?
DOES IT NO LONGER MATTER HOW YOU DIE? HALF-HEARTED SUICIDE BY MOUNTAIN OR BEAR?
BAH! THE WOMAN I ONCE CALLED FRIEND MAY HAVE BEEN A FOOL BUT HER LIFE HAD MEANING. SHE HAD HONOR! FOR HERSELF, FOR HER FRIENDS, AND FOR JUSTICE.
I AM HERE ASKING YOU TO FULFILL THE BLOOD OATH WE SWORE TO EACH OTHER.
YOU'VE AGED INTO A SPINELESS COWARD BY YOUR OWN ADMISSION, BUT ARE YOU ALSO A LIAR?
YOU'RE DONE TALKING ABOUT THIS, GASPAR.
GIRL! GO TO THE BARN AND BRING ME MY SHOVEL.
WHAT?

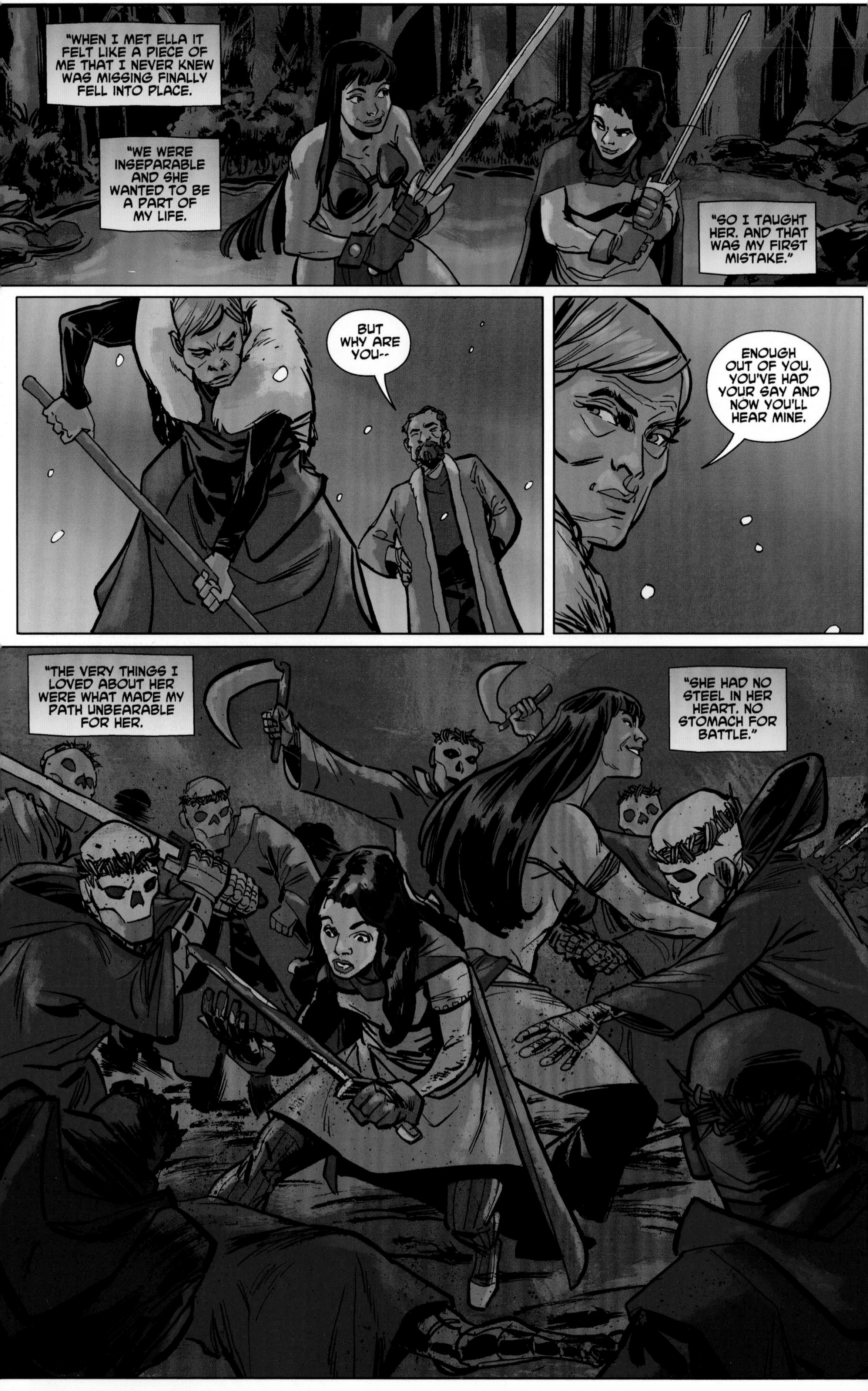
"WHEN I MET ELLA IT FELT LIKE A PIECE OF ME THAT I NEVER KNEW WAS MISSING FINALLY FELL INTO PLACE.
"WE WERE INSEPARABLE AND SHE WANTED TO BE A PART OF MY LIFE.
"SO I TAUGHT HER. AND THAT WAS MY FIRST MISTAKE."
BUT WHY ARE YOU--
ENOUGH OUT OF YOU. YOU'VE HAD YOUR SAY AND NOW YOU'LL HEAR MINE.
"THE VERY THINGS I LOVED ABOUT HER WERE WHAT MADE MY PATH UNBEARABLE FOR HER.
"SHE HAD NO STEEL IN HER HEART. NO STOMACH FOR BATTLE."

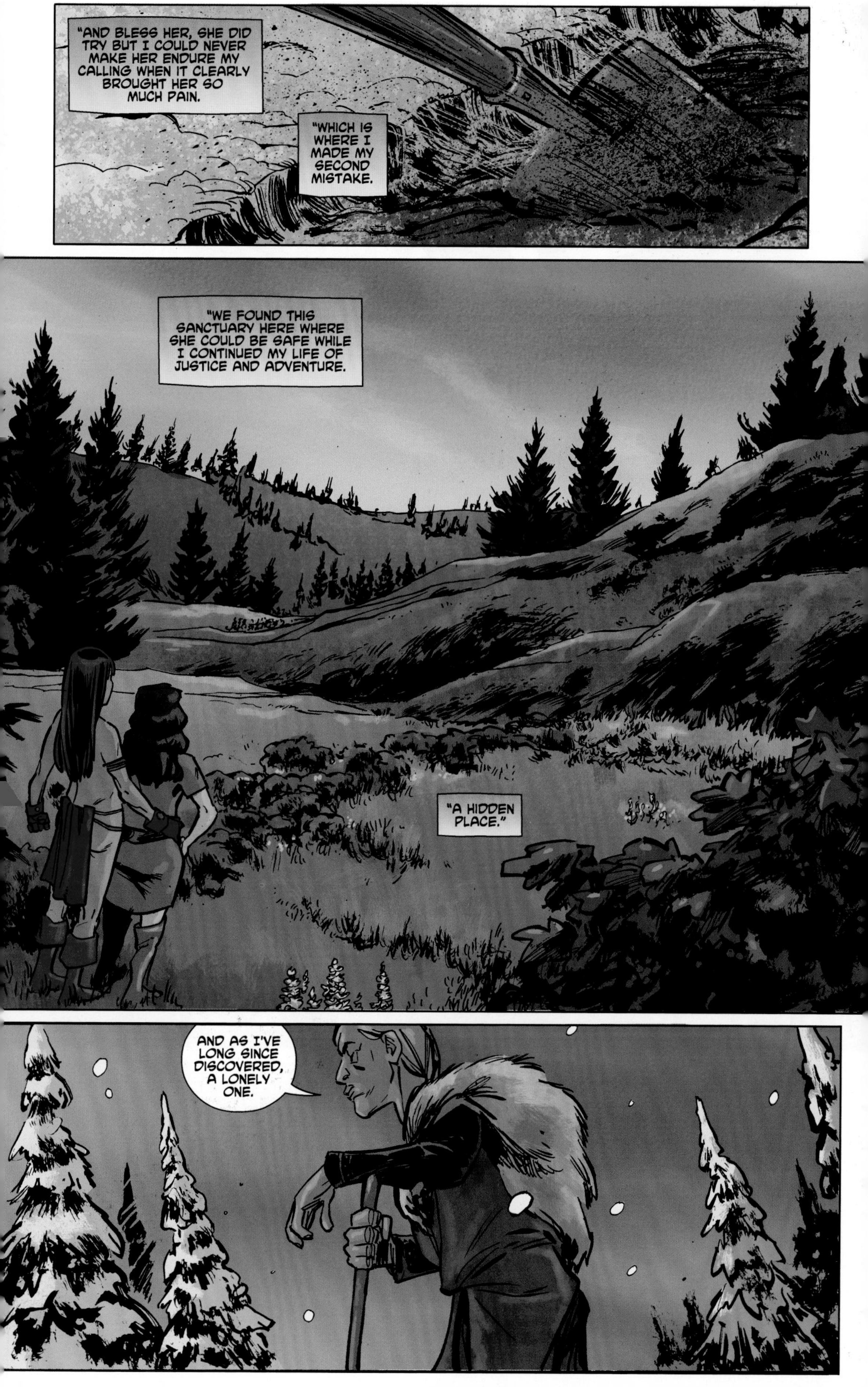
"AND BLESS HER, SHE DID TRY BUT I COULD NEVER MAKE HER ENDURE MY CALLING WHEN IT CLEARLY BROUGHT HER SO MUCH PAIN.
"WHICH IS WHERE I MADE MY SECOND MISTAKE.
"WE FOUND THIS SANCTUARY HERE WHERE SHE COULD BE SAFE WHILE I CONTINUED MY LIFE OF JUSTICE AND ADVENTURE.
"A HIDDEN PLACE."
AND AS I'VE LONG SINCE DISCOVERED, A LONELY ONE.

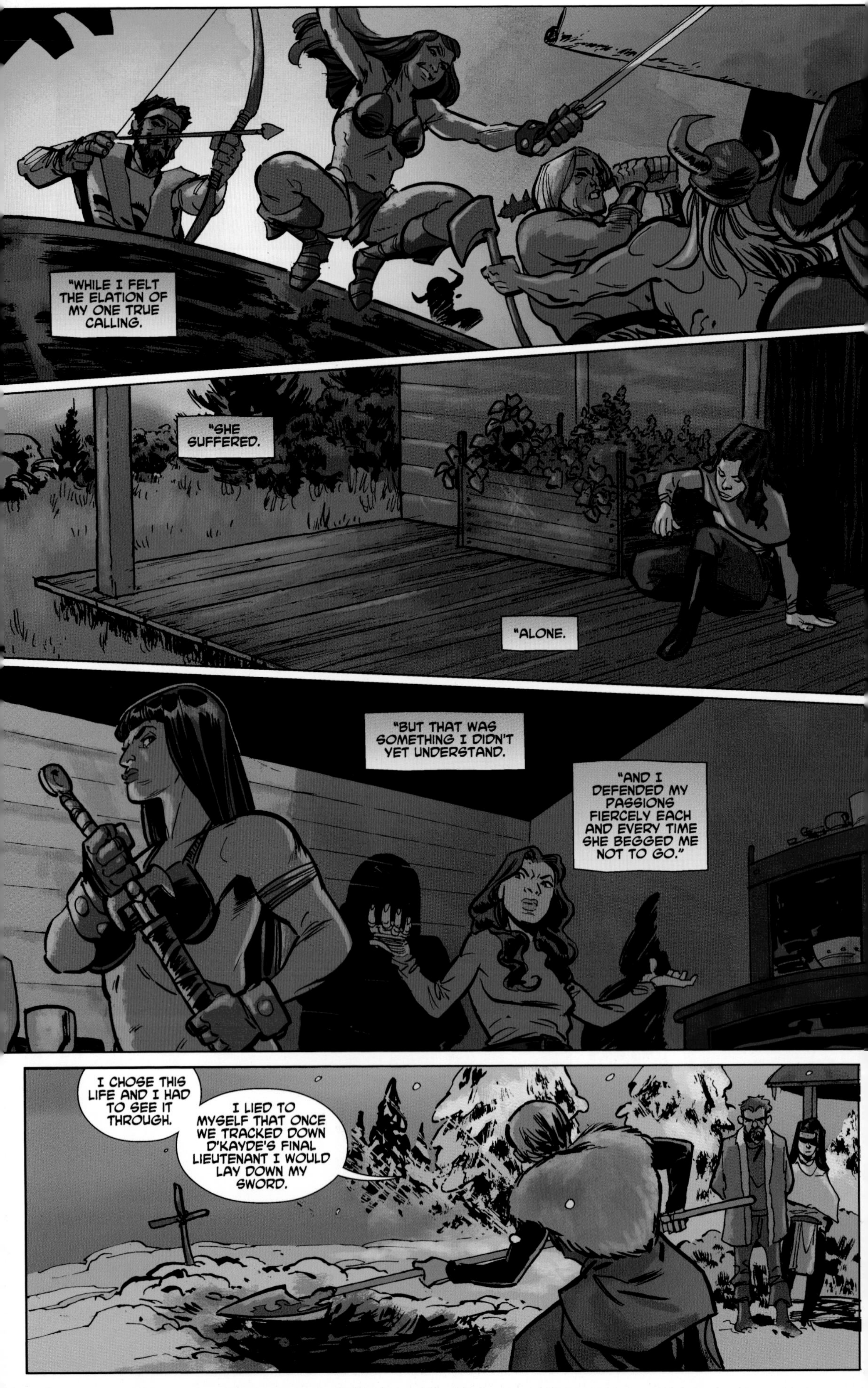
"WHILE I FELT THE ELATION OF MY ONE TRUE CALLING.
"SHE SUFFERED.
"ALONE.
"BUT THAT WAS SOMETHING I DIDN'T YET UNDERSTAND.
"AND I DEFENDED MY PASSIONS FIERCELY EACH AND EVERY TIME SHE BEGGED ME NOT TO GO."
I CHOSE THIS LIFE AND I HAD TO SEE IT THROUGH.
I LIED TO MYSELF THAT ONCE WE TRACKED DOWN D'KAYDE'S FINAL LIEUTENANT I WOULD LAY DOWN MY SWORD.

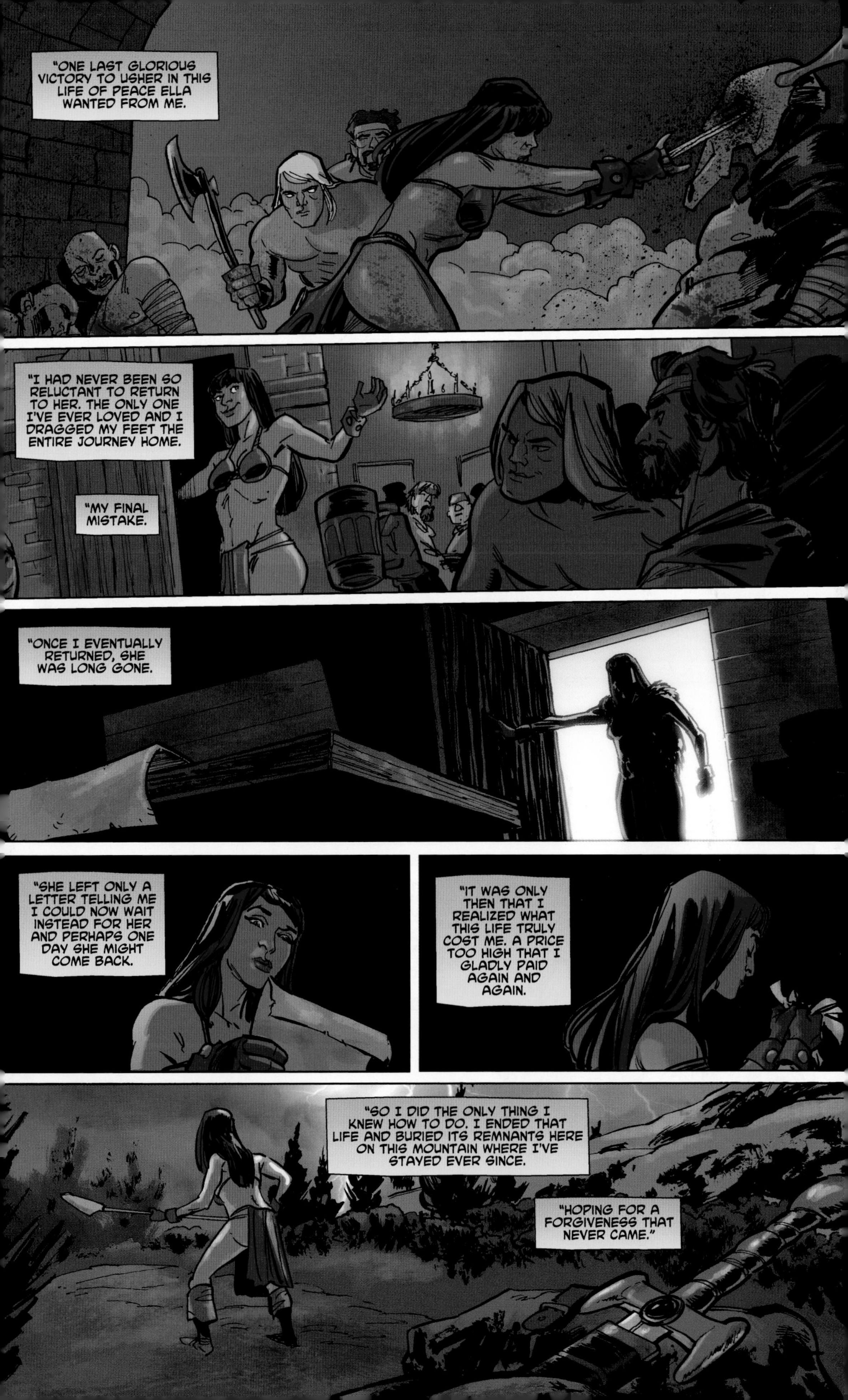
"ONE LAST GLORIOUS VICTORY TO USHER IN THIS LIFE OF PEACE ELLA WANTED FROM ME.
"I HAD NEVER BEEN SO RELUCTANT TO RETURN TO HER. THE ONLY ONE I'VE EVER LOVED AND I DRAGGED MY FEET THE ENTIRE JOURNEY HOME.
"MY FINAL MISTAKE.
"ONCE I EVENTUALLY RETURNED, SHE WAS LONG GONE.
"SHE LEFT ONLY A LETTER TELLING ME I COULD NOW WAIT INSTEAD FOR HER AND PERHAPS ONE DAY SHE MIGHT COME BACK.
"IT WAS ONLY THEN THAT I REALIZED WHAT THIS LIFE TRULY COST ME. A PRICE TOO HIGH THAT I GLADLY PAID AGAIN AND AGAIN.
"SO I DID THE ONLY THING I KNEW HOW TO DO. I ENDED THAT LIFE AND BURIED ITS REMNANTS HERE ON THIS MOUNTAIN WHERE I'VE STAYED EVER SINCE.
"HOPING FOR A FORGIVENESS THAT NEVER CAME."

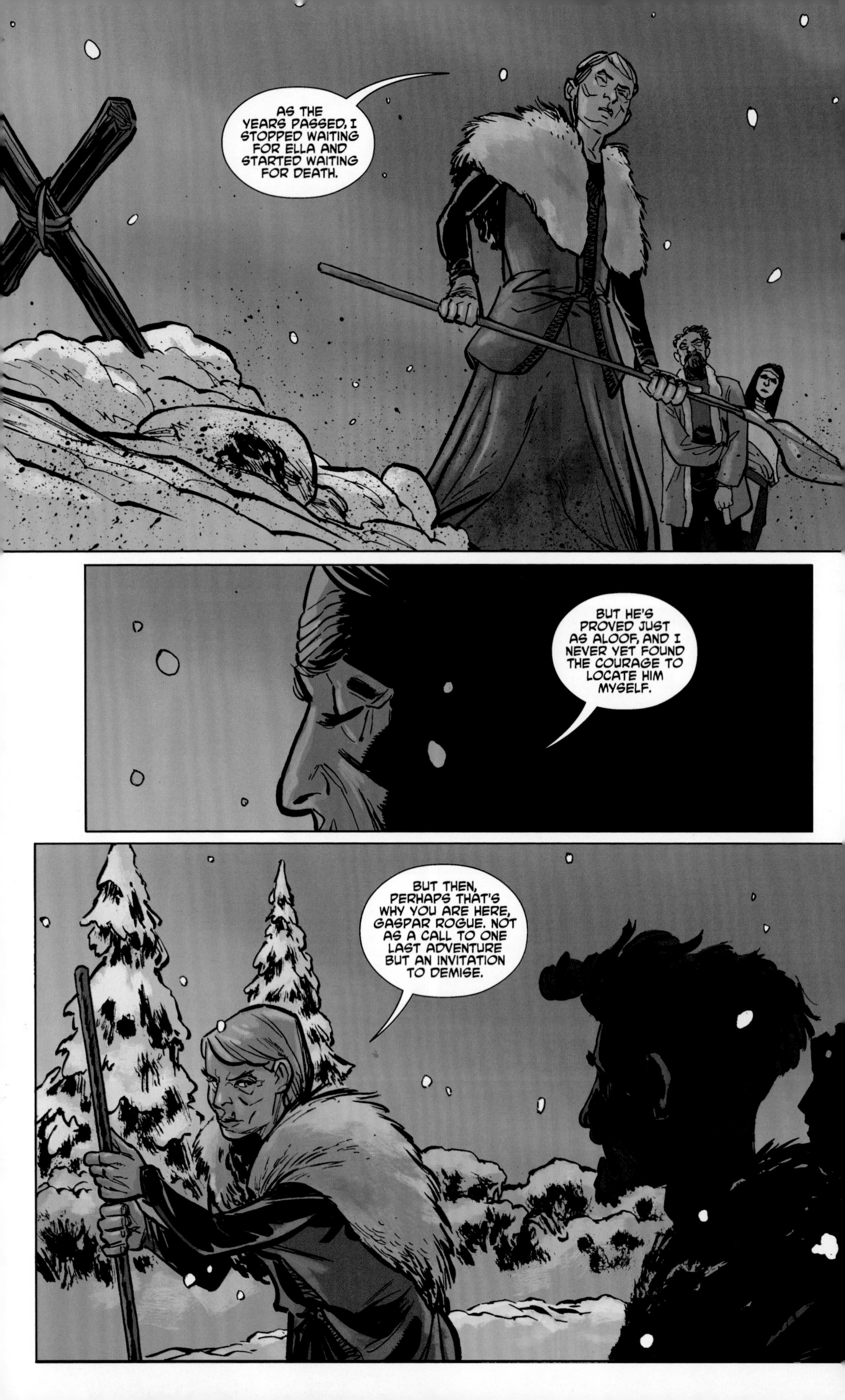
AS THE YEARS PASSED, I STOPPED WAITING FOR ELLA AND STARTED WAITING FOR DEATH.
BUT HE'S PROVED JUST AS ALOOF, AND I NEVER YET FOUND THE COURAGE TO LOCATE HIM MYSELF.
BUT THEN, PERHAPS THAT'S WHY YOU ARE HERE, GASPAR ROGUE. NOT AS A CALL TO ONE LAST ADVENTURE BUT AN INVITATION TO DEMISE.

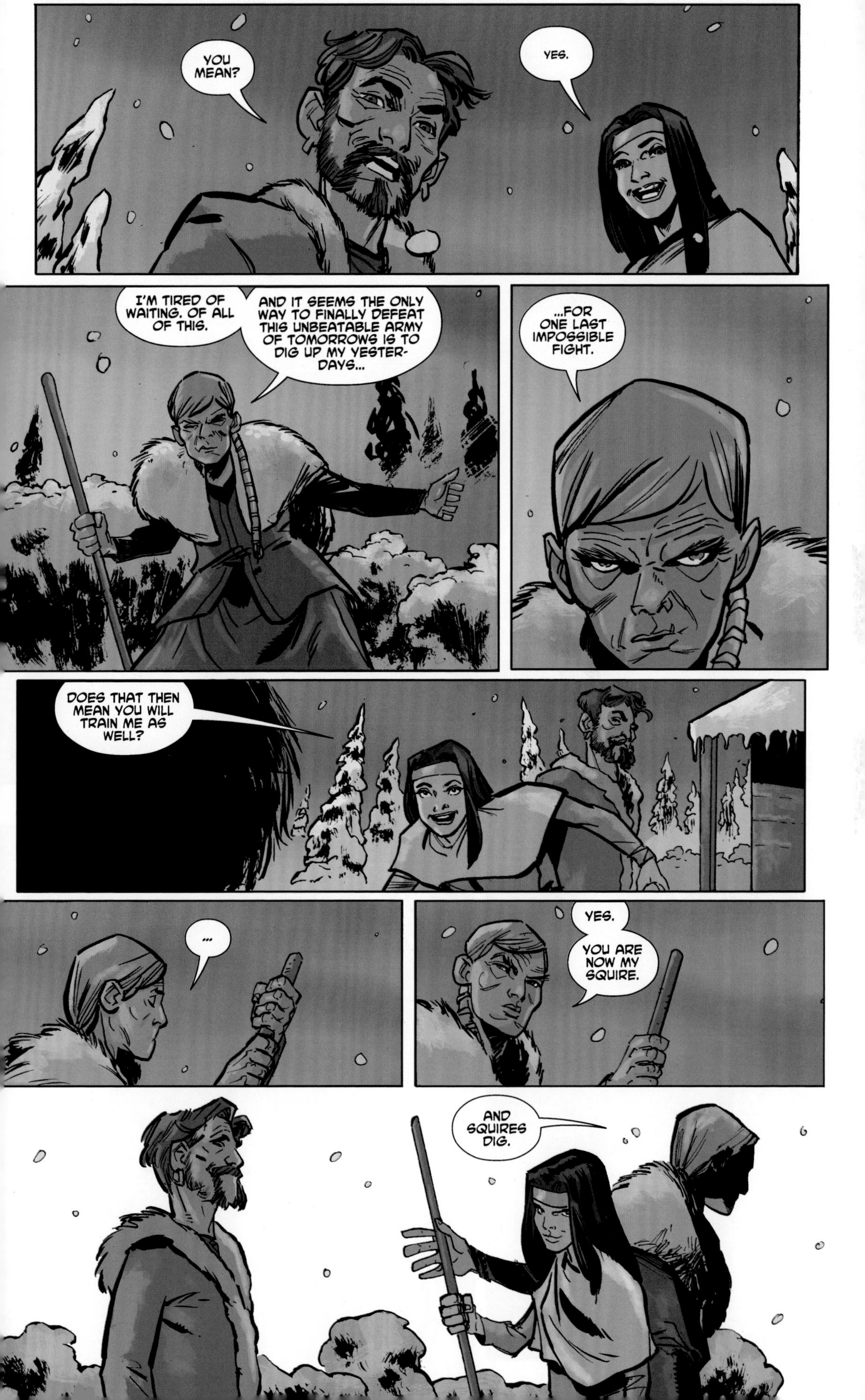
YOU MEAN?
YES.
I'M TIRED OF WAITING. OF ALL OF THIS.
AND IT SEEMS THE ONLY WAY TO FINALLY DEFEAT THIS UNBEATABLE ARMY OF TOMORROWS IS TO DIG UP MY YESTER-DAYS...
...FOR ONE LAST IMPOSSIBLE FIGHT.
DOES THAT THEN MEAN YOU WILL TRAIN ME AS WELL?
...
YES.
YOU ARE NOW MY SQUIRE.
AND SQUIRES DIG.

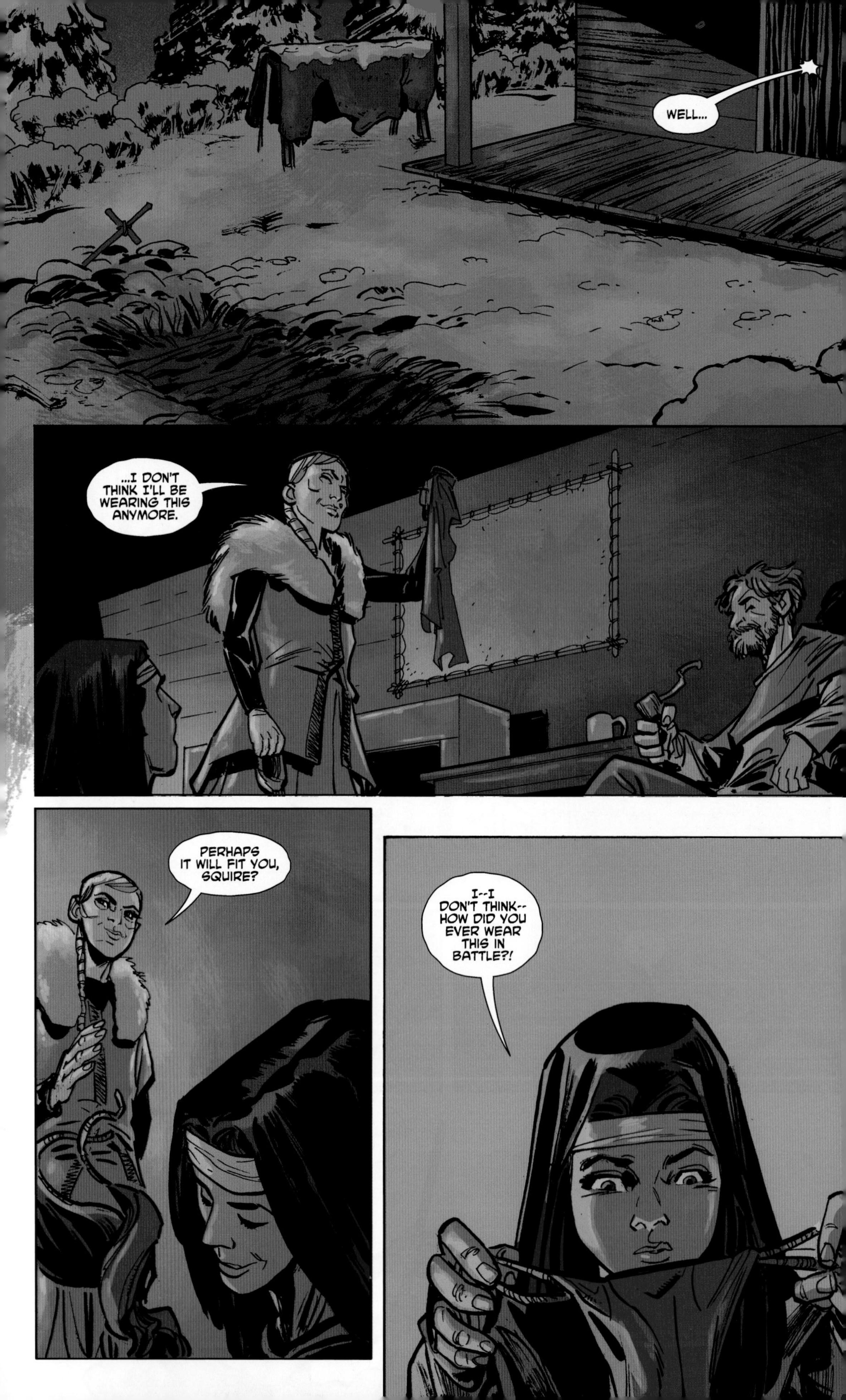
WELL...
...I DON'T THINK I'LL BE WEARING THIS ANYMORE.
PERHAPS IT WILL FIT YOU, SQUIRE?
I--I DON'T THINK-- HOW DID YOU EVER WEAR THIS IN BATTLE?!

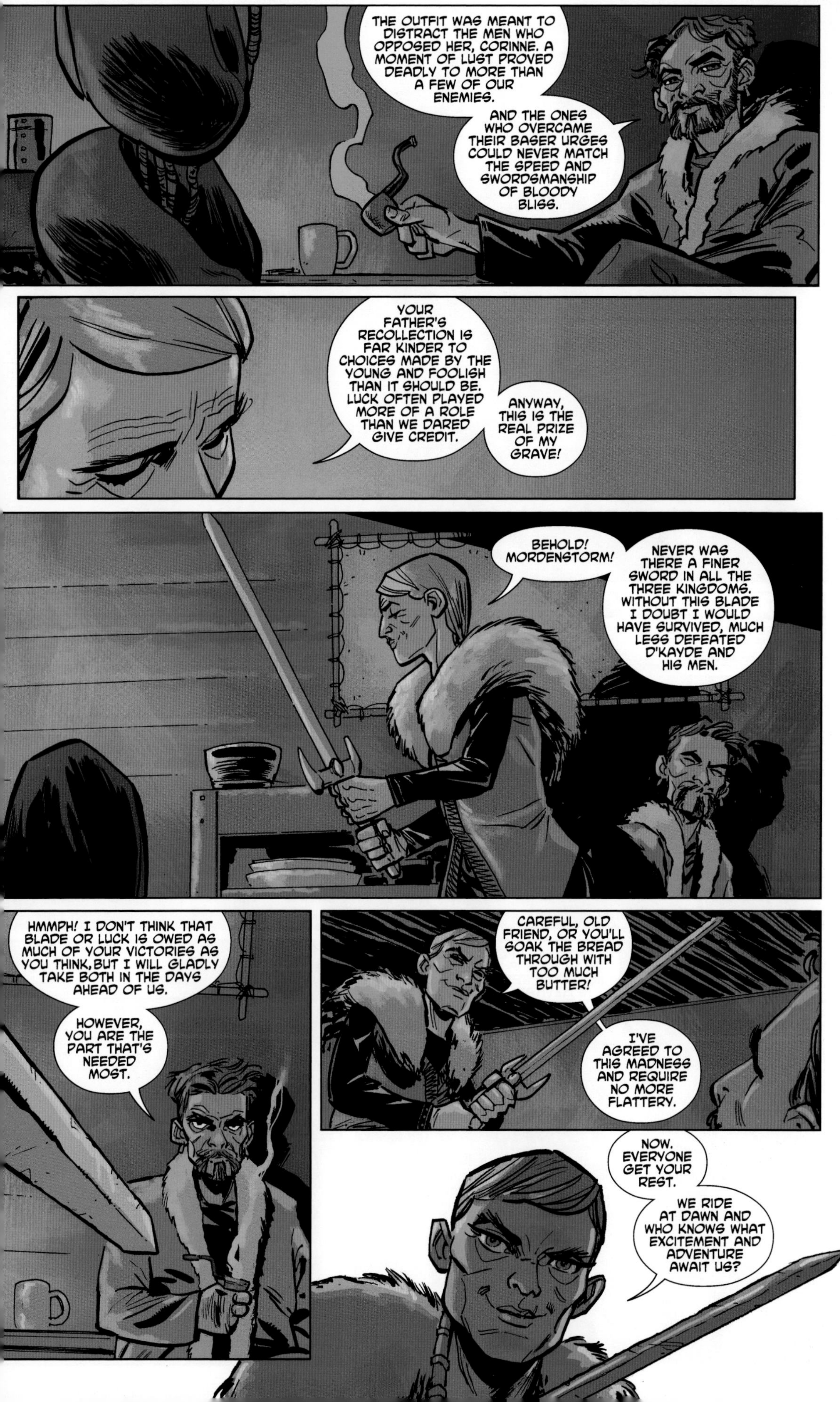
THE OUTFIT WAS MEANT TO DISTRACT THE MEN WHO OPPOSED HER, CORINNE. A MOMENT OF LUST PROVED DEADLY TO MORE THAN A FEW OF OUR ENEMIES.
AND THE ONES WHO OVERCAME THEIR BASER URGES COULD NEVER MATCH THE SPEED AND SWORDSMANSHIP OF BLOODY BLISS.
YOUR FATHER'S RECOLLECTION IS FAR KINDER TO CHOICES MADE BY THE YOUNG AND FOOLISH THAN IT SHOULD BE. LUCK OFTEN PLAYED MORE OF A ROLE THAN WE DARED GIVE CREDIT.
ANYWAY, THIS IS THE REAL PRIZE OF MY GRAVE!
BEHOLD! MORDENSTORM!
NEVER WAS THERE A FINER SWORD IN ALL THE THREE KINGDOMS. WITHOUT THIS BLADE I DOUBT I WOULD HAVE SURVIVED, MUCH LESS DEFEATED D'KAYDE AND HIS MEN.
HMMPH! I DON'T THINK THAT BLADE OR LUCK IS OWED AS MUCH OF YOUR VICTORIES AS YOU THINK, BUT I WILL GLADLY TAKE BOTH IN THE DAYS AHEAD OF US.
HOWEVER, YOU ARE THE PART THAT'S NEEDED MOST.
CAREFUL, OLD FRIEND, OR YOU'LL SOAK THE BREAD THROUGH WITH TOO MUCH BUTTER!
I'VE AGREED TO THIS MADNESS AND REQUIRE NO MORE FLATTERY.
NOW. EVERYONE GET YOUR REST.
WE RIDE AT DAWN AND WHO KNOWS WHAT EXCITEMENT AND ADVENTURE AWAIT US?

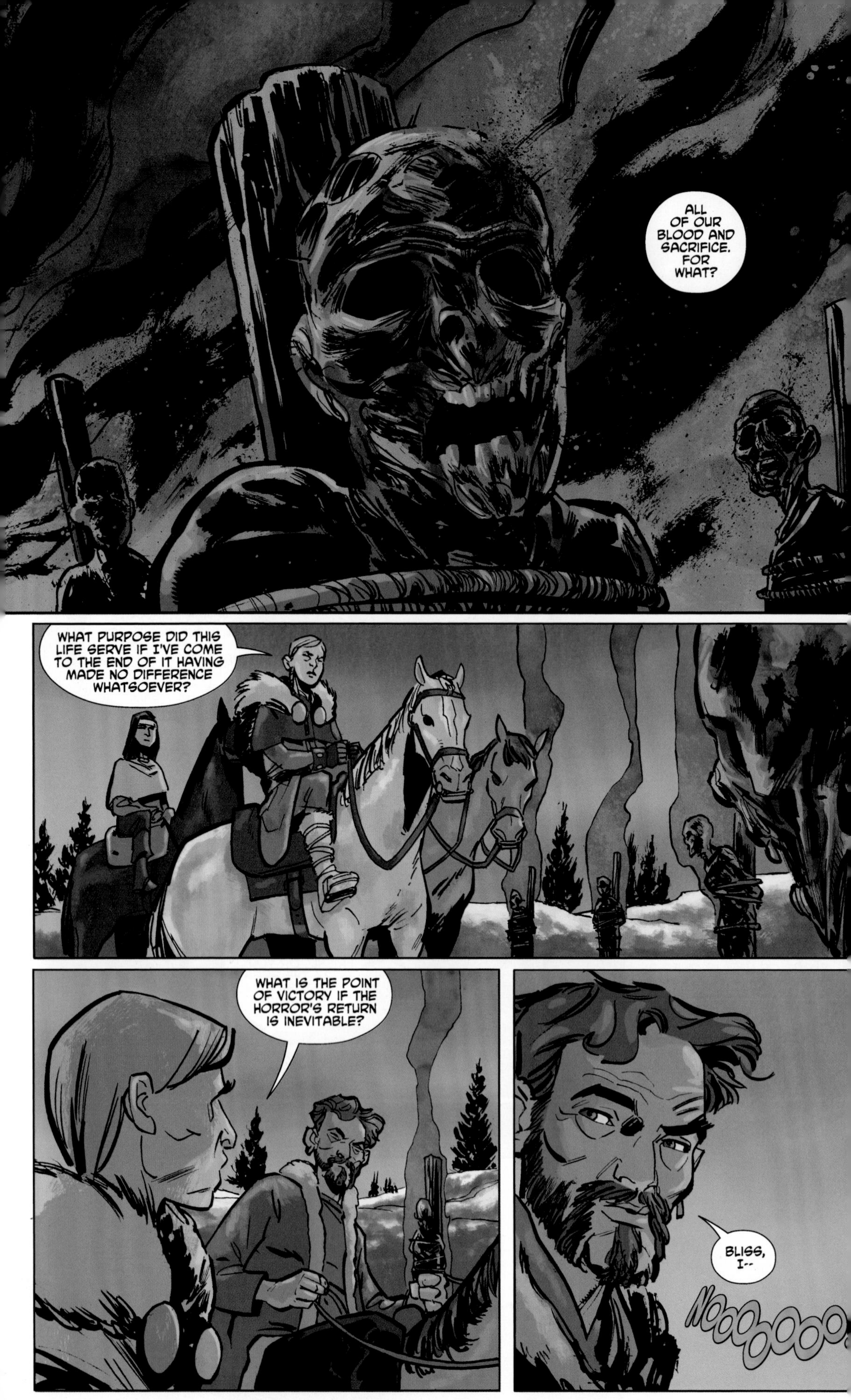
ALL OF OUR BLOOD AND SACRIFICE. FOR WHAT?
WHAT PURPOSE DID THIS LIFE SERVE IF I'VE COME TO THE END OF IT HAVING MADE NO DIFFERENCE WHATSOEVER?
WHAT IS THE POINT OF VICTORY IF THE HORROR'S RETURN IS INEVITABLE?
BLISS, I--
NOOOOOOOO

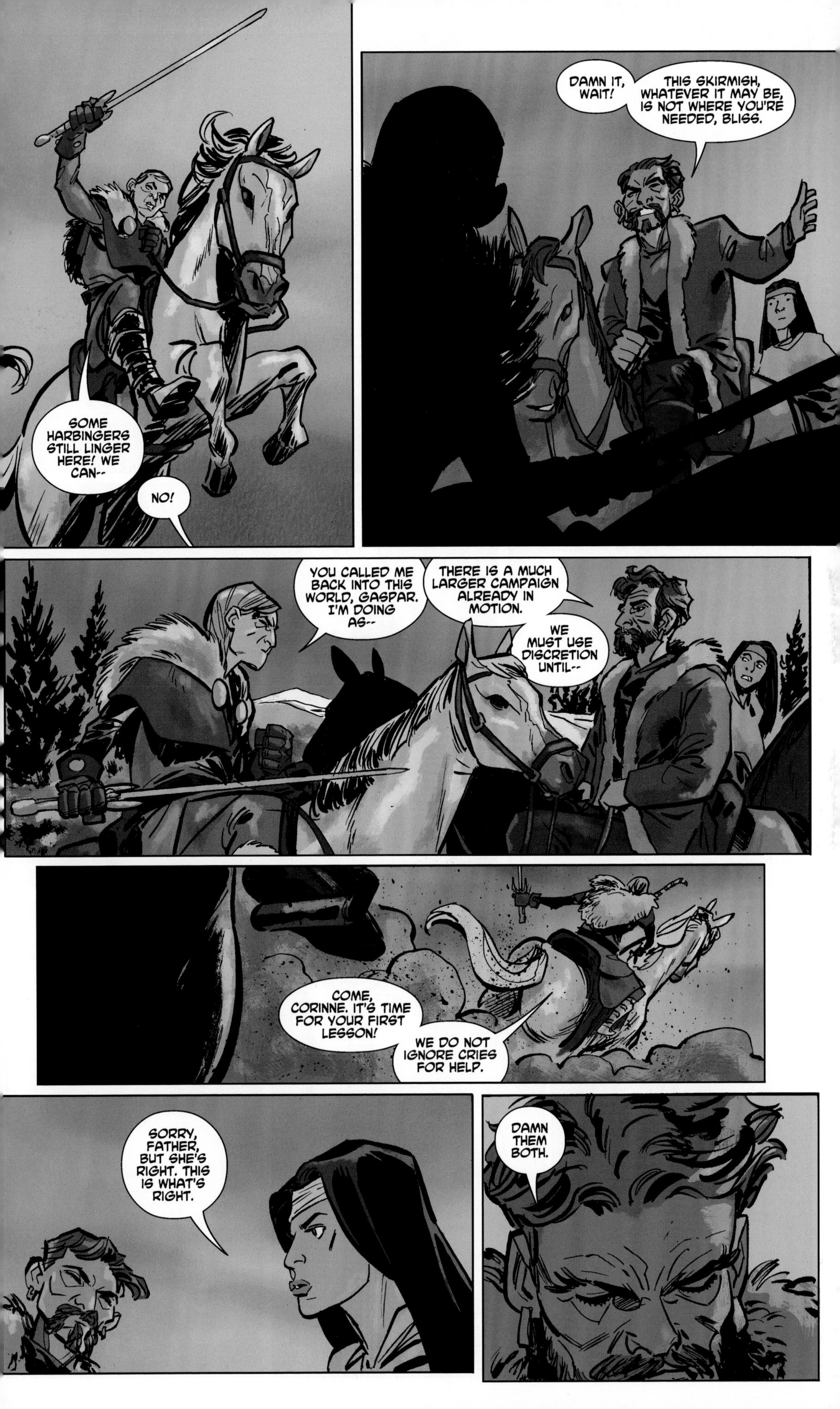
SOME HARBINGERS STILL LINGER HERE! WE CAN--
NO!
DAMN IT, WAIT!
THIS SKIRMISH, WHATEVER IT MAY BE, IS NOT WHERE YOU'RE NEEDED, BLISS.
YOU CALLED ME BACK INTO THIS WORLD, GASPAR. I'M DOING AS--
THERE IS A MUCH LARGER CAMPAIGN ALREADY IN MOTION.
WE MUST USE DISCRETION UNTIL--
COME, CORINNE. IT'S TIME FOR YOUR FIRST LESSON!
WE DO NOT IGNORE CRIES FOR HELP.
SORRY, FATHER, BUT SHE'S RIGHT. THIS IS WHAT'S RIGHT.
DAMN THEM BOTH.

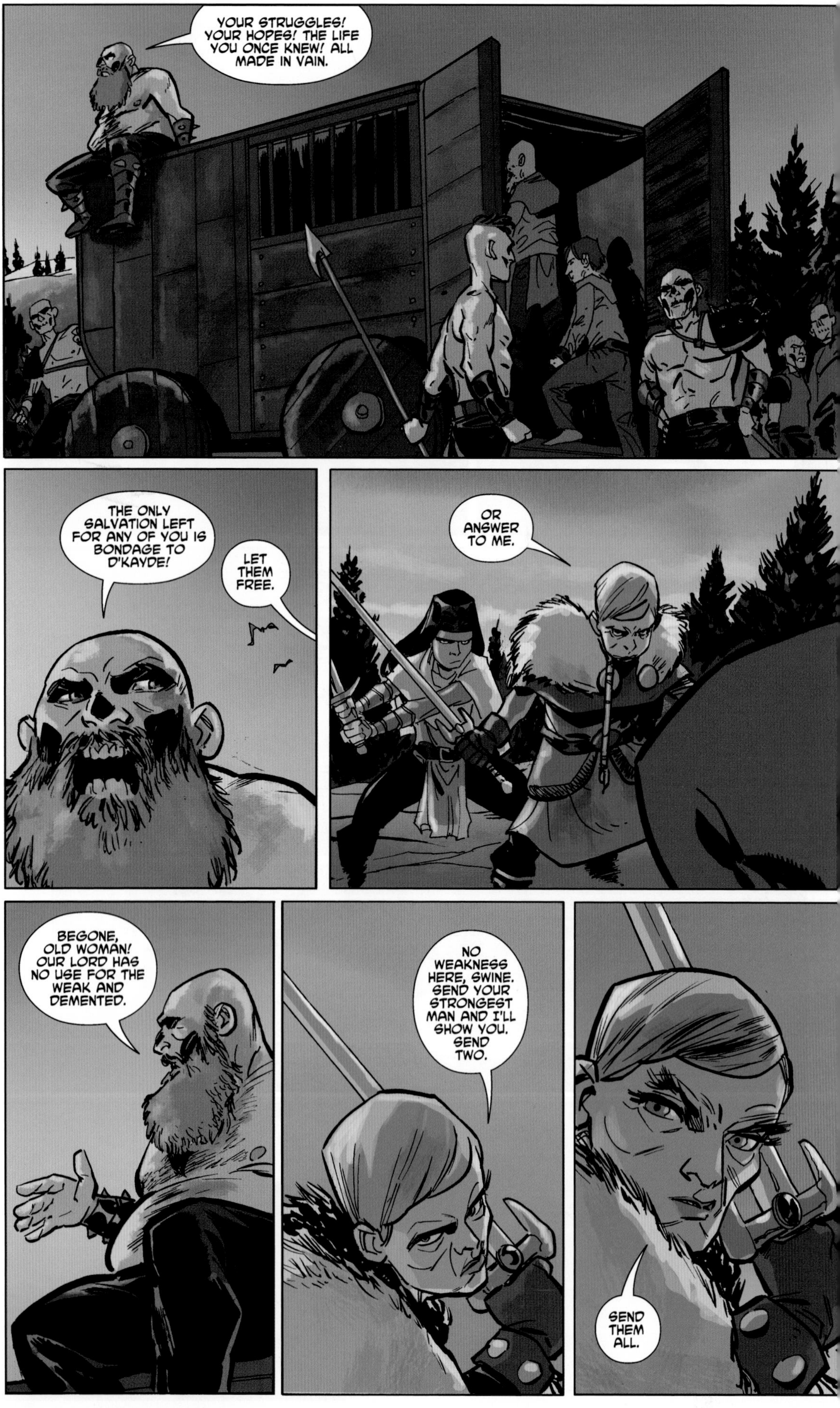

YOUR STRUGGLES! YOUR HOPES! THE LIFE YOU ONCE KNEW! ALL MADE IN VAIN.
THE ONLY SALVATION LEFT FOR ANY OF YOU IS BONDAGE TO D'KAYDE!
LET THEM FREE.
OR ANSWER TO ME.
BEGONE, OLD WOMAN! OUR LORD HAS NO USE FOR THE WEAK AND DEMENTED.
NO WEAKNESS HERE, SWINE. SEND YOUR STRONGEST MAN AND I'LL SHOW YOU. SEND TWO.
SEND THEM ALL.

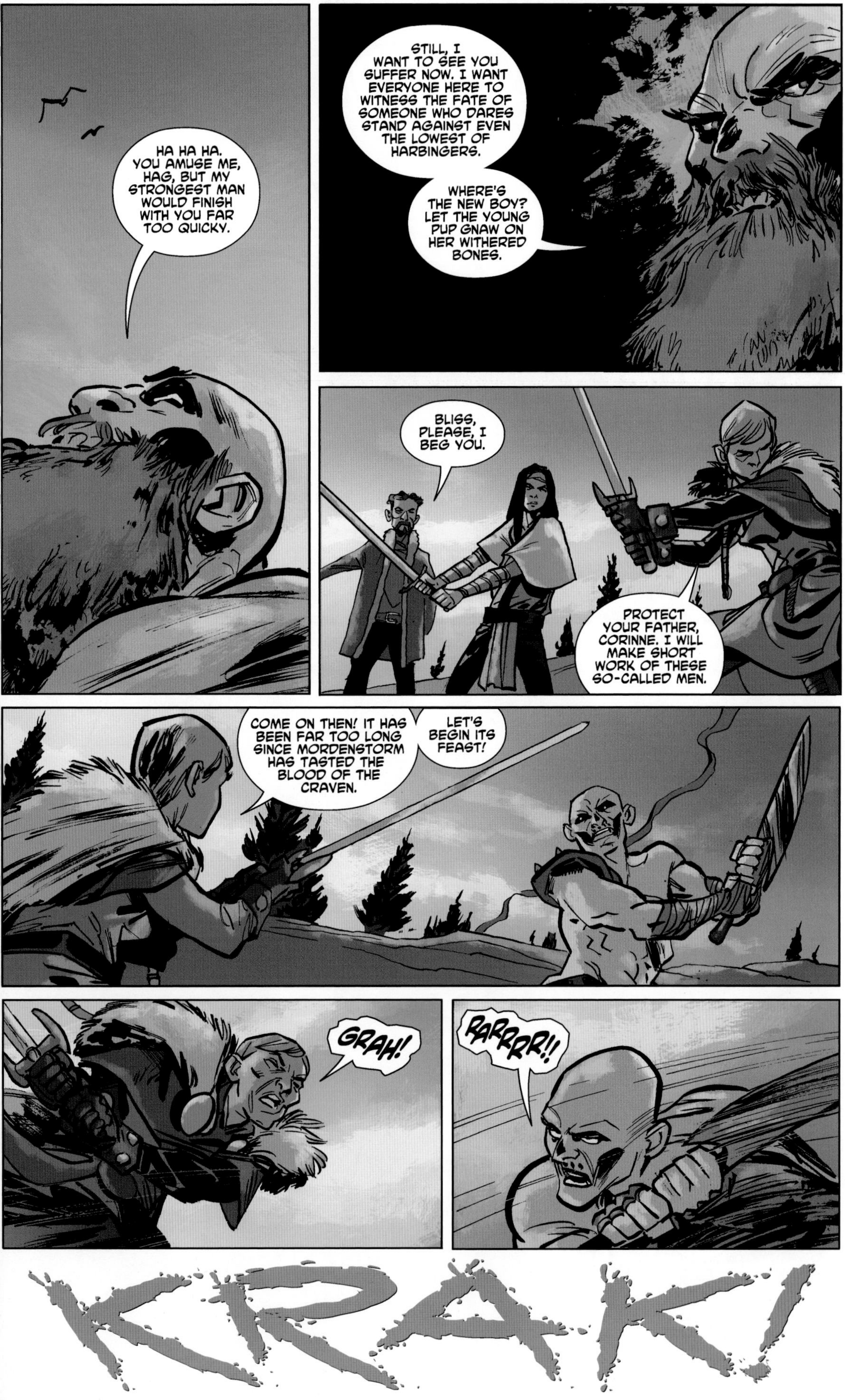
HA HA HA. YOU AMUSE ME, HAG, BUT MY STRONGEST MAN WOULD FINISH WITH YOU FAR TOO QUICKY.
STILL, I WANT TO SEE YOU SUFFER NOW. I WANT EVERYONE HERE TO WITNESS THE FATE OF SOMEONE WHO DARES STAND AGAINST EVEN THE LOWEST OF HARBINGERS.
WHERE'S THE NEW BOY? LET THE YOUNG PUP GNAW ON HER WITHERED BONES.
BLISS, PLEASE, I BEG YOU.
PROTECT YOUR FATHER, CORINNE. I WILL MAKE SHORT WORK OF THESE SO-CALLED MEN.
COME ON THEN! IT HAS BEEN FAR TOO LONG SINCE MORDENSTORM HAS TASTED THE BLOOD OF THE CRAVEN.
LET'S BEGIN ITS FEAST!
GRAH!
RARRRR!!
KRAK!

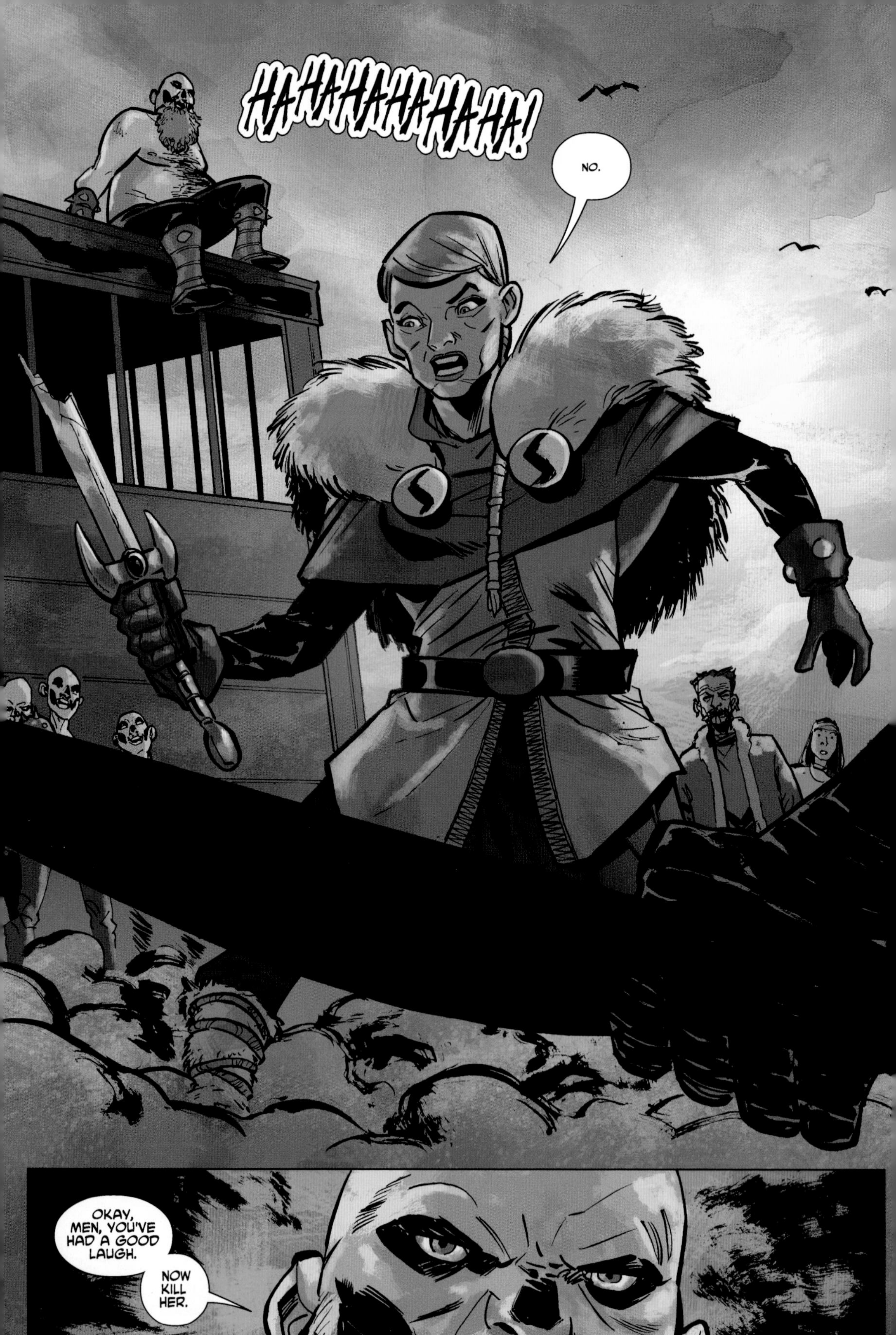
HAHAHAHAHAHAHA!
NO.

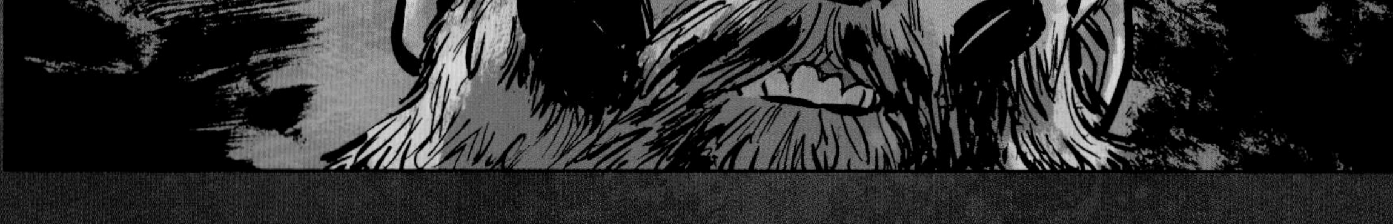
OKAY, MEN, YOU'VE HAD A GOOD LAUGH.
NOW KILL HER.

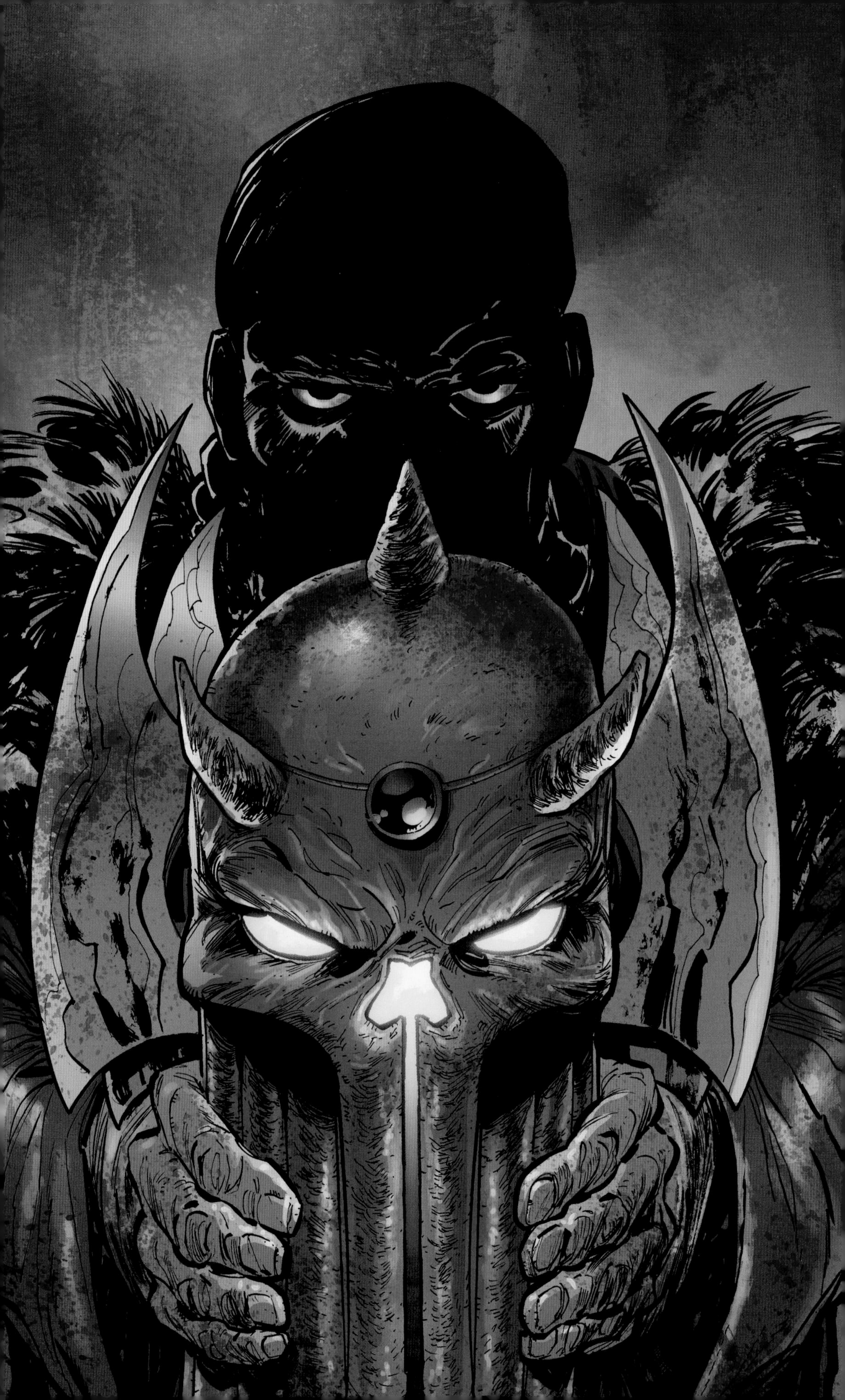

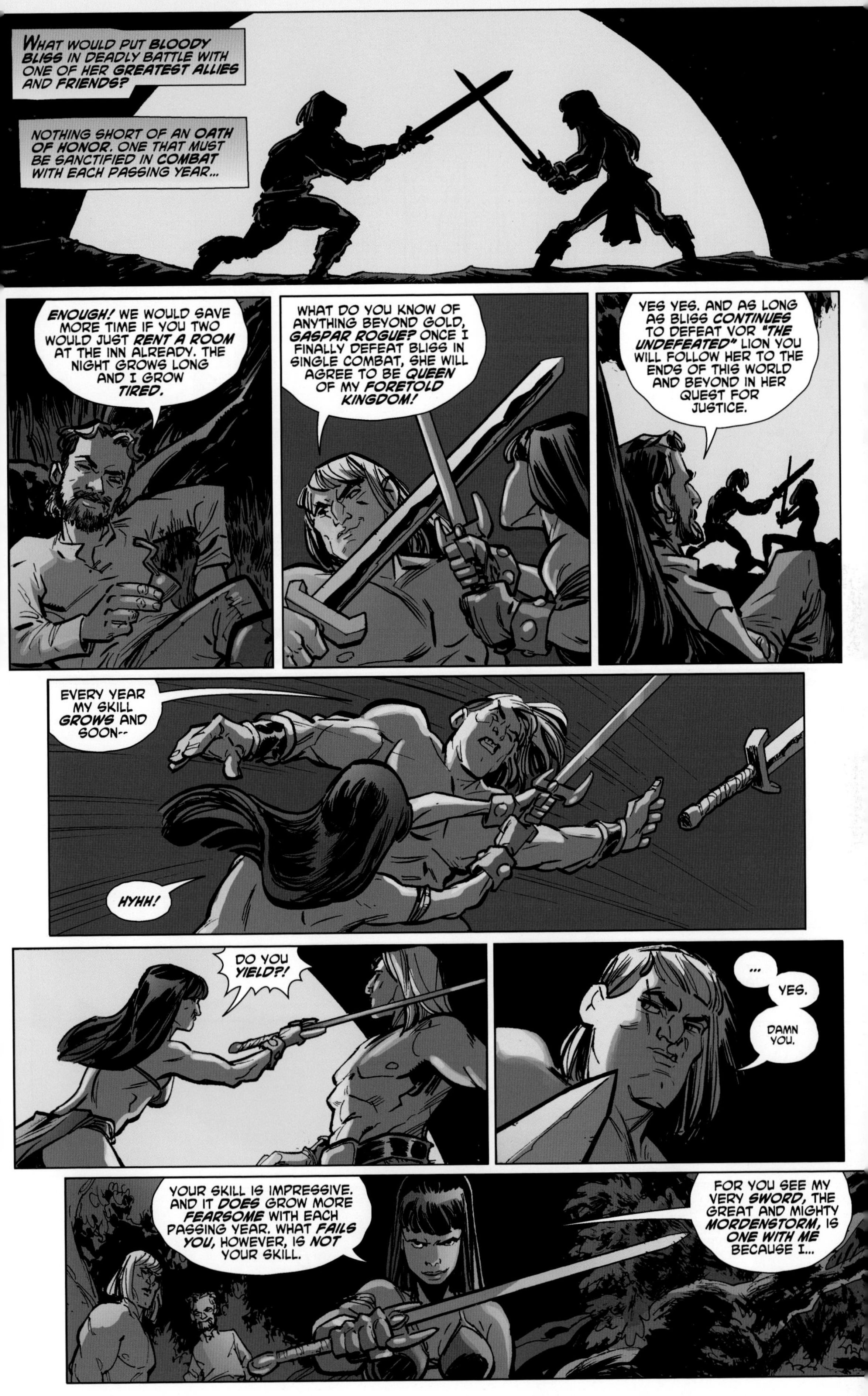
WHAT WOULD PUT BLOODY BLISS IN DEADLY BATTLE WITH ONE OF HER GREATEST ALLIES AND FRIENDS?
NOTHING SHORT OF AN OATH OF HONOR. ONE THAT MUST BE SANCTIFIED IN COMBAT WITH EACH PASSING YEAR...
ENOUGH! WE WOULD SAVE MORE TIME IF YOU TWO WOULD JUST RENT A ROOM AT THE INN ALREADY. THE NIGHT GROWS LONG AND I GROW TIRED.
WHAT DO YOU KNOW OF ANYTHING BEYOND GOLD, GASPAR ROGUE? ONCE I FINALLY DEFEAT BLISS IN SINGLE COMBAT, SHE WILL AGREE TO BE QUEEN OF MY FORETOLD KINGDOM!
YES YES. AND AS LONG AS BLISS CONTINUES TO DEFEAT VOR "THE UNDEFEATED" LION YOU WILL FOLLOW HER TO THE ENDS OF THIS WORLD AND BEYOND IN HER QUEST FOR JUSTICE.
EVERY YEAR MY SKILL GROWS AND SOON--
HYHH!
DO YOU YIELD?!
...
YES.
DAMN YOU.
YOUR SKILL IS IMPRESSIVE. AND IT DOES GROW MORE FEARSOME WITH EACH PASSING YEAR. WHAT FAILS YOU, HOWEVER, IS NOT YOUR SKILL.
FOR YOU SEE MY VERY SWORD, THE GREAT AND MIGHTY MORDENSTORM, IS ONE WITH ME BECAUSE I...

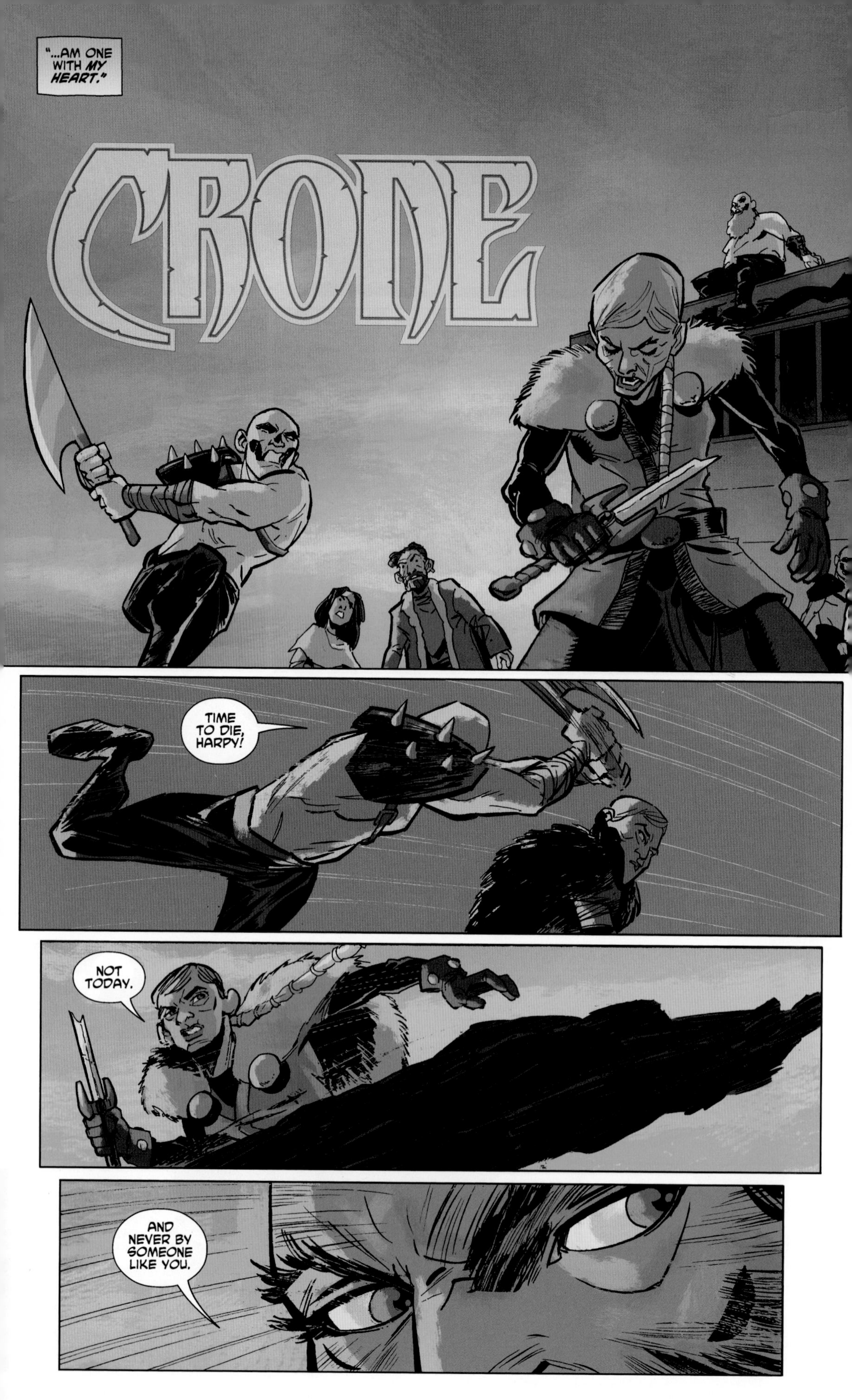
"...AM ONE WITH MY HEART."
CRONE
TIME TO DIE, HARPY!
NOT TODAY.
AND NEVER BY SOMEONE LIKE YOU.

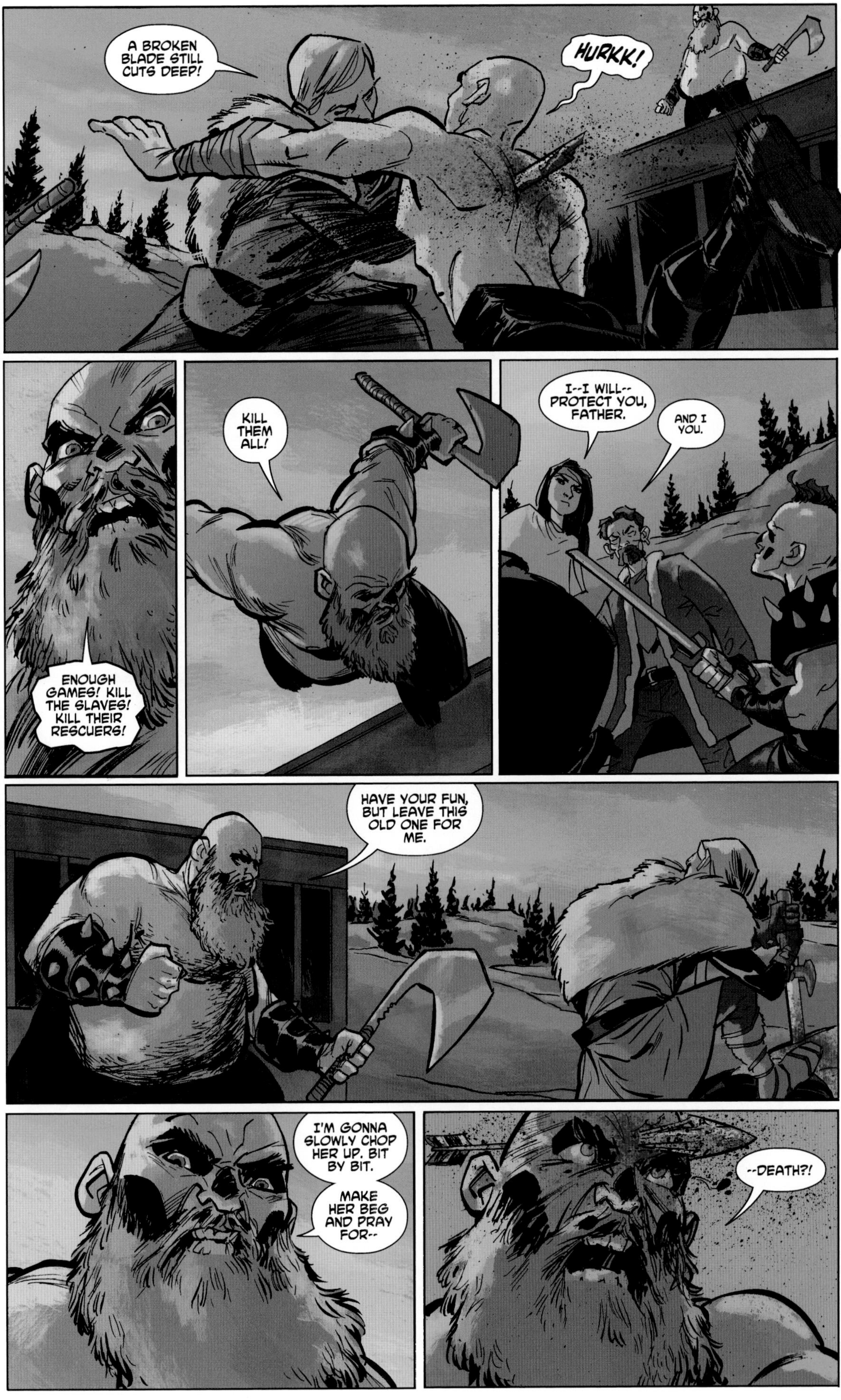
A BROKEN BLADE STILL CUTS DEEP!
HURKK!
ENOUGH GAMES! KILL THE SLAVES! KILL THEIR RESCUERS!
KILL THEM ALL!
I--I WILL--PROTECT YOU, FATHER.
AND I YOU.
HAVE YOUR FUN, BUT LEAVE THIS OLD ONE FOR ME.
I'M GONNA SLOWLY CHOP HER UP. BIT BY BIT.
MAKE HER BEG AND PRAY FOR--
--DEATH?!

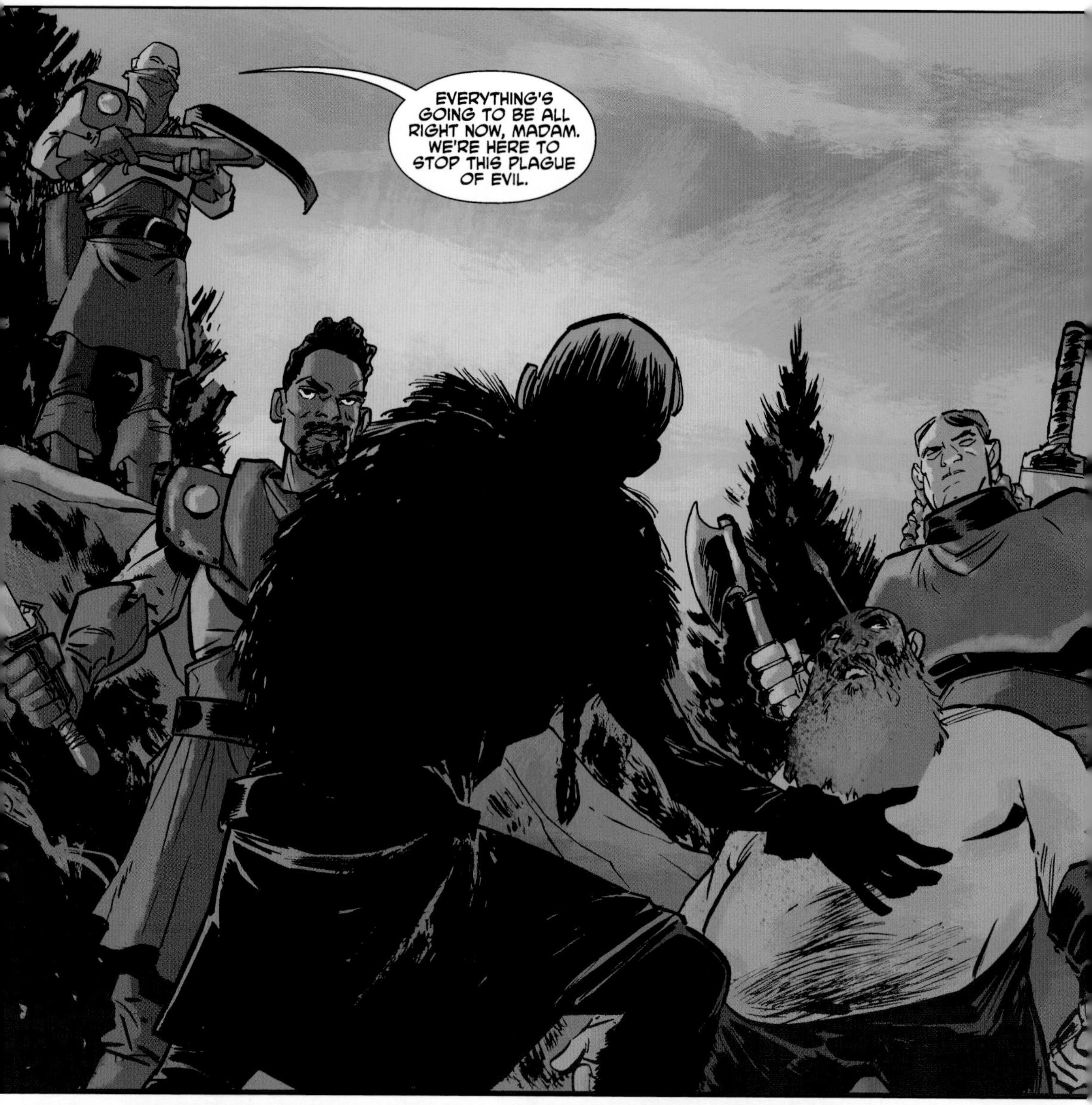
EVERYTHING'S GOING TO BE ALL RIGHT NOW, MADAM. WE'RE HERE TO STOP THIS PLAGUE OF EVIL.

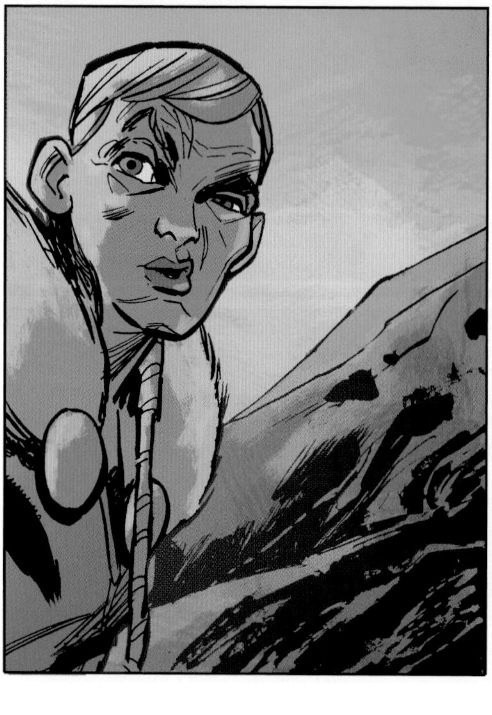

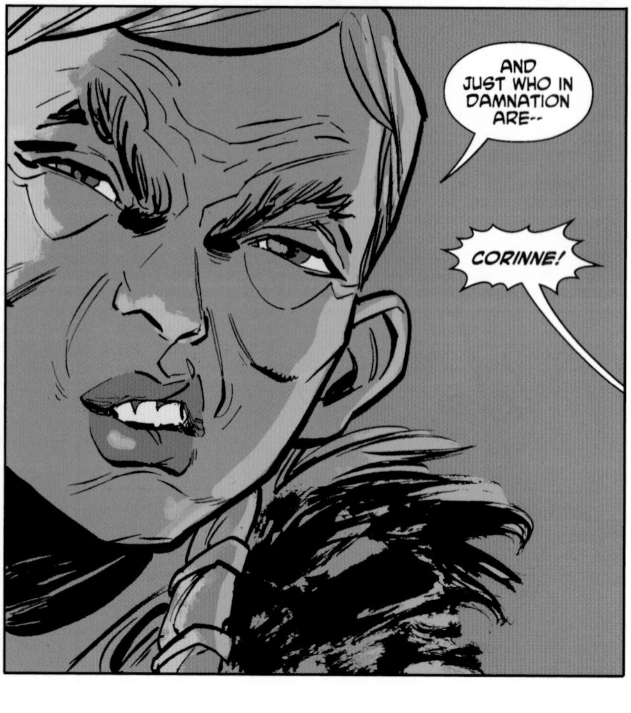
AND JUST WHO IN DAMNATION ARE--
CORINNE!

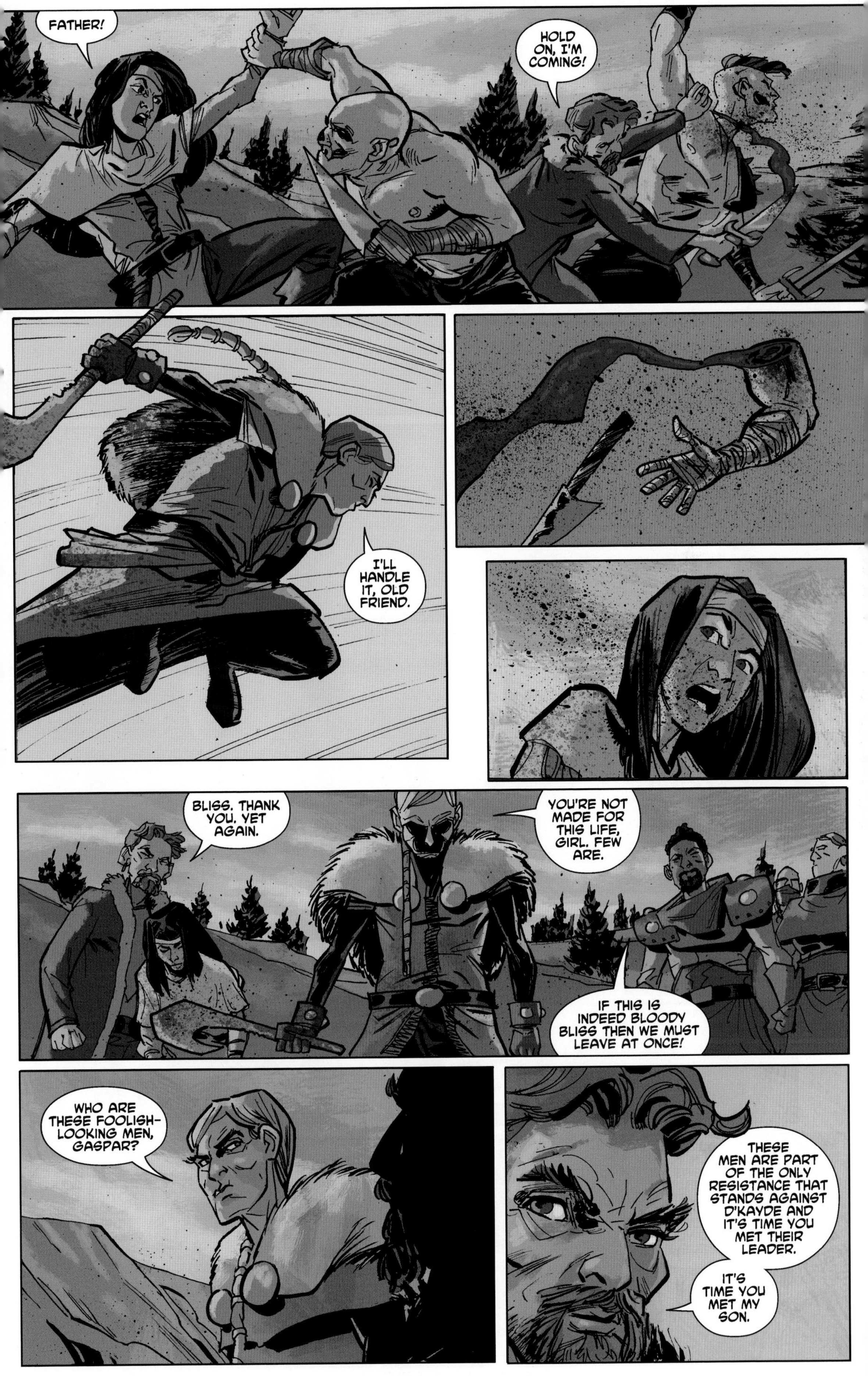
FATHER!
HOLD ON, I'M COMING!
I'LL HANDLE IT, OLD FRIEND.
BLISS. THANK YOU. YET AGAIN.
YOU'RE NOT MADE FOR THIS LIFE, GIRL. FEW ARE.
IF THIS IS INDEED BLOODY BLISS THEN WE MUST LEAVE AT ONCE!
WHO ARE THESE FOOLISH-LOOKING MEN, GASPAR?
THESE MEN ARE PART OF THE ONLY RESISTANCE THAT STANDS AGAINST D'KAYDE AND IT'S TIME YOU MET THEIR LEADER.
IT'S TIME YOU MET MY SON.

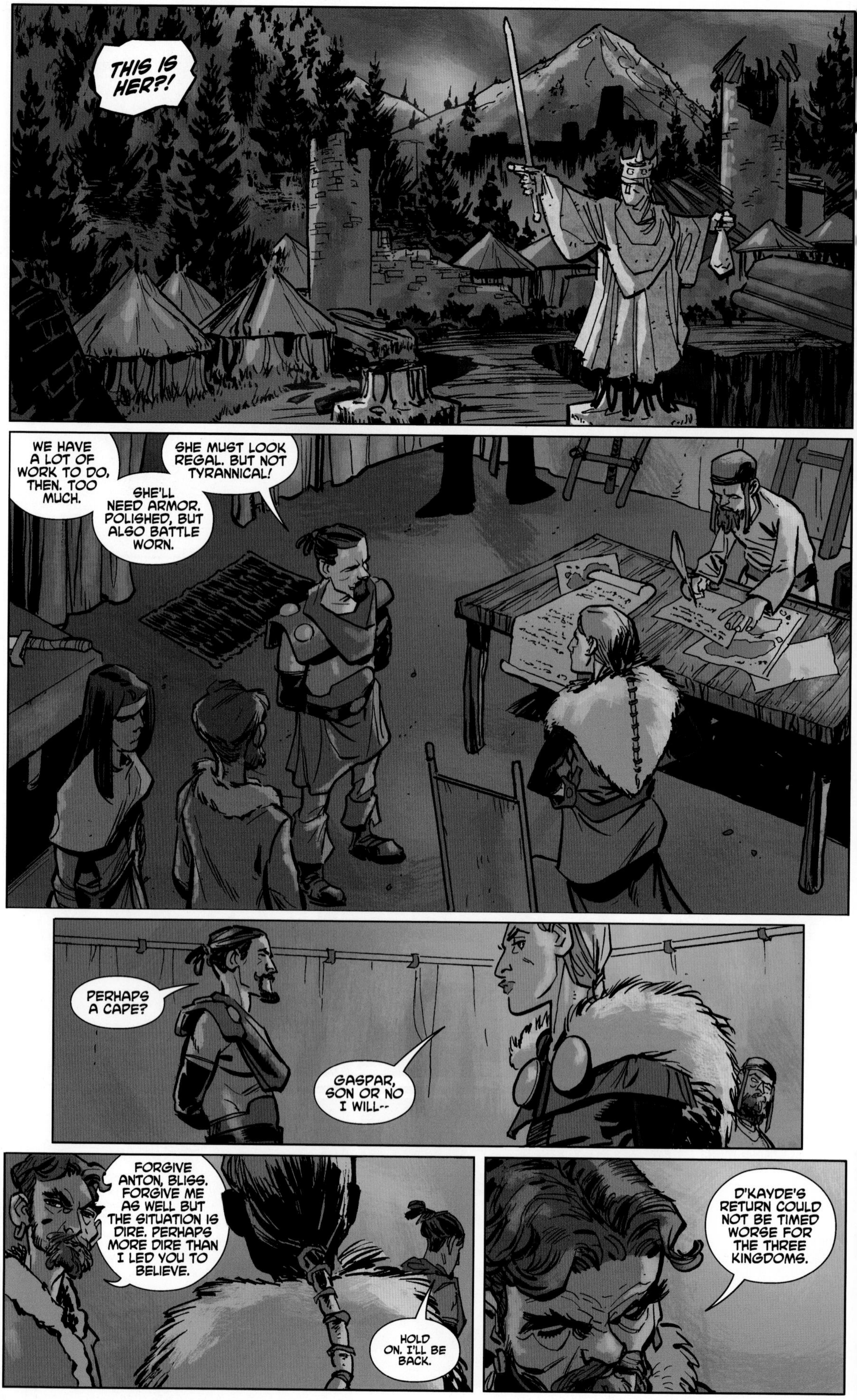
THIS IS HER?!
WE HAVE A LOT OF WORK TO DO, THEN. TOO MUCH.
SHE MUST LOOK REGAL. BUT NOT TYRANNICAL!
SHE'LL NEED ARMOR. POLISHED, BUT ALSO BATTLE WORN.
PERHAPS A CAPE?
GASPAR, SON OR NO I WILL--
FORGIVE ANTON, BLISS. FORGIVE ME AS WELL BUT THE SITUATION IS DIRE. PERHAPS MORE DIRE THAN I LED YOU TO BELIEVE.
HOLD ON. I'LL BE BACK.
D'KAYDE'S RETURN COULD NOT BE TIMED WORSE FOR THE THREE KINGDOMS.

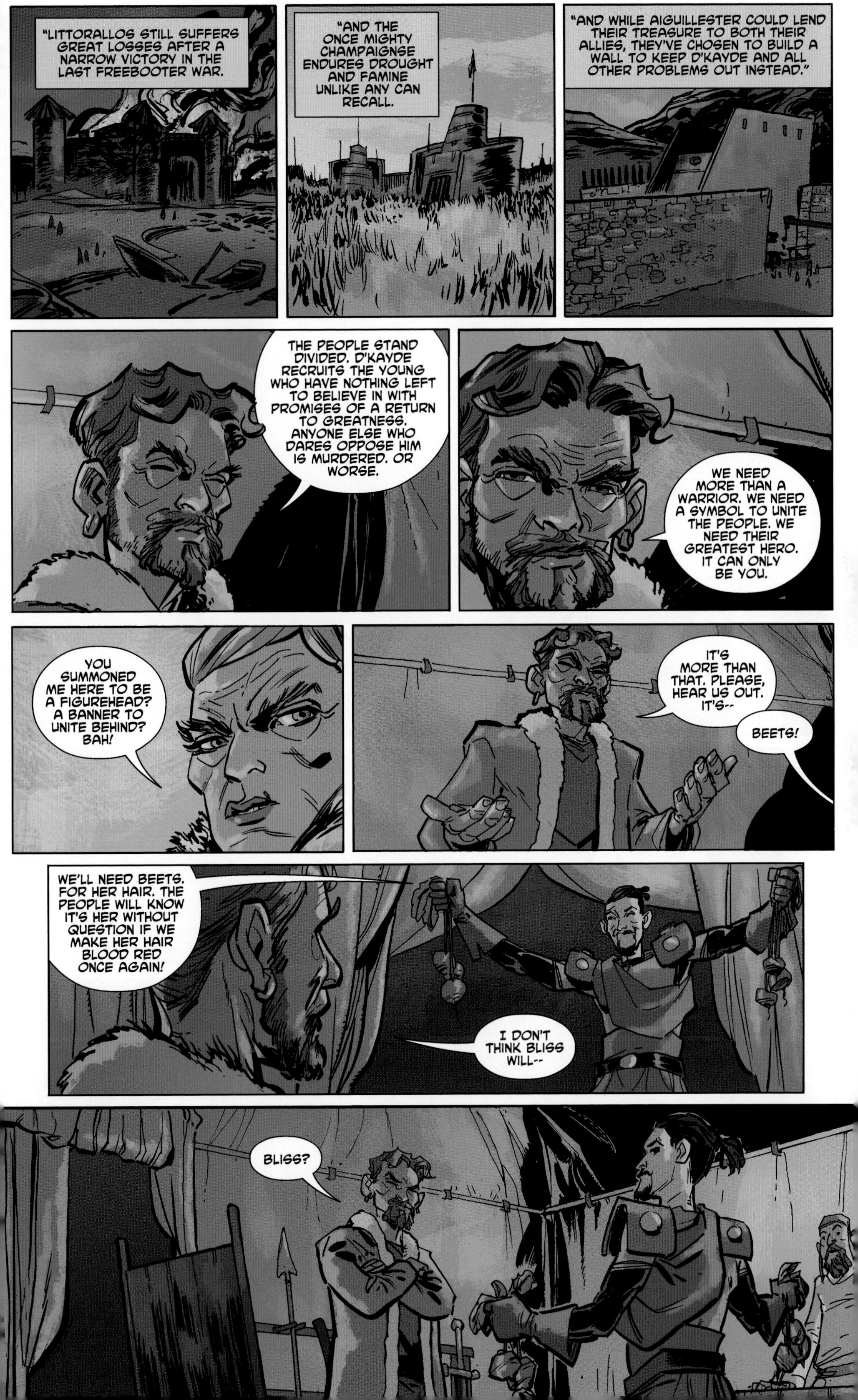
"LITTORALLOS STILL SUFFERS GREAT LOSSES AFTER A NARROW VICTORY IN THE LAST FREEBOOTER WAR.
"AND THE ONCE MIGHTY CHAMPAIGNSE ENDURES DROUGHT AND FAMINE UNLIKE ANY CAN RECALL.
"AND WHILE AIGUILLESTER COULD LEND THEIR TREASURE TO BOTH THEIR ALLIES, THEY'VE CHOSEN TO BUILD A WALL TO KEEP D'KAYDE AND ALL OTHER PROBLEMS OUT INSTEAD."
THE PEOPLE STAND DIVIDED. D'KAYDE RECRUITS THE YOUNG WHO HAVE NOTHING LEFT TO BELIEVE IN WITH PROMISES OF A RETURN TO GREATNESS. ANYONE ELSE WHO DARES OPPOSE HIM IS MURDERED. OR WORSE.
WE NEED MORE THAN A WARRIOR. WE NEED A SYMBOL TO UNITE THE PEOPLE. WE NEED THEIR GREATEST HERO. IT CAN ONLY BE YOU.
YOU SUMMONED ME HERE TO BE A FIGUREHEAD? A BANNER TO UNITE BEHIND? BAH!
IT'S MORE THAN THAT. PLEASE, HEAR US OUT. IT'S--
BEETS!
WE'LL NEED BEETS. FOR HER HAIR. THE PEOPLE WILL KNOW IT'S HER WITHOUT QUESTION IF WE MAKE HER HAIR BLOOD RED ONCE AGAIN!
I DON'T THINK BLISS WILL--
BLISS?

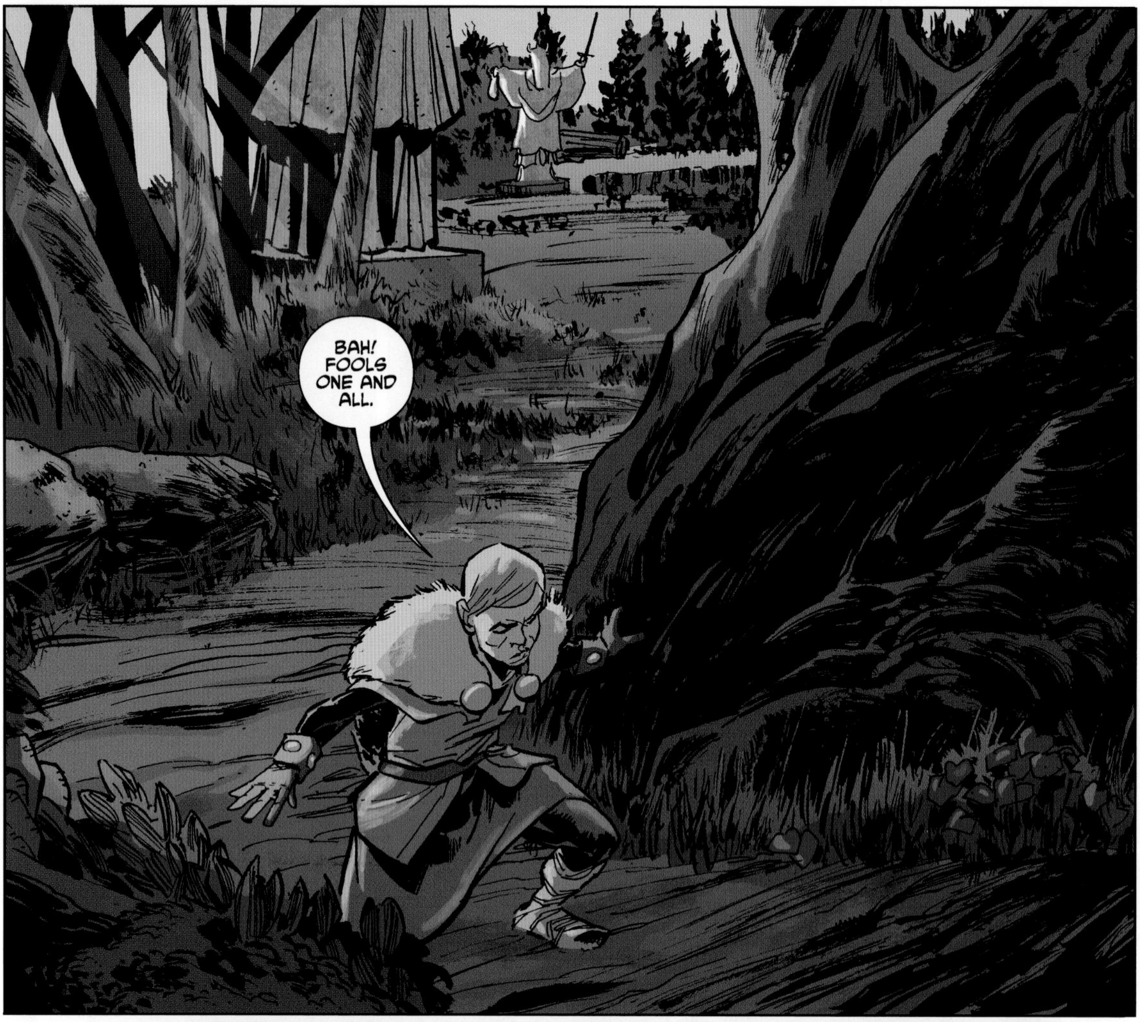
BAH! FOOLS ONE AND ALL.

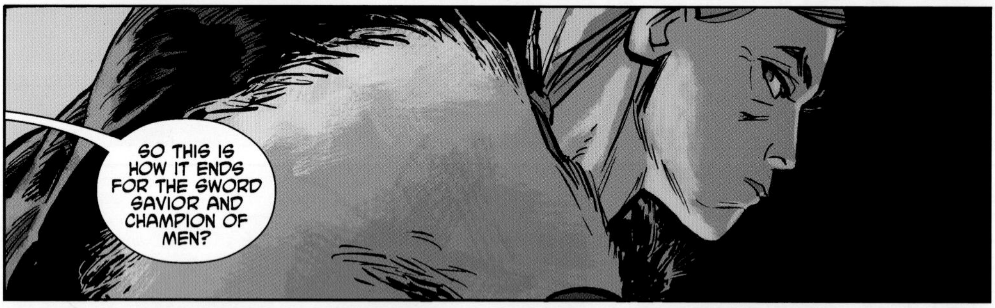
SO THIS IS HOW IT ENDS FOR THE SWORD SAVIOR AND CHAMPION OF MEN?

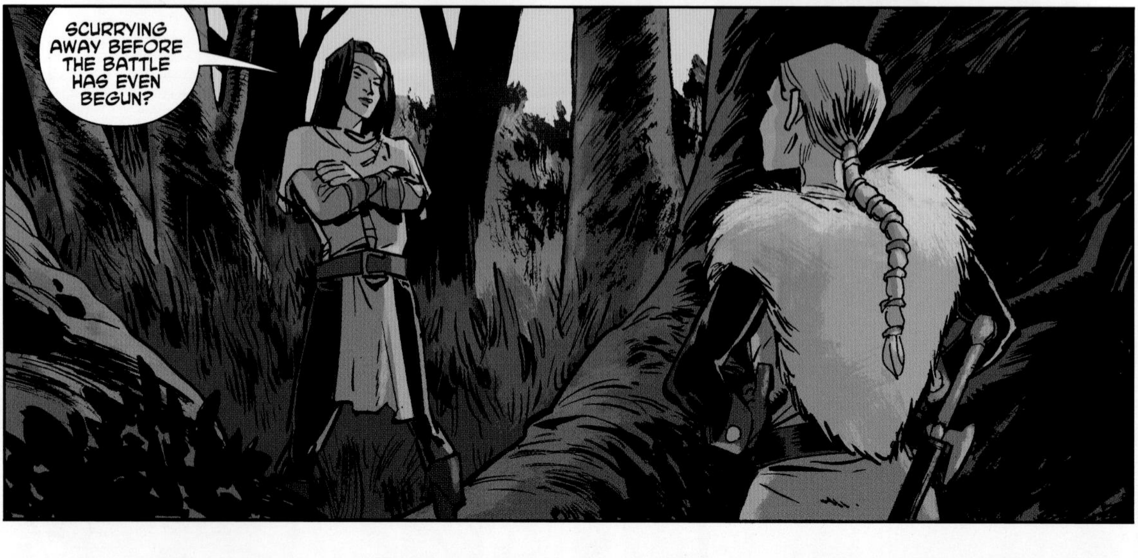
SCURRYING AWAY BEFORE THE BATTLE HAS EVEN BEGUN?

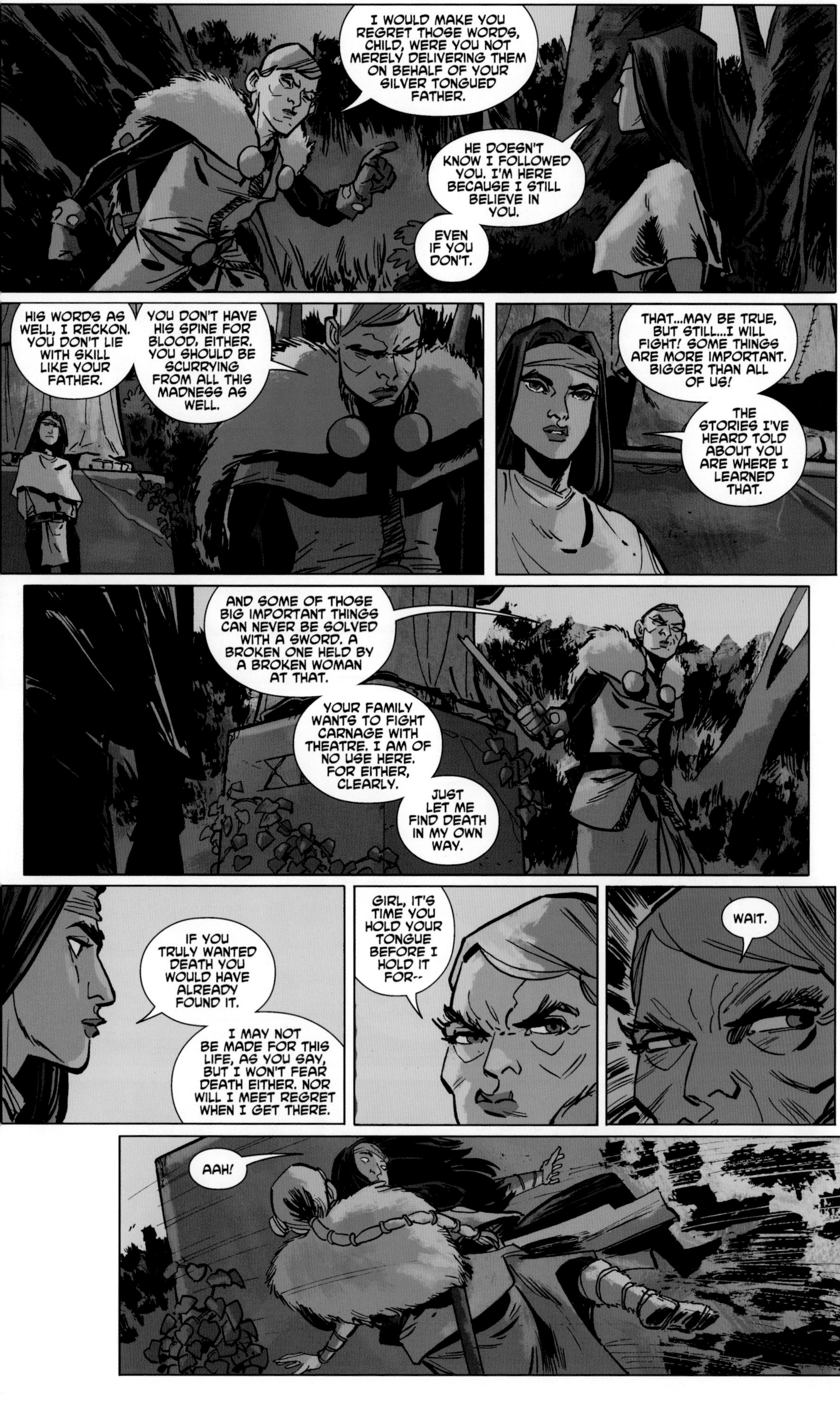
I WOULD MAKE YOU REGRET THOSE WORDS, CHILD, WERE YOU NOT MERELY DELIVERING THEM ON BEHALF OF YOUR SILVER TONGUED FATHER.
HE DOESN'T KNOW I FOLLOWED YOU. I'M HERE BECAUSE I STILL BELIEVE IN YOU.
EVEN IF YOU DON'T.
HIS WORDS AS WELL, I RECKON. YOU DON'T LIE WITH SKILL LIKE YOUR FATHER.
YOU DON'T HAVE HIS SPINE FOR BLOOD, EITHER. YOU SHOULD BE SCURRYING FROM ALL THIS MADNESS AS WELL.
THAT...MAY BE TRUE, BUT STILL...I WILL FIGHT! SOME THINGS ARE MORE IMPORTANT. BIGGER THAN ALL OF US!
THE STORIES I'VE HEARD TOLD ABOUT YOU ARE WHERE I LEARNED THAT.
AND SOME OF THOSE BIG IMPORTANT THINGS CAN NEVER BE SOLVED WITH A SWORD. A BROKEN ONE HELD BY A BROKEN WOMAN AT THAT.
YOUR FAMILY WANTS TO FIGHT CARNAGE WITH THEATRE. I AM OF NO USE HERE. FOR EITHER, CLEARLY.
JUST LET ME FIND DEATH IN MY OWN WAY.
IF YOU TRULY WANTED DEATH YOU WOULD HAVE ALREADY FOUND IT.
I MAY NOT BE MADE FOR THIS LIFE, AS YOU SAY, BUT I WON'T FEAR DEATH EITHER. NOR WILL I MEET REGRET WHEN I GET THERE.
GIRL, IT'S TIME YOU HOLD YOUR TONGUE BEFORE I HOLD IT FOR--
WAIT.
AAH!

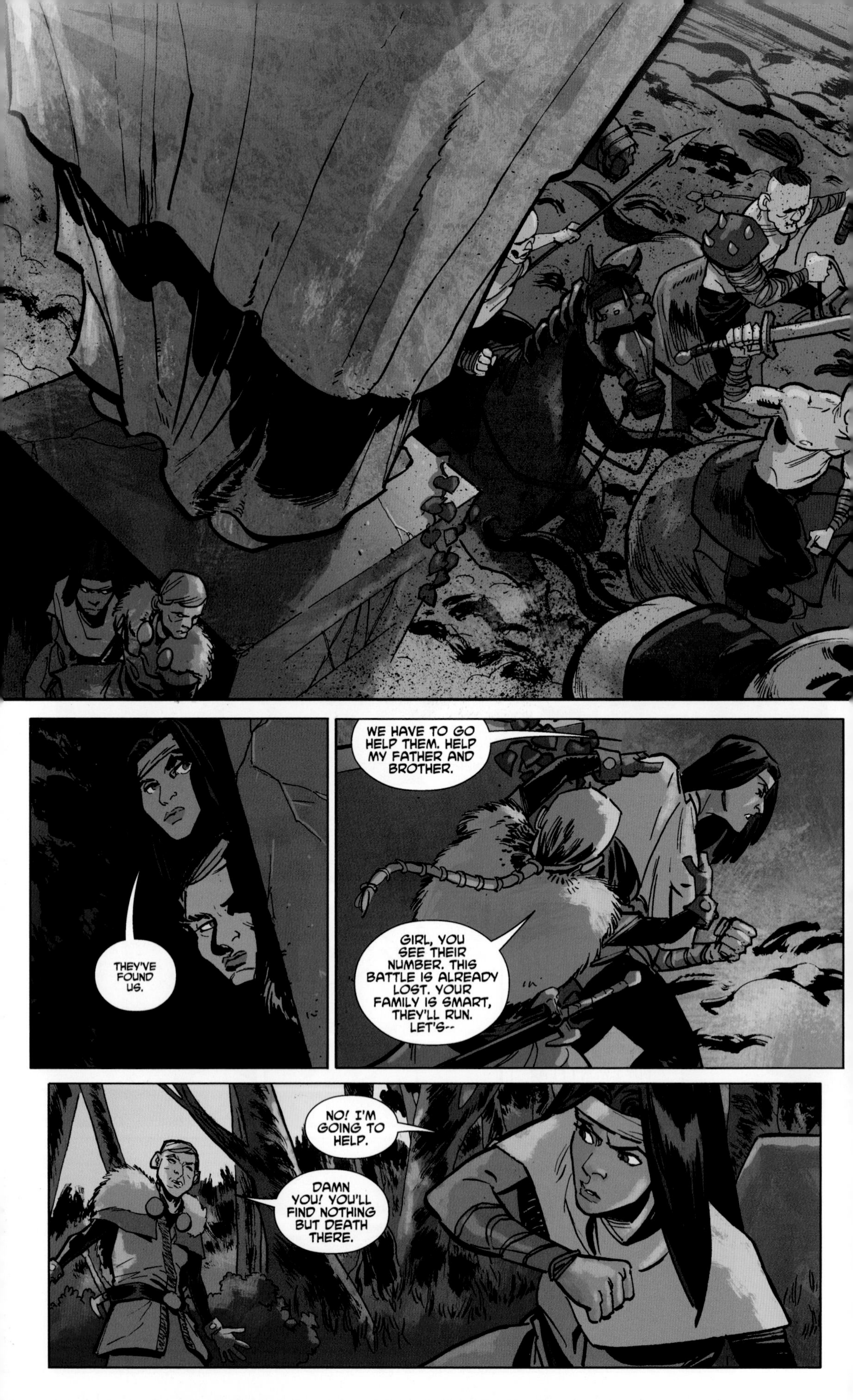
THEY'VE FOUND US.
WE HAVE TO GO HELP THEM. HELP MY FATHER AND BROTHER.
GIRL, YOU SEE THEIR NUMBER. THIS BATTLE IS ALREADY LOST. YOUR FAMILY IS SMART, THEY'LL RUN. LET'S--
NO! I'M GOING TO HELP.
DAMN YOU! YOU'LL FIND NOTHING BUT DEATH THERE.

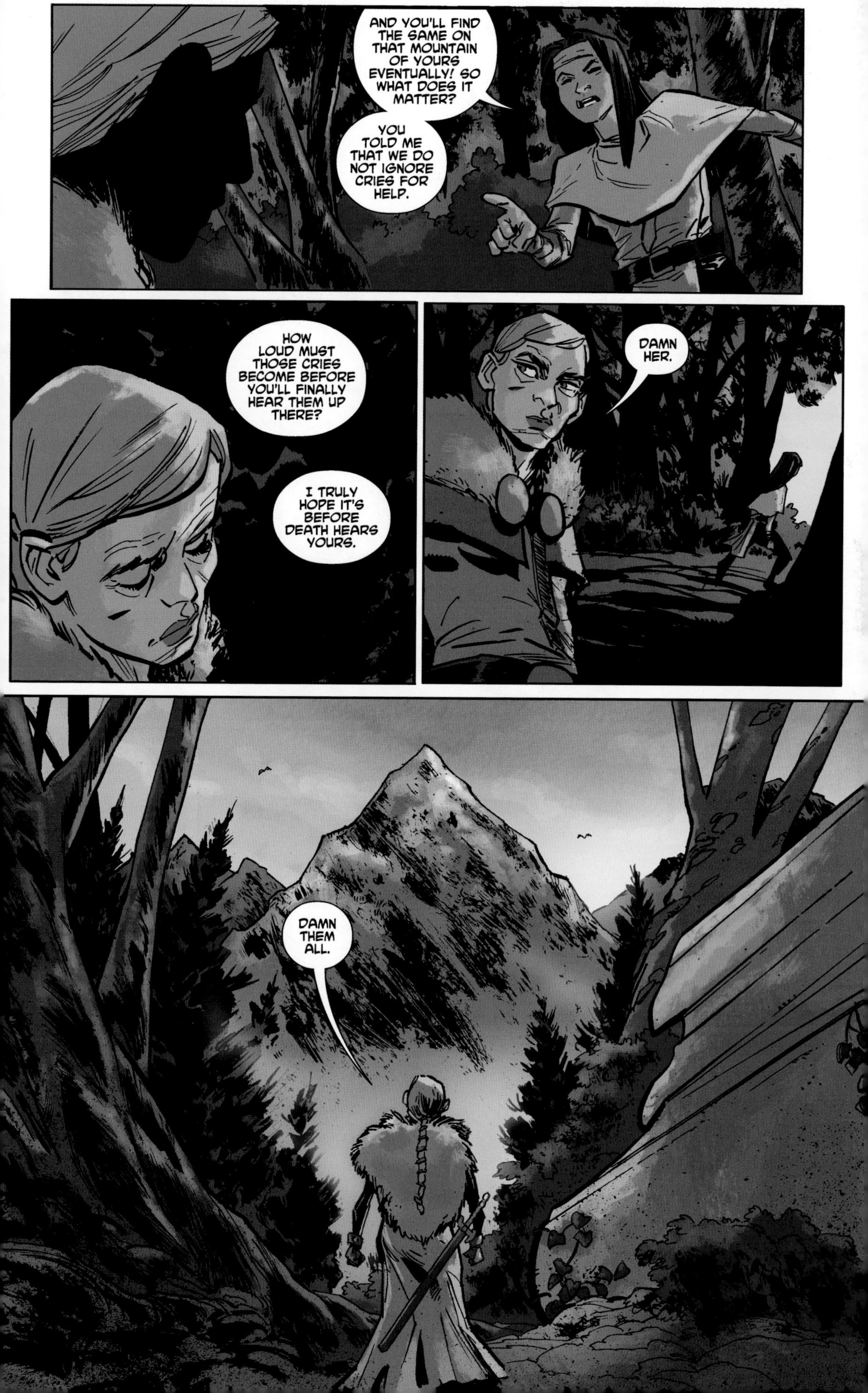
AND YOU'LL FIND THE SAME ON THAT MOUNTAIN OF YOURS EVENTUALLY! SO WHAT DOES IT MATTER?
YOU TOLD ME THAT WE DO NOT IGNORE CRIES FOR HELP.
HOW LOUD MUST THOSE CRIES BECOME BEFORE YOU'LL FINALLY HEAR THEM UP THERE?
I TRULY HOPE IT'S BEFORE DEATH HEARS YOURS.
DAMN HER.
DAMN THEM ALL.

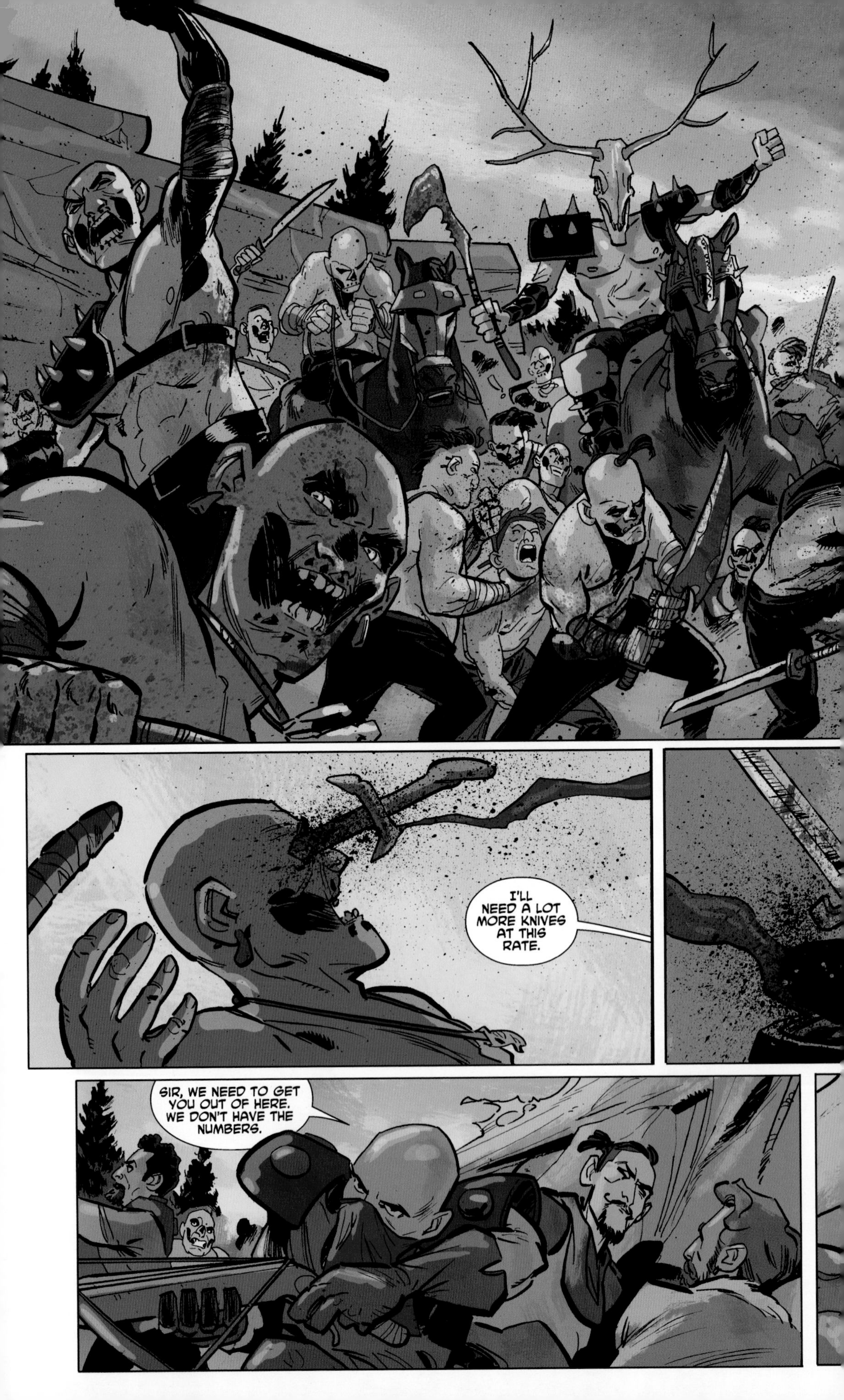
I'LL NEED A LOT MORE KNIVES AT THIS RATE.
SIR, WE NEED TO GET YOU OUT OF HERE. WE DON'T HAVE THE NUMBERS.

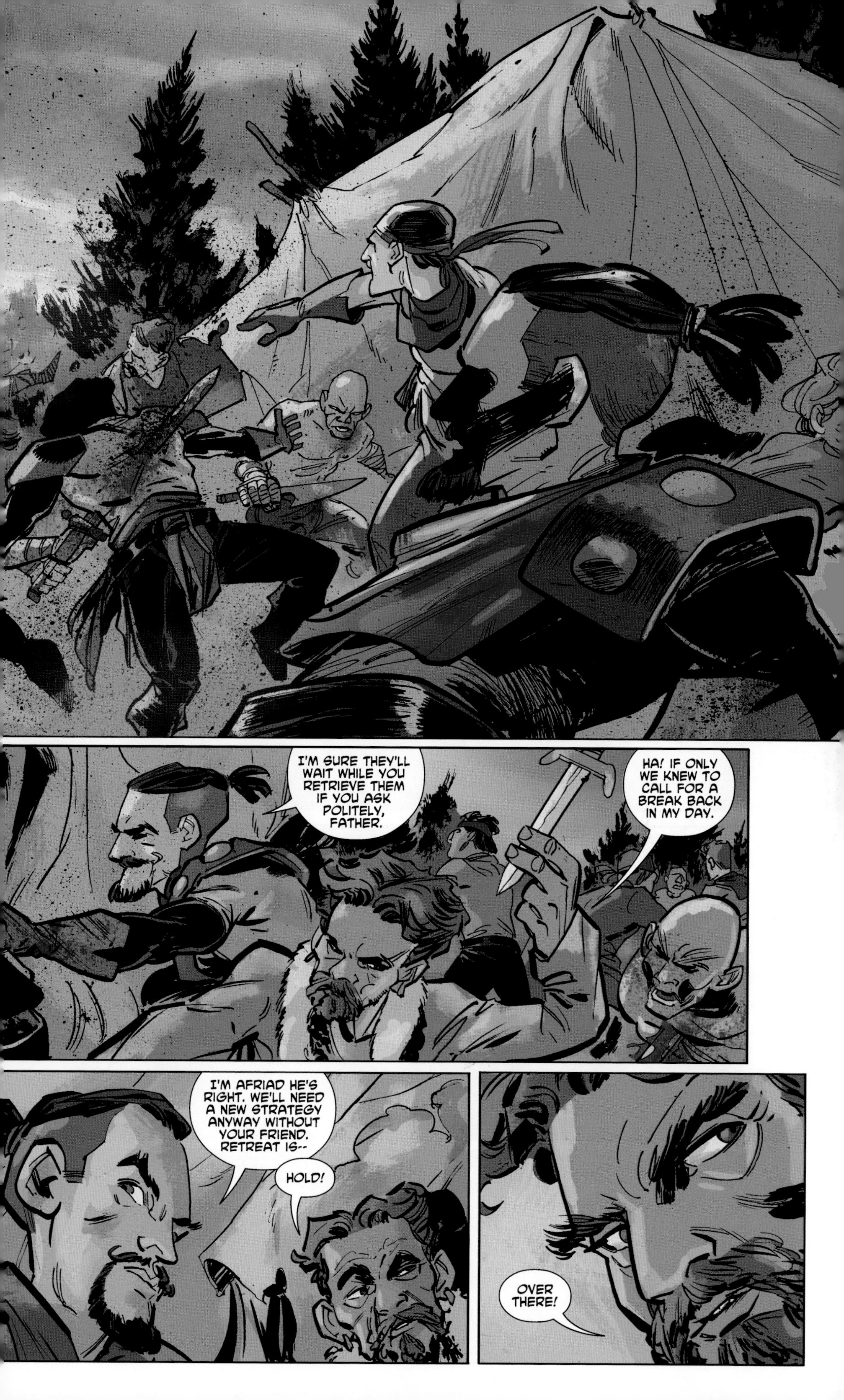
I'M SURE THEY'LL WAIT WHILE YOU RETRIEVE THEM IF YOU ASK POLITELY, FATHER.
HA! IF ONLY WE KNEW TO CALL FOR A BREAK BACK IN MY DAY.
I'M AFRIAD HE'S RIGHT. WE'LL NEED A NEW STRATEGY ANYWAY WITHOUT YOUR FRIEND. RETREAT IS--
HOLD!
OVER THERE!

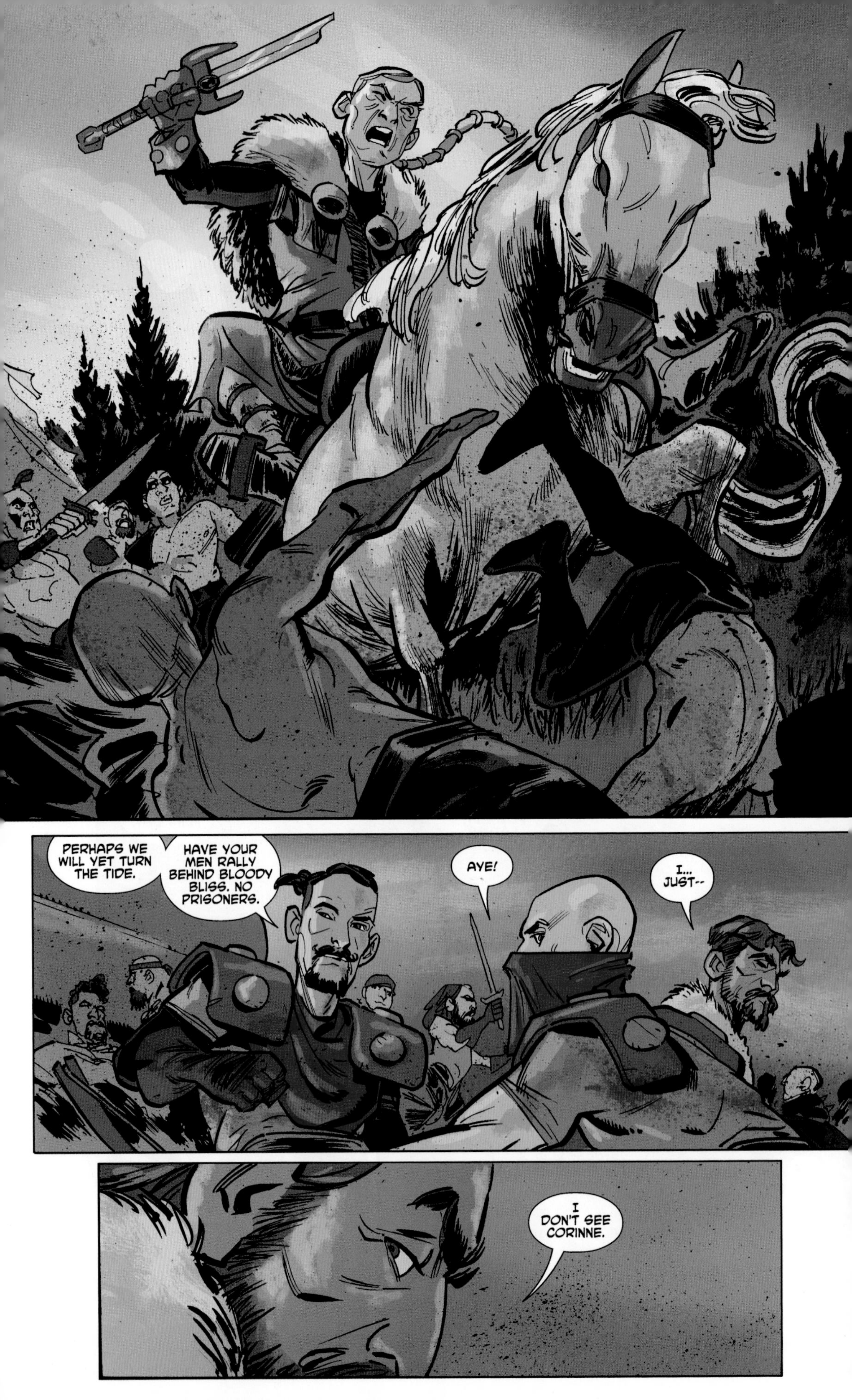
PERHAPS WE WILL YET TURN THE TIDE.
HAVE YOUR MEN RALLY BEHIND BLOODY BLISS. NO PRISONERS.
AYE!
I... JUST--
I DON'T SEE CORINNE.

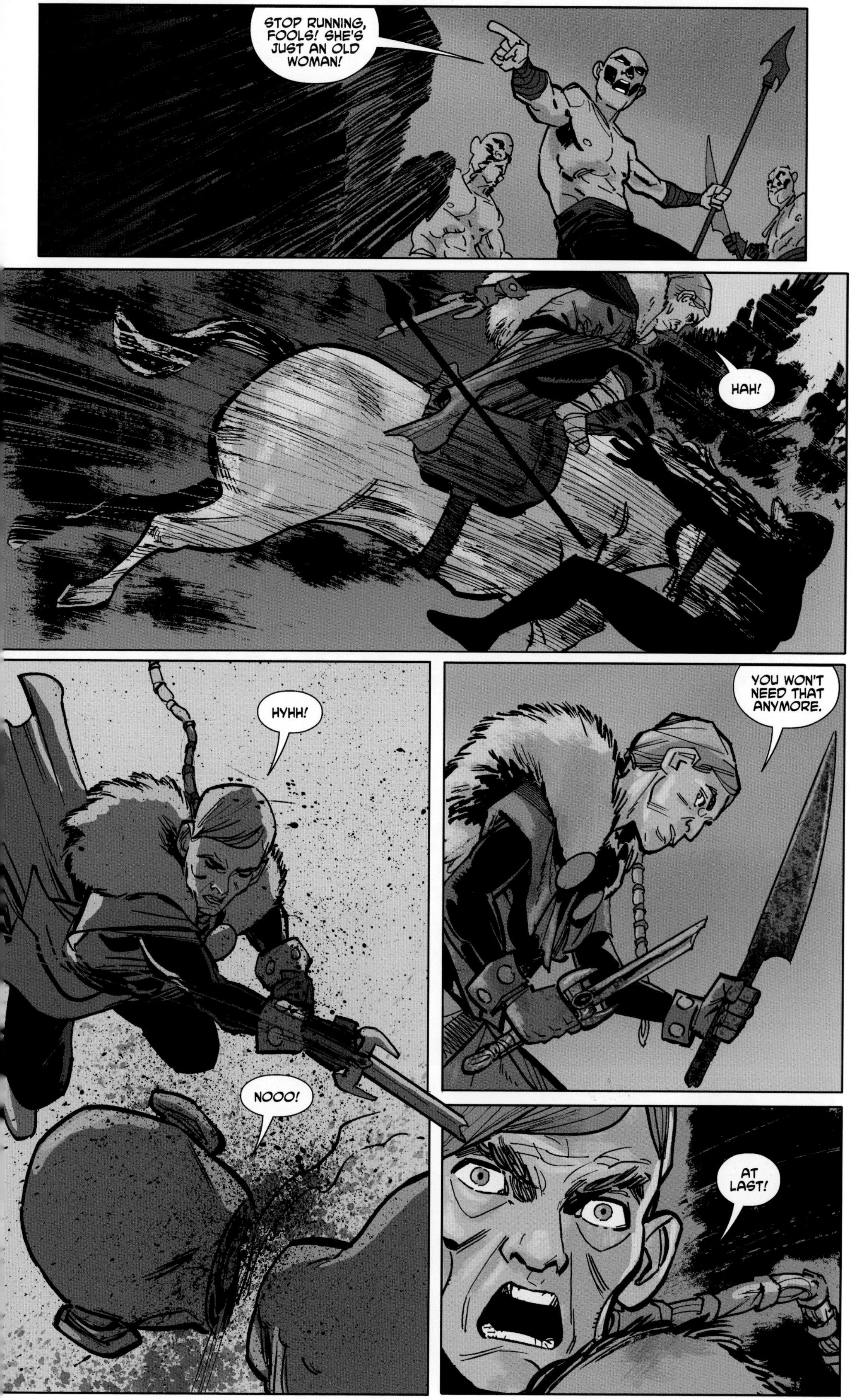
STOP RUNNING, FOOLS! SHE'S JUST AN OLD WOMAN!
HAH!
HYHH!
NOOO!
YOU WON'T NEED THAT ANYMORE.
AT LAST!

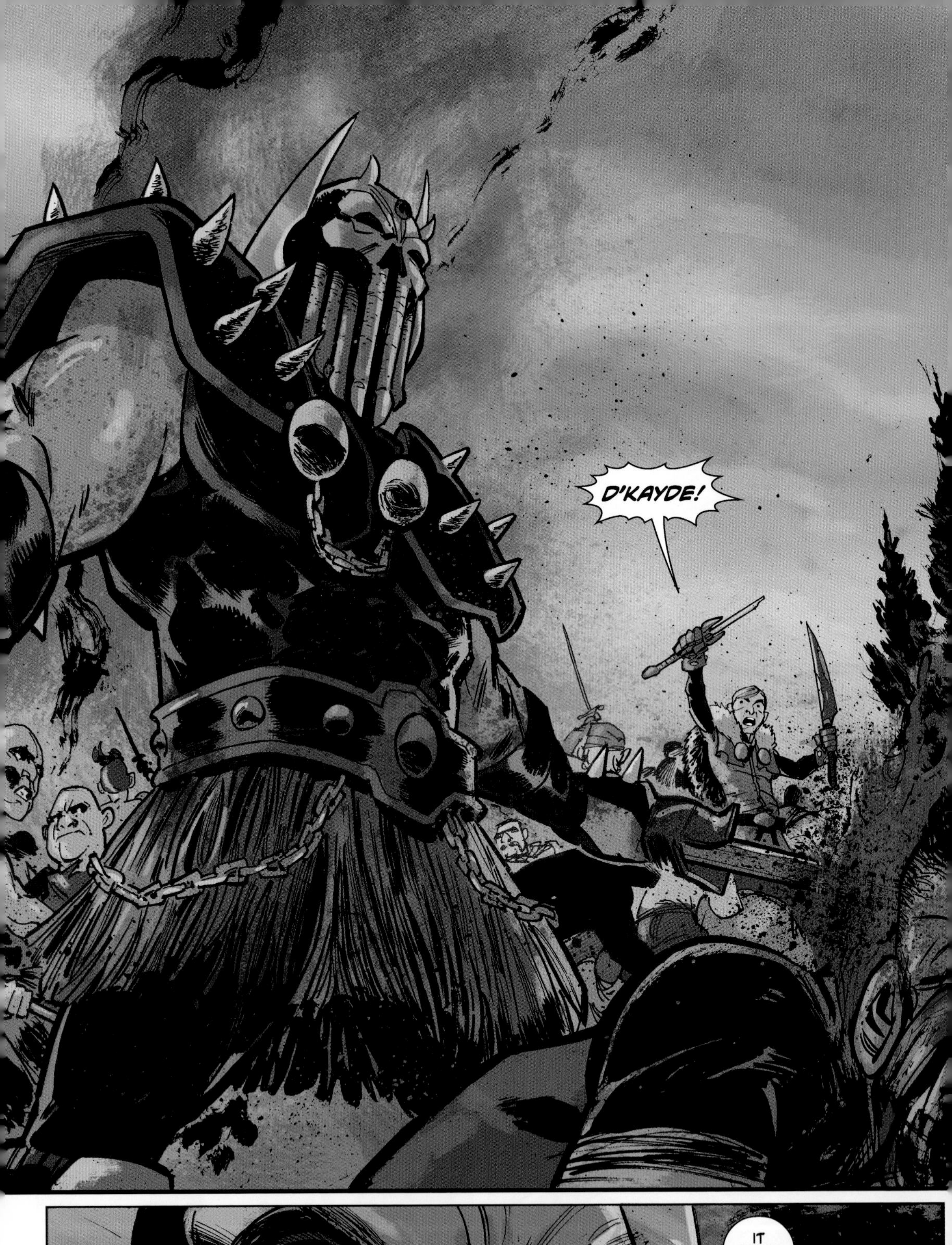
D'KAYDE!

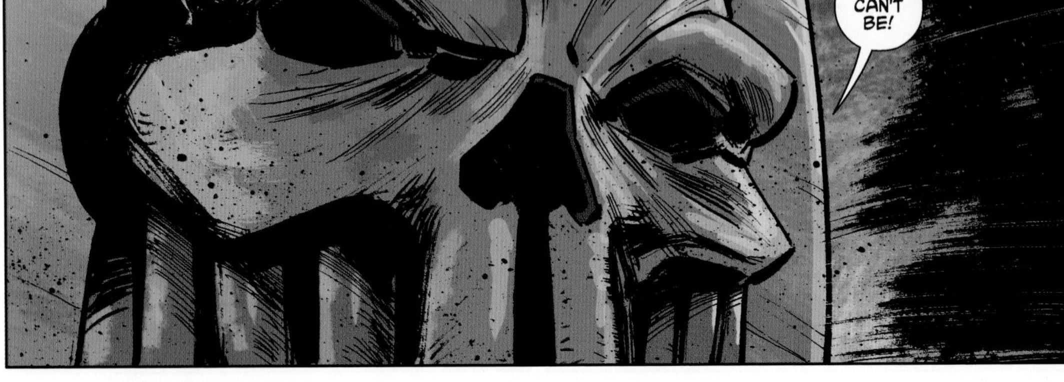
IT CAN'T BE!

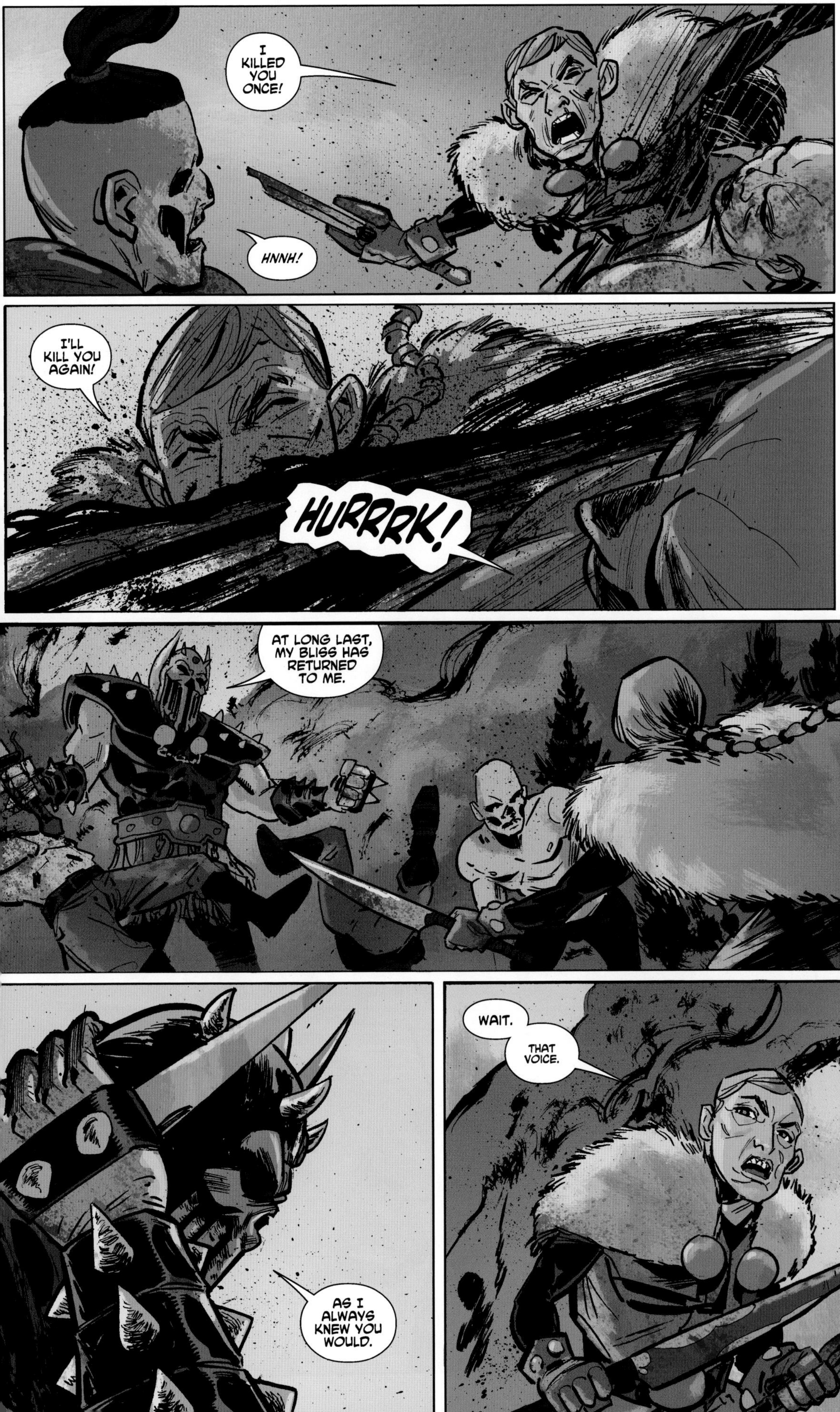
I KILLED YOU ONCE!
HNNH!
I'LL KILL YOU AGAIN!
HURRRK!
AT LONG LAST, MY BLISS HAS RETURNED TO ME.
AS I ALWAYS KNEW YOU WOULD.
WAIT.
THAT VOICE.

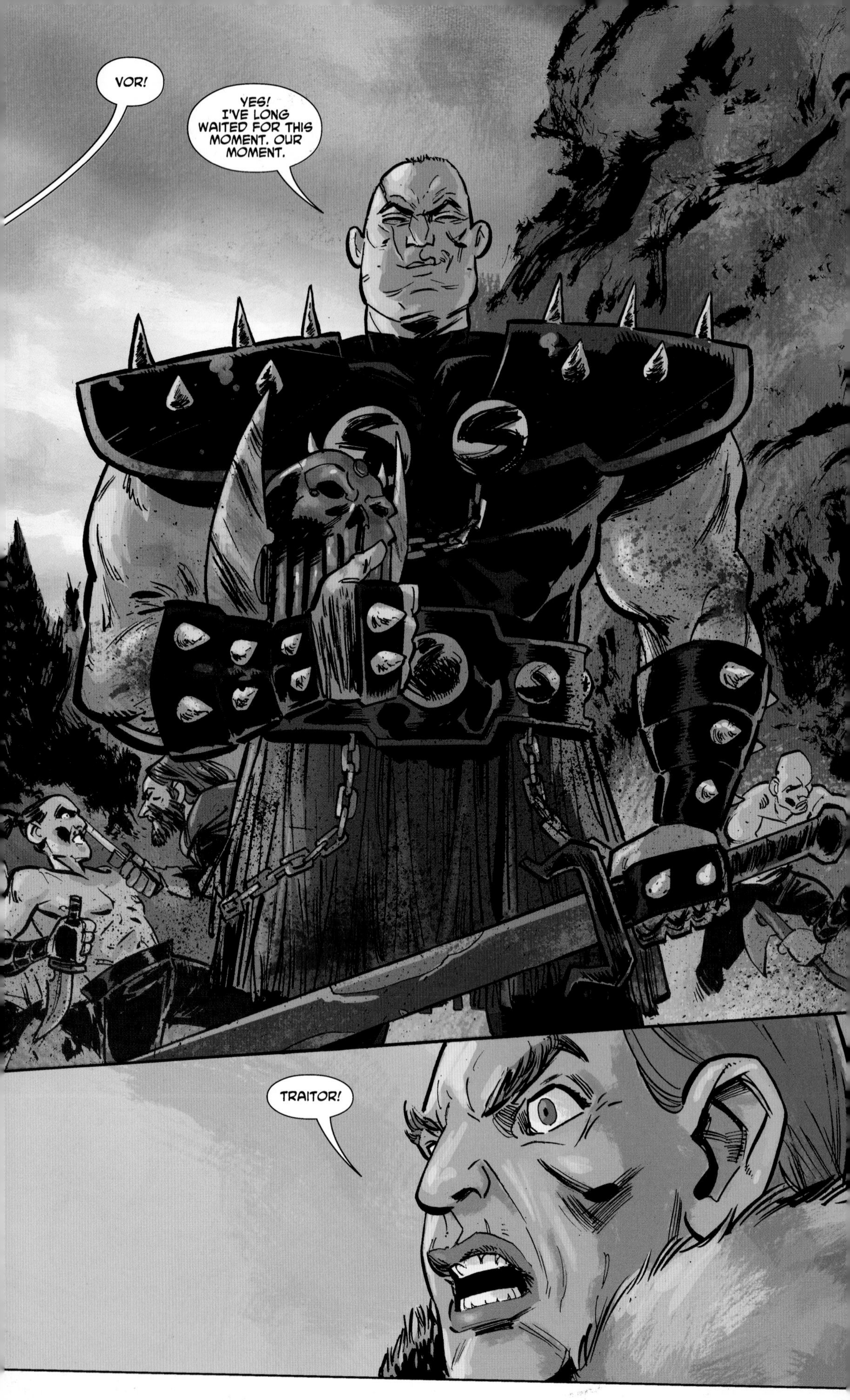
VOR!
YES! I'VE LONG WAITED FOR THIS MOMENT. OUR MOMENT.
TRAITOR!

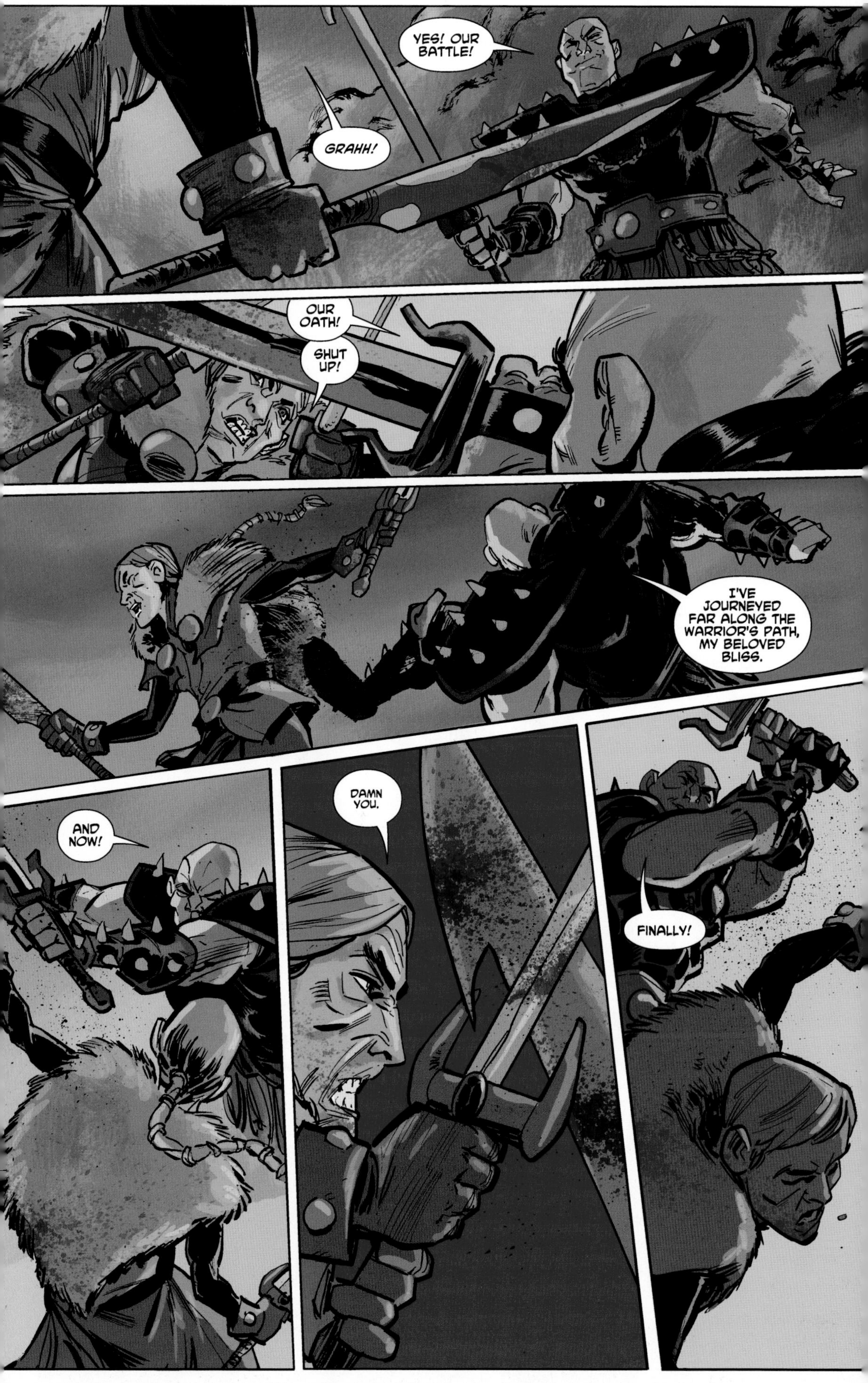
YES! OUR BATTLE!
GRAHH!
OUR OATH!
SHUT UP!
I'VE JOURNEYED FAR ALONG THE WARRIOR'S PATH, MY BELOVED BLISS.
AND NOW!
DAMN YOU.
FINALLY!

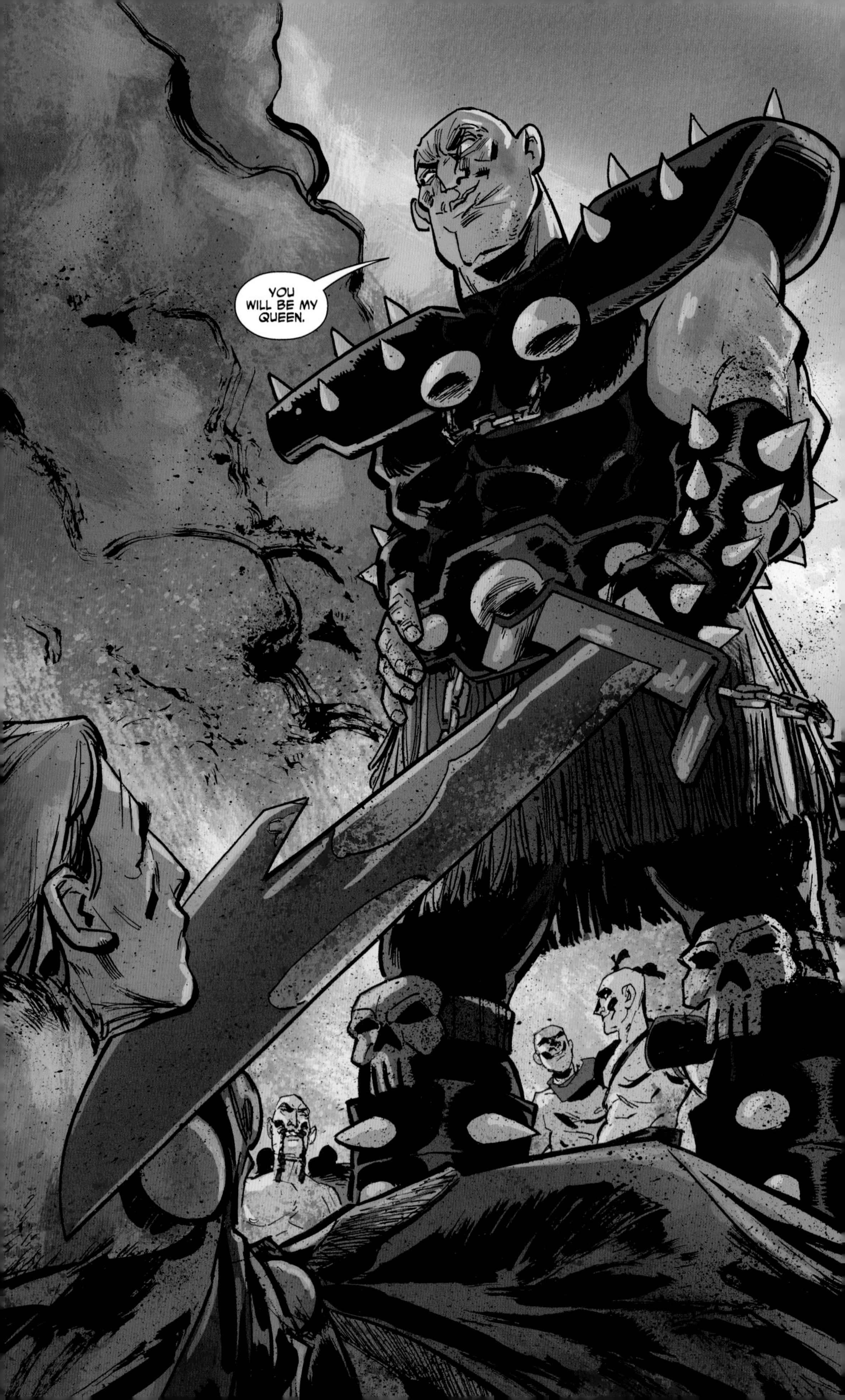
YOU WILL BE MY QUEEN.

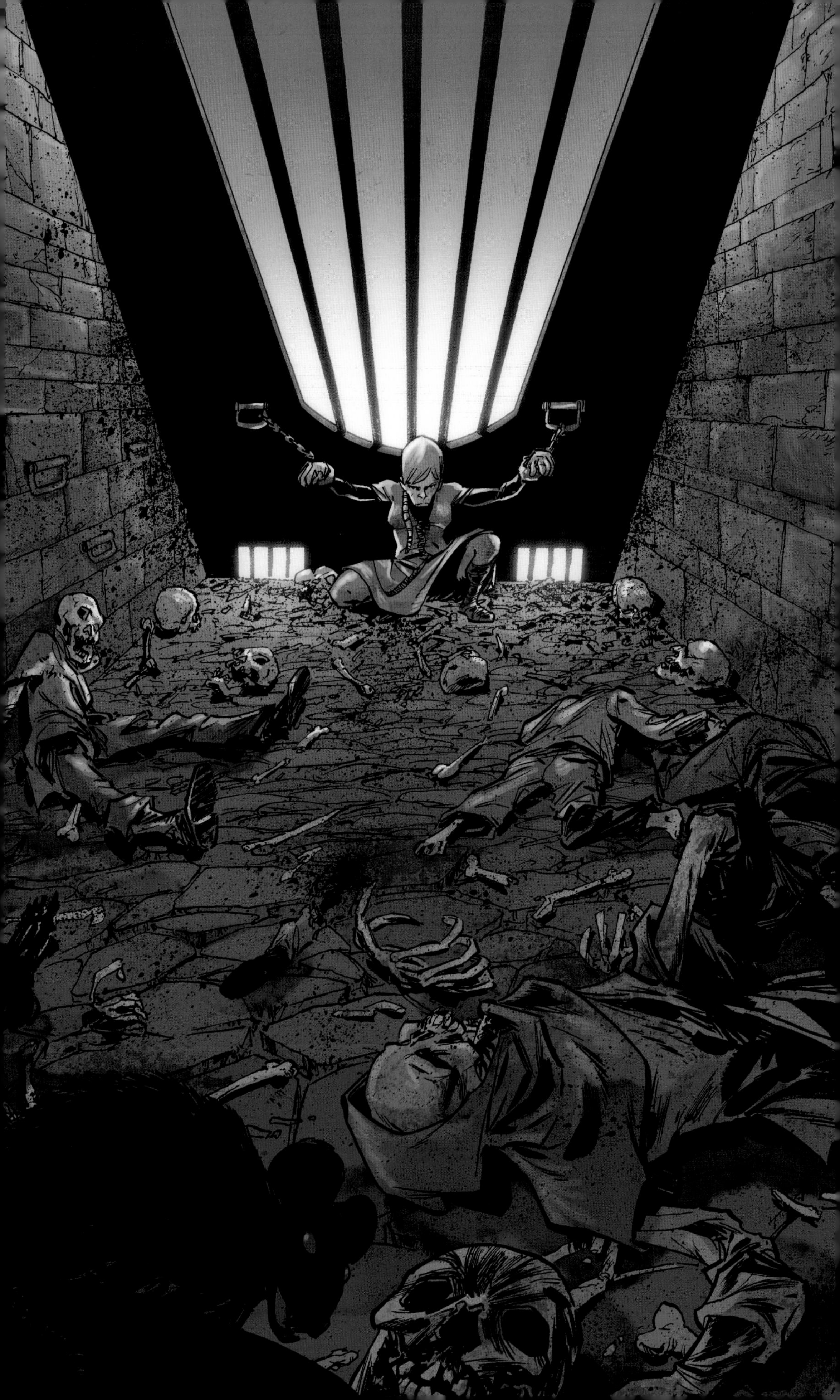

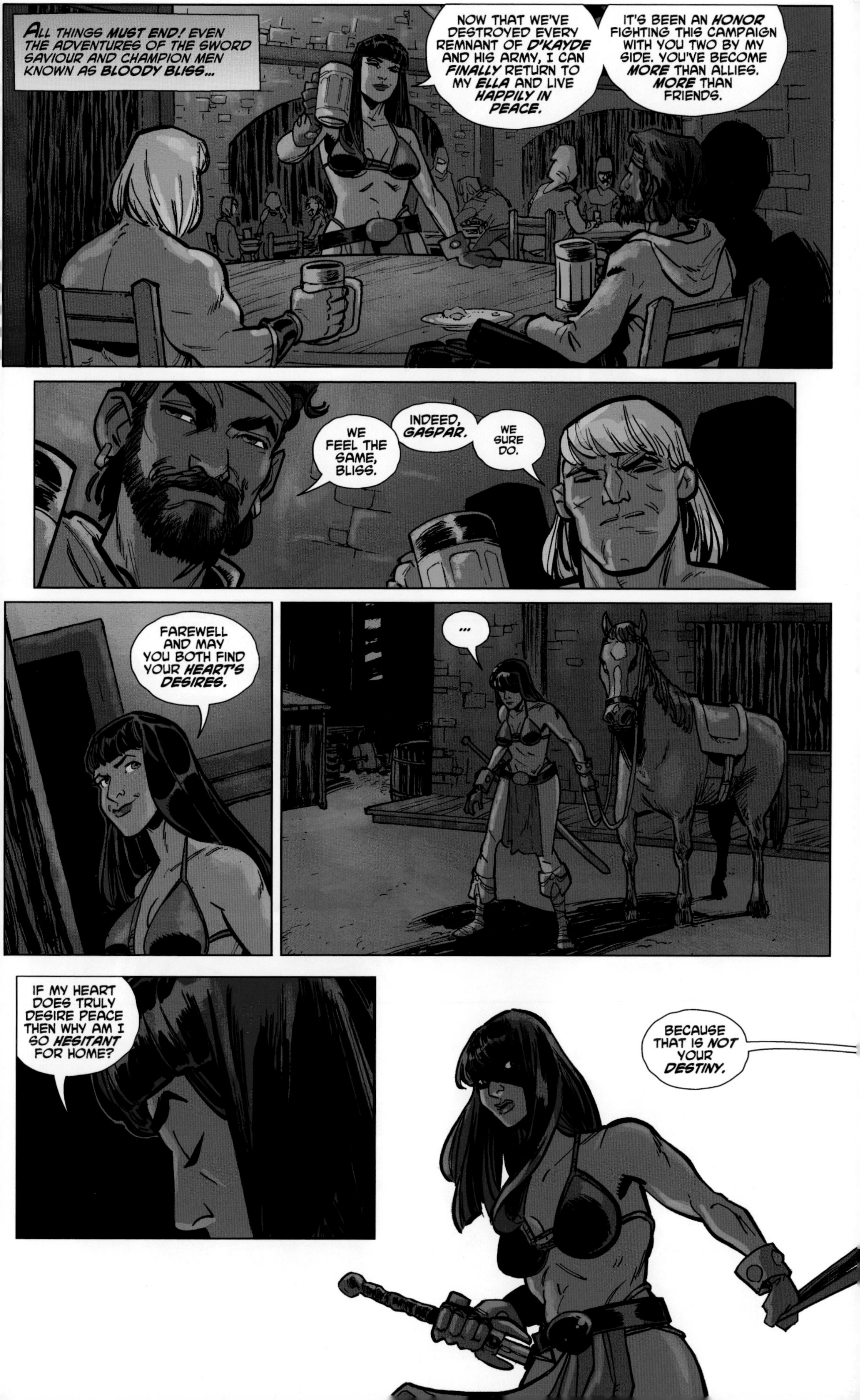
ALL THINGS MUST END! EVEN THE ADVENTURES OF THE SWORD SAVIOUR AND CHAMPION MEN KNOWN AS BLOODY BLISS...
NOW THAT WE'VE DESTROYED EVERY REMNANT OF D'KAYDE AND HIS ARMY, I CAN FINALLY RETURN TO MY ELLA AND LIVE HAPPILY IN PEACE.
IT'S BEEN AN HONOR FIGHTING THIS CAMPAIGN WITH YOU TWO BY MY SIDE. YOU'VE BECOME MORE THAN ALLIES. MORE THAN FRIENDS.
WE FEEL THE SAME, BLISS.
INDEED, GASPAR.
WE SURE DO.
FAREWELL AND MAY YOU BOTH FIND YOUR HEART'S DESIRES.
...
IF MY HEART DOES TRULY DESIRE PEACE THEN WHY AM I SO HESITANT FOR HOME?
BECAUSE THAT IS NOT YOUR DESTINY.

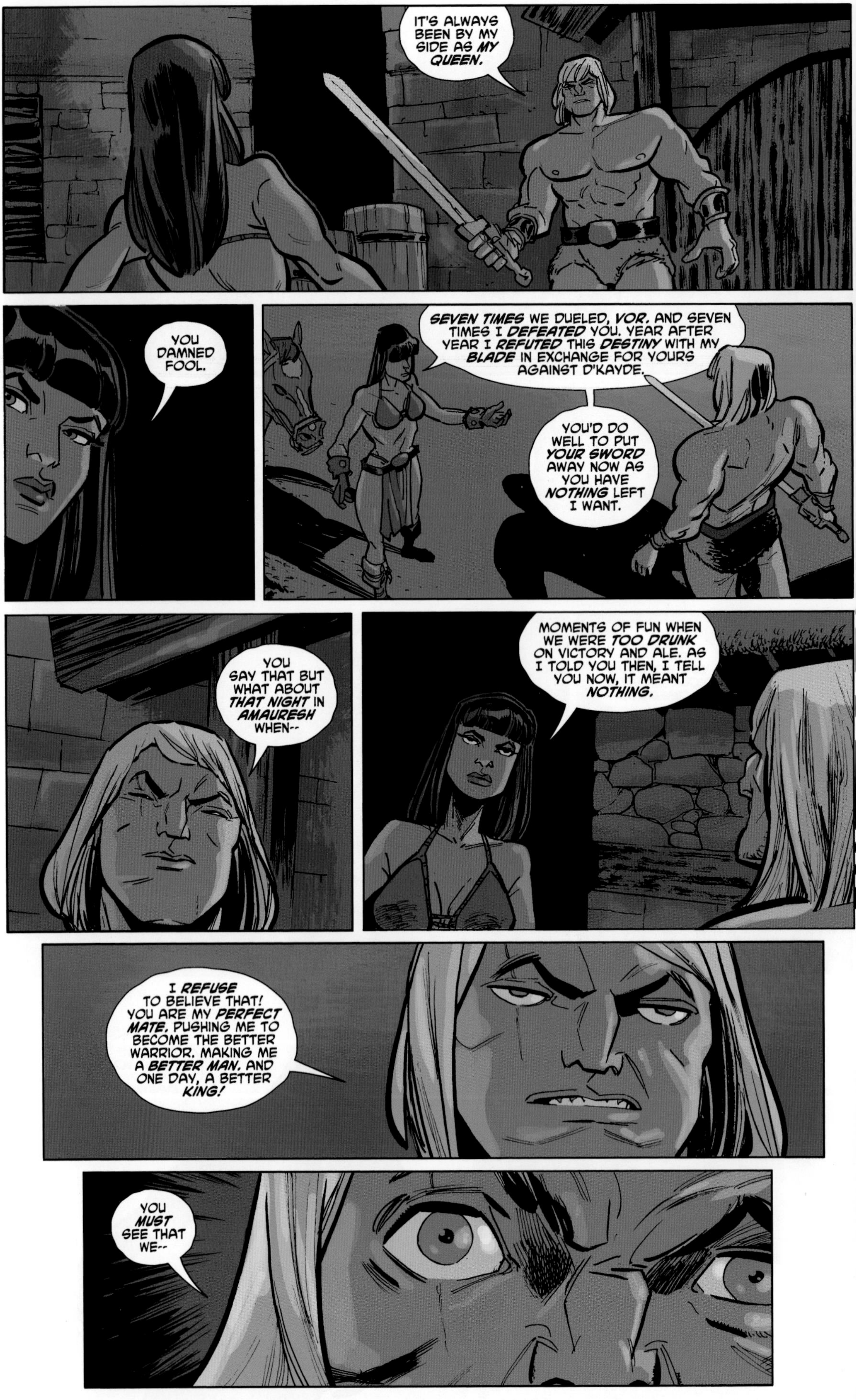
IT'S ALWAYS BEEN BY MY SIDE AS MY QUEEN.
YOU DAMNED FOOL.
SEVEN TIMES WE DUELED, VOR, AND SEVEN TIMES I DEFEATED YOU. YEAR AFTER YEAR I REFUTED THIS DESTINY WITH MY BLADE IN EXCHANGE FOR YOURS AGAINST D'KAYDE.
YOU'D DO WELL TO PUT YOUR SWORD AWAY NOW AS YOU HAVE NOTHING LEFT I WANT.
YOU SAY THAT BUT WHAT ABOUT THAT NIGHT IN AMAURESH WHEN--
MOMENTS OF FUN WHEN WE WERE TOO DRUNK ON VICTORY AND ALE. AS I TOLD YOU THEN, I TELL YOU NOW, IT MEANT NOTHING.
I REFUSE TO BELIEVE THAT! YOU ARE MY PERFECT MATE, PUSHING ME TO BECOME THE BETTER WARRIOR. MAKING ME A BETTER MAN. AND ONE DAY, A BETTER KING!
YOU MUST SEE THAT WE--

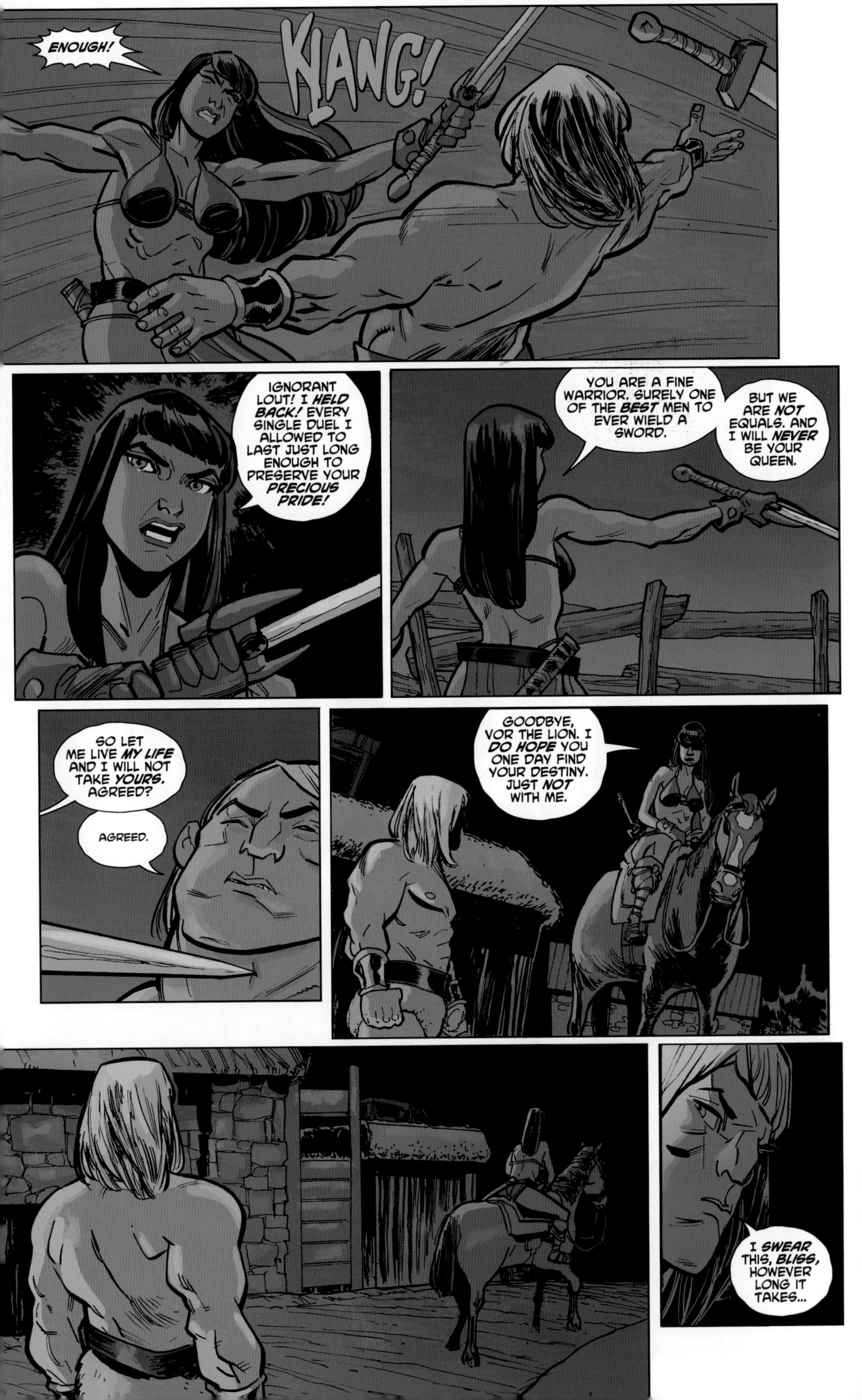

ENOUGH!
KLANG!
IGNORANT LOUT! I HELD BACK! EVERY SINGLE DUEL I ALLOWED TO LAST JUST LONG ENOUGH TO PRESERVE YOUR PRECIOUS PRIDE!
YOU ARE A FINE WARRIOR. SURELY ONE OF THE BEST MEN TO EVER WIELD A SWORD.
BUT WE ARE NOT EQUALS. AND I WILL NEVER BE YOUR QUEEN.
SO LET ME LIVE MY LIFE AND I WILL NOT TAKE YOURS. AGREED?
AGREED.
GOODBYE, VOR THE LION. I DO HOPE YOU ONE DAY FIND YOUR DESTINY. JUST NOT WITH ME.
I SWEAR THIS, BLISS, HOWEVER LONG IT TAKES...

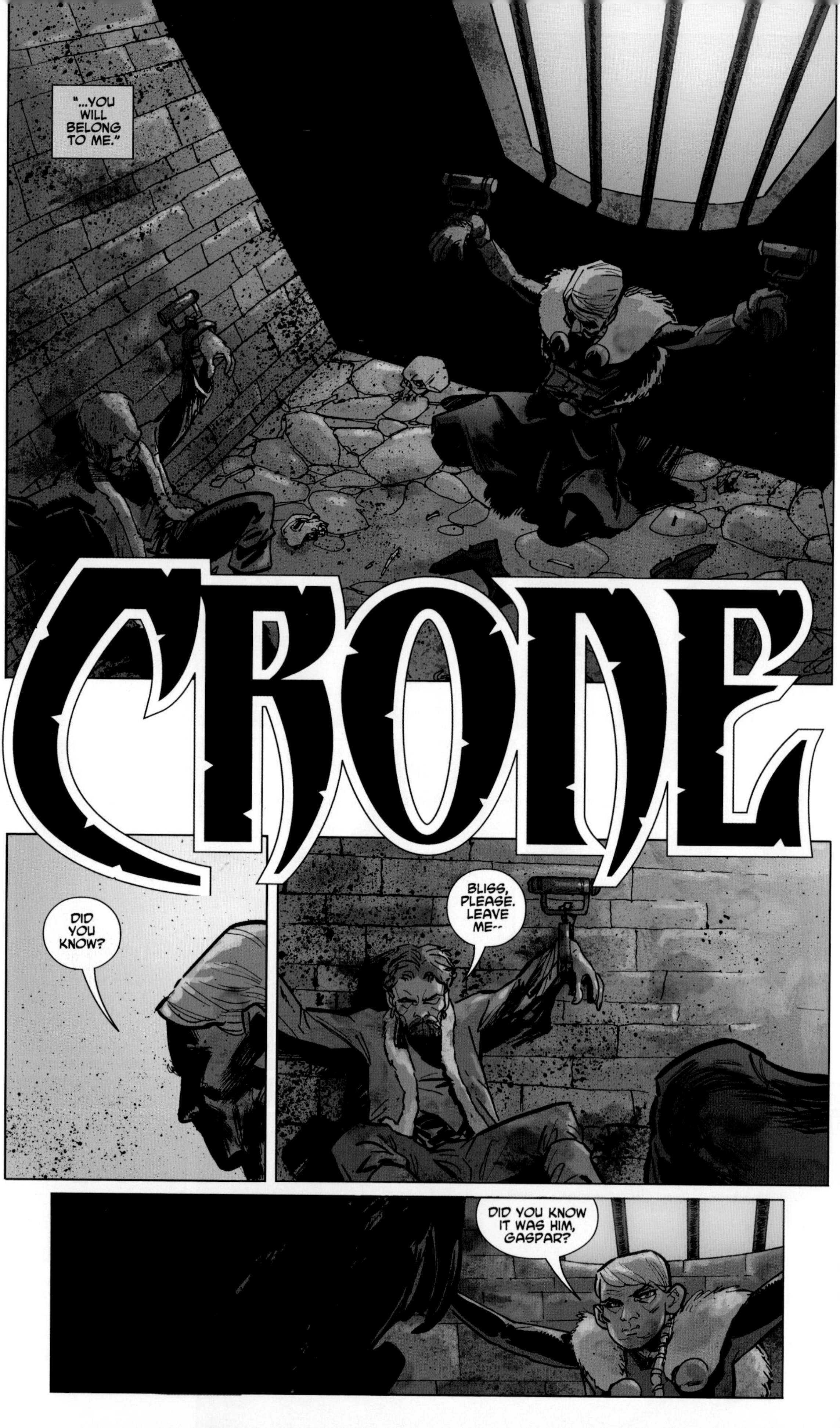
"...YOU WILL BELONG TO ME."
CRONE
DID YOU KNOW?
BLISS, PLEASE. LEAVE ME--
DID YOU KNOW IT WAS HIM, GASPAR?

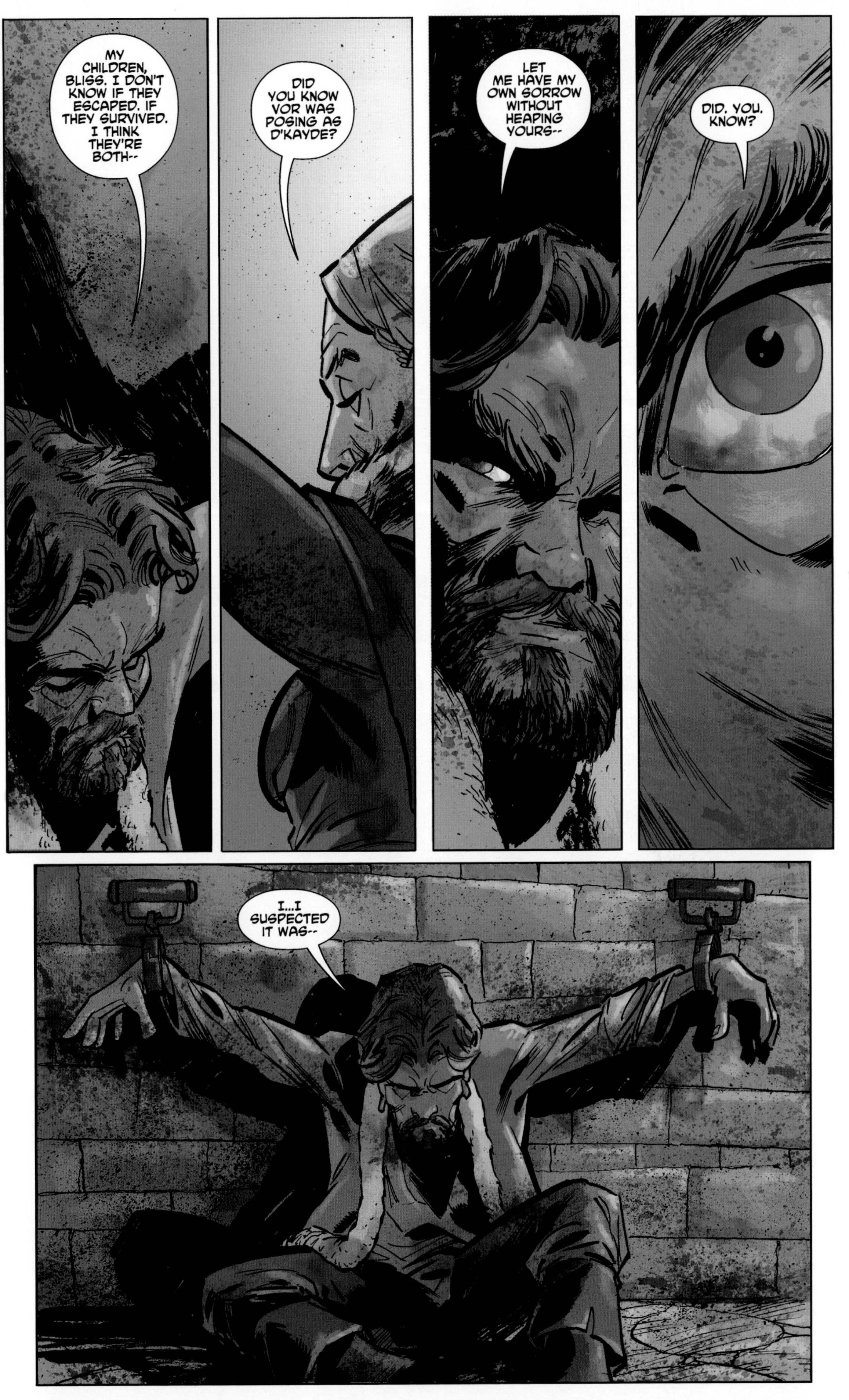
MY CHILDREN, BLISS. I DON'T KNOW IF THEY ESCAPED. IF THEY SURVIVED. I THINK THEY'RE BOTH--
DID YOU KNOW VOR WAS POSING AS D'KAYDE?
LET ME HAVE MY OWN SORROW WITHOUT HEAPING YOURS--
DID. YOU. KNOW?
I...I SUSPECTED IT WAS--

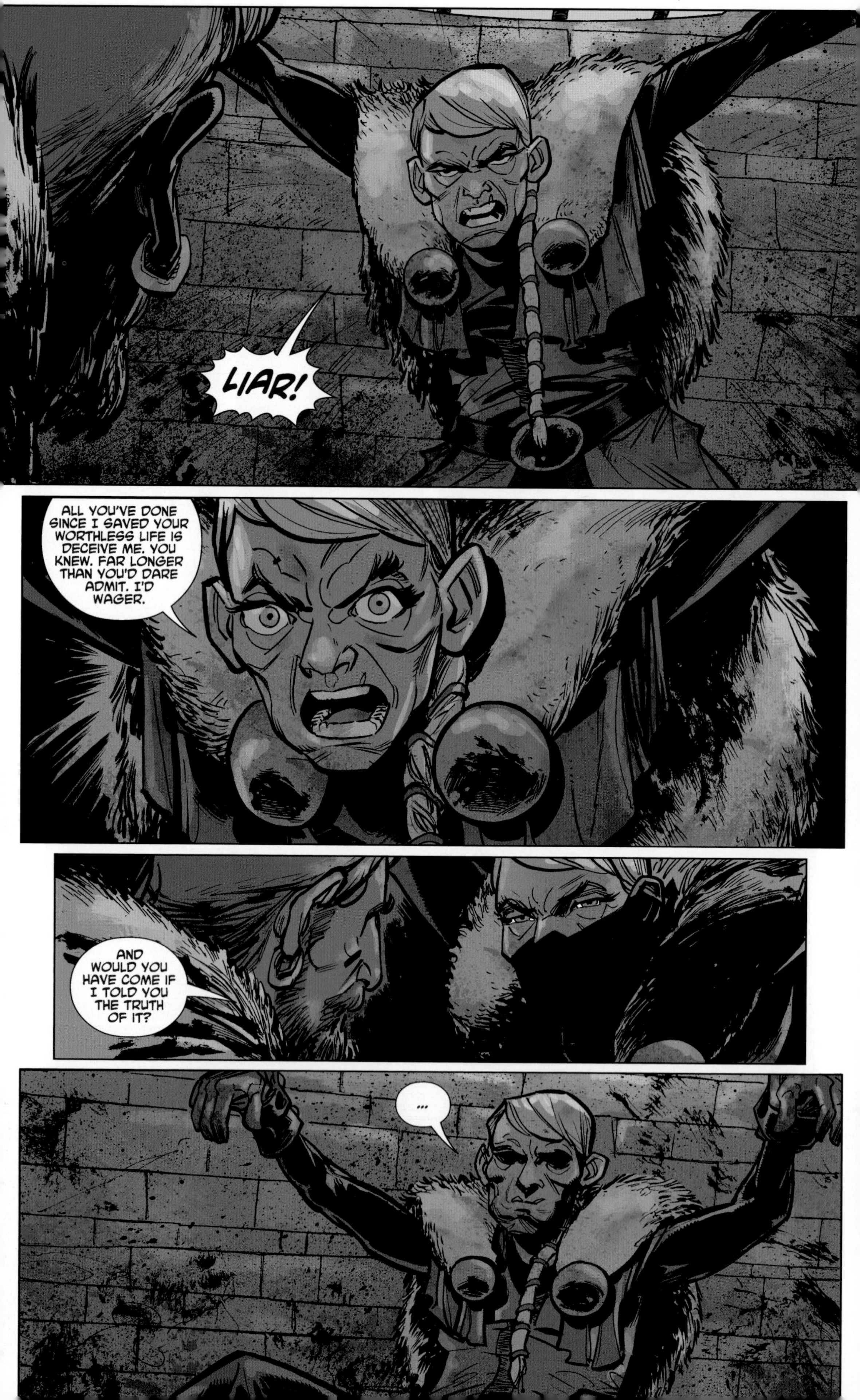
LIAR!
ALL YOU'VE DONE SINCE I SAVED YOUR WORTHLESS LIFE IS DECEIVE ME. YOU KNEW. FAR LONGER THAN YOU'D DARE ADMIT, I'D WAGER.
AND WOULD YOU HAVE COME IF I TOLD YOU THE TRUTH OF IT?
...

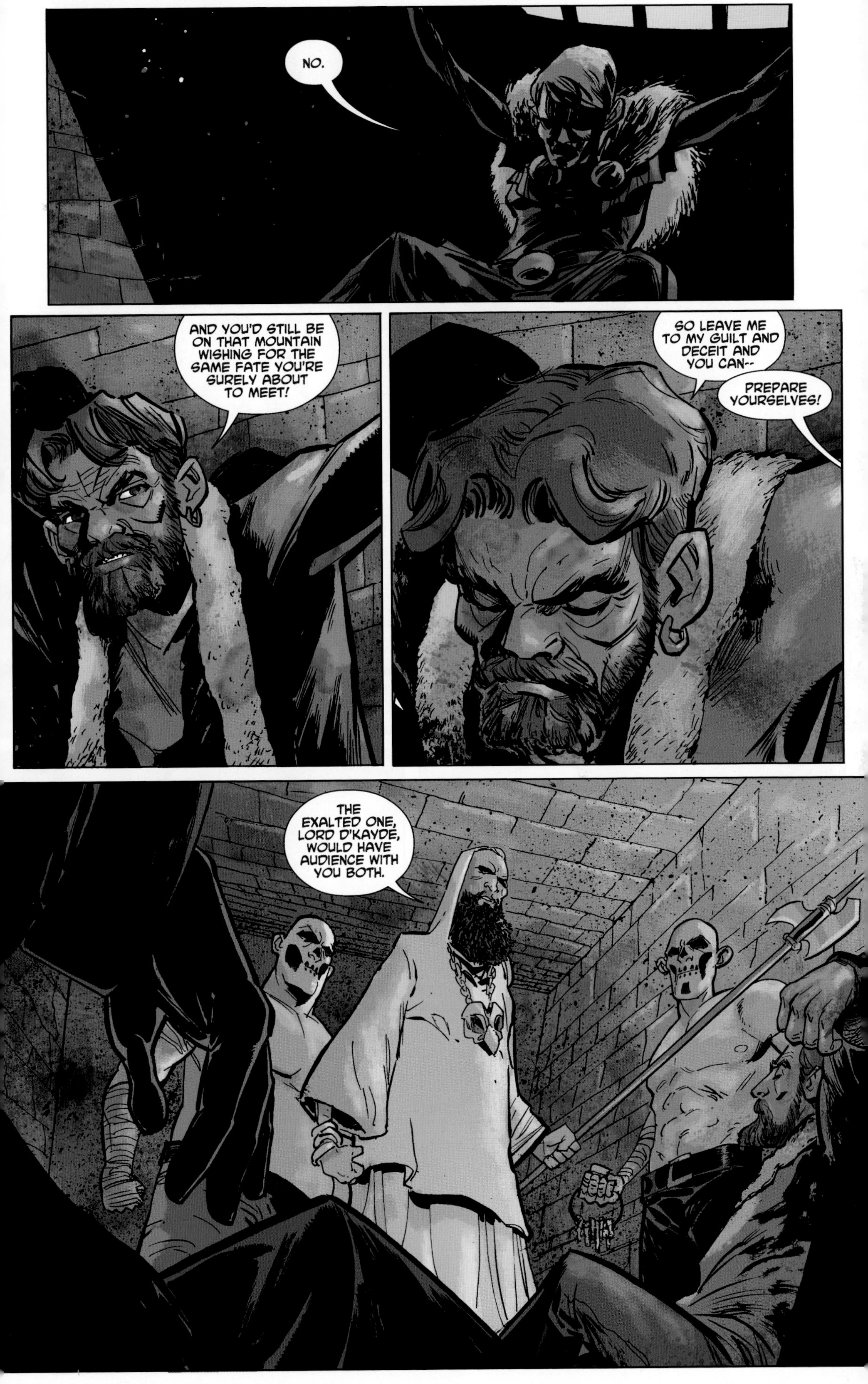
NO.
AND YOU'D STILL BE ON THAT MOUNTAIN WISHING FOR THE SAME FATE YOU'RE SURELY ABOUT TO MEET!
SO LEAVE ME TO MY GUILT AND DECEIT AND YOU CAN--
PREPARE YOURSELVES!
THE EXALTED ONE, LORD D'KAYDE, WOULD HAVE AUDIENCE WITH YOU BOTH.

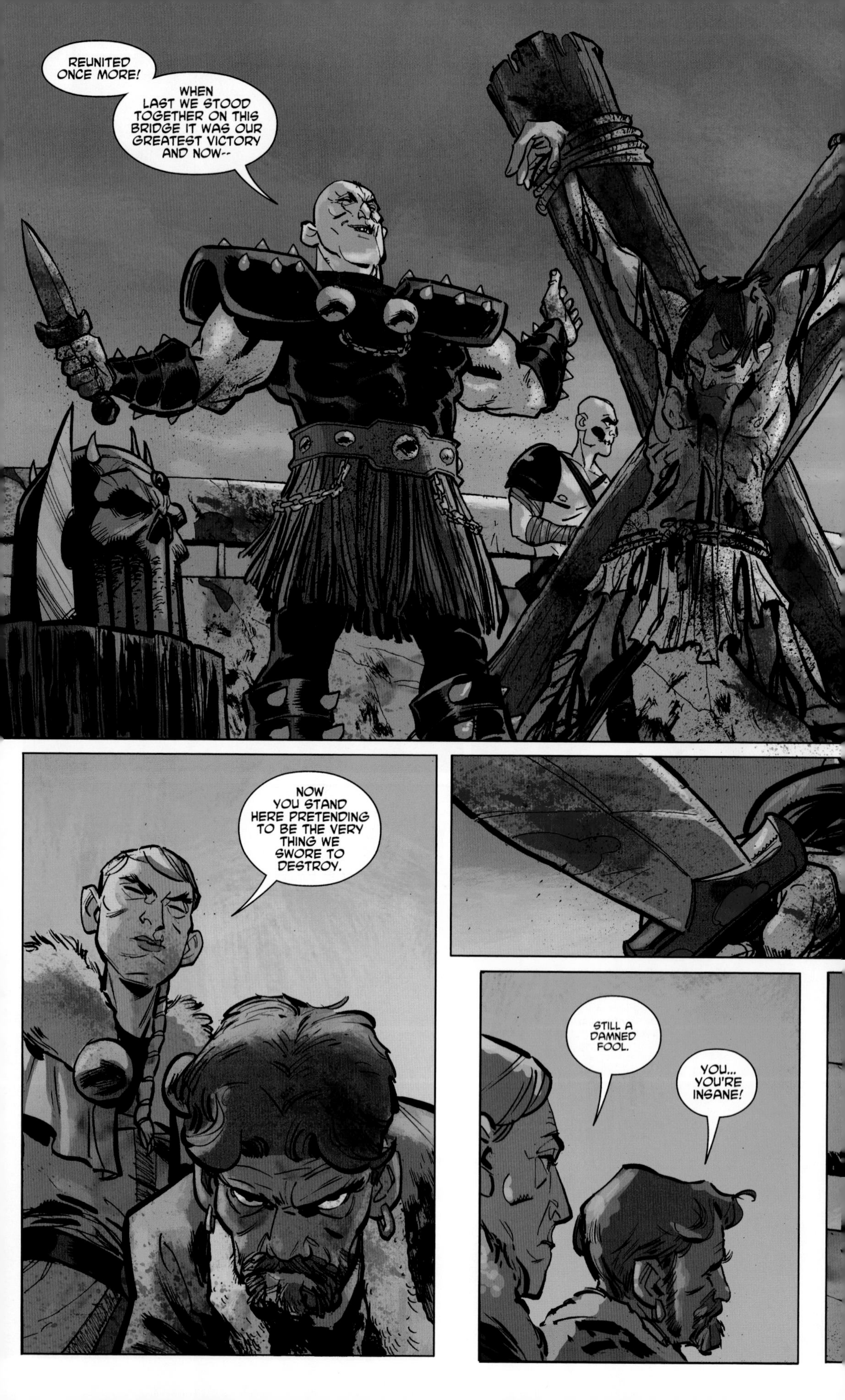
REUNITED ONCE MORE!
WHEN LAST WE STOOD TOGETHER ON THIS BRIDGE IT WAS OUR GREATEST VICTORY AND NOW--
NOW YOU STAND HERE PRETENDING TO BE THE VERY THING WE SWORE TO DESTROY.
STILL A DAMNED FOOL.
YOU... YOU'RE INSANE!

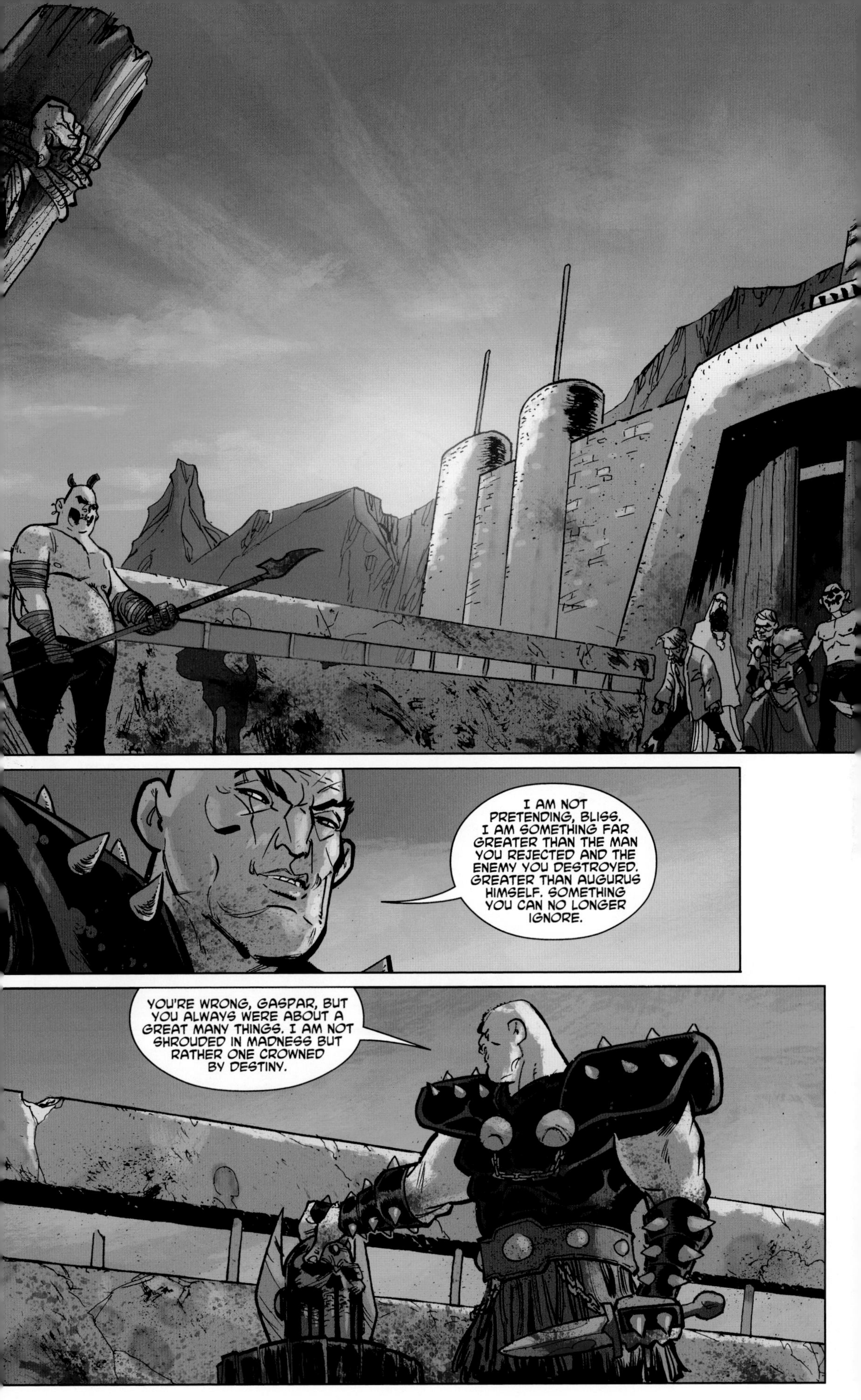
I AM NOT PRETENDING, BLISS. I AM SOMETHING FAR GREATER THAN THE MAN YOU REJECTED AND THE ENEMY YOU DESTROYED. GREATER THAN AUGURUS HIMSELF. SOMETHING YOU CAN NO LONGER IGNORE.
YOU'RE WRONG, GASPAR, BUT YOU ALWAYS WERE ABOUT A GREAT MANY THINGS. I AM NOT SHROUDED IN MADNESS BUT RATHER ONE CROWNED BY DESTINY.

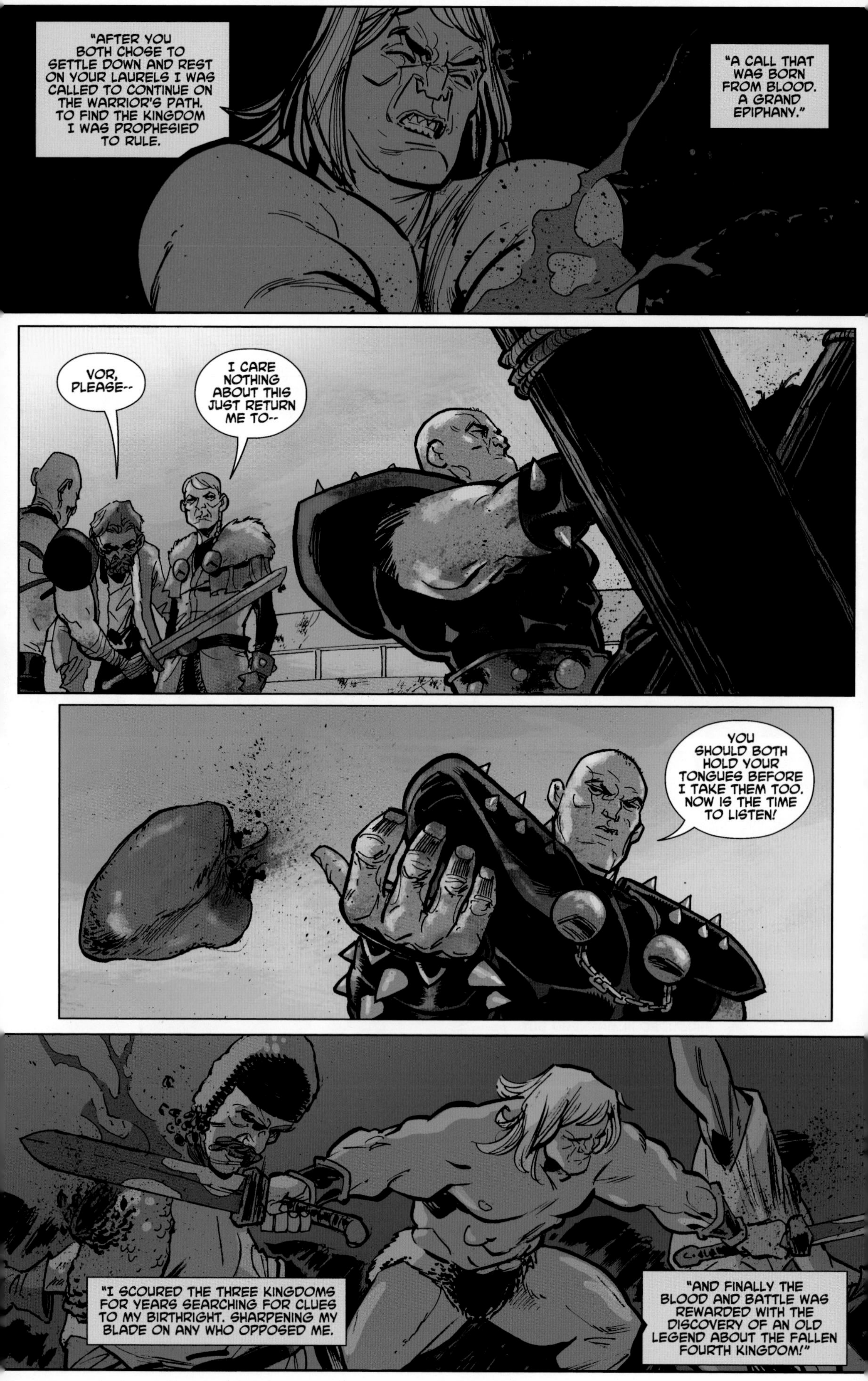
"AFTER YOU BOTH CHOSE TO SETTLE DOWN AND REST ON YOUR LAURELS I WAS CALLED TO CONTINUE ON THE WARRIOR'S PATH. TO FIND THE KINGDOM I WAS PROPHESIED TO RULE.
"A CALL THAT WAS BORN FROM BLOOD. A GRAND EPIPHANY."
VOR, PLEASE--
I CARE NOTHING ABOUT THIS JUST RETURN ME TO--
YOU SHOULD BOTH HOLD YOUR TONGUES BEFORE I TAKE THEM TOO. NOW IS THE TIME TO LISTEN!
"I SCOURED THE THREE KINGDOMS FOR YEARS SEARCHING FOR CLUES TO MY BIRTHRIGHT. SHARPENING MY BLADE ON ANY WHO OPPOSED ME.
"AND FINALLY THE BLOOD AND BATTLE WAS REWARDED WITH THE DISCOVERY OF AN OLD LEGEND ABOUT THE FALLEN FOURTH KINGDOM!"

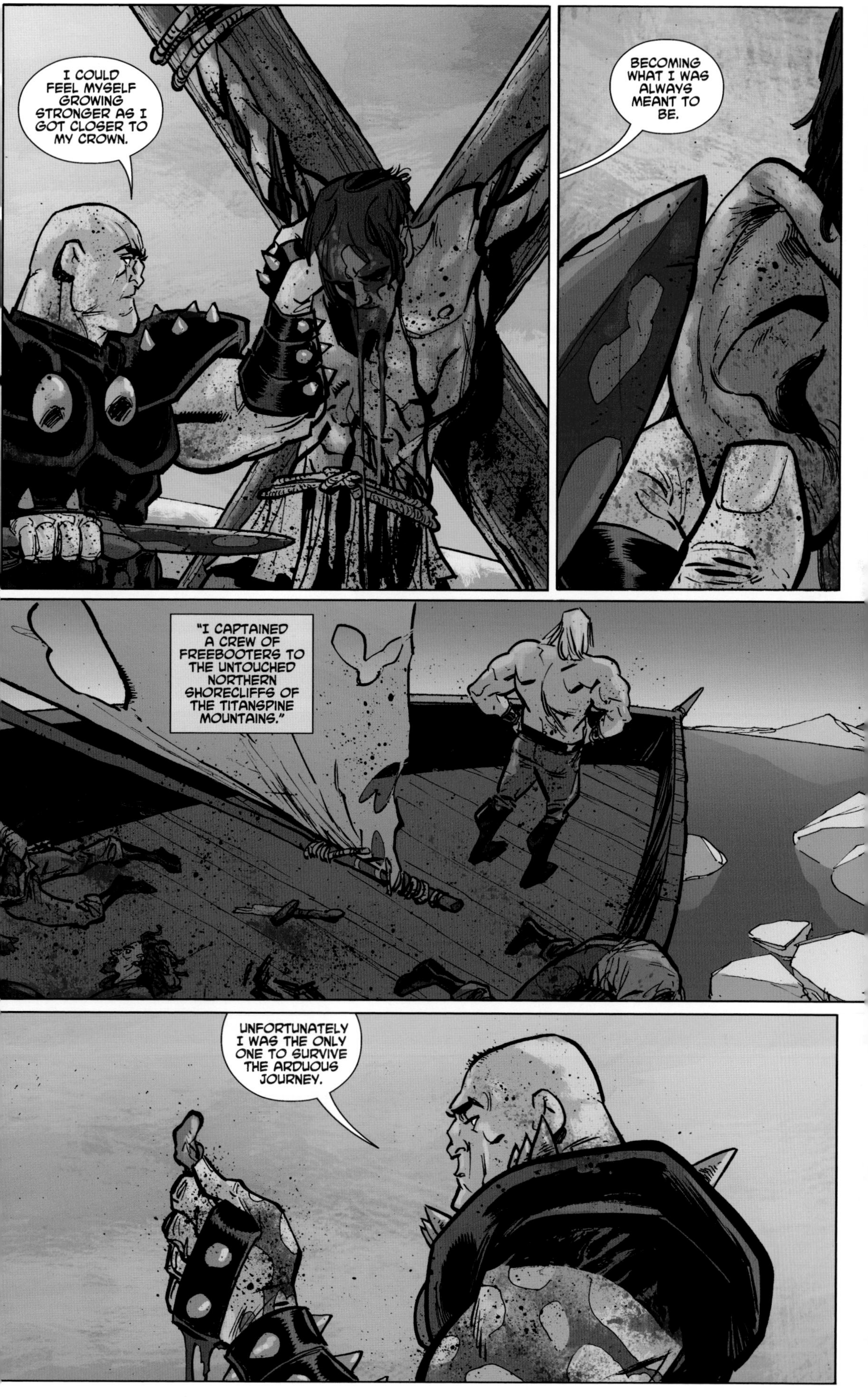
I COULD FEEL MYSELF GROWING STRONGER AS I GOT CLOSER TO MY CROWN.
BECOMING WHAT I WAS ALWAYS MEANT TO BE.
"I CAPTAINED A CREW OF FREEBOOTERS TO THE UNTOUCHED NORTHERN SHORECLIFFS OF THE TITANSPINE MOUNTAINS."
UNFORTUNATELY I WAS THE ONLY ONE TO SURVIVE THE ARDUOUS JOURNEY.

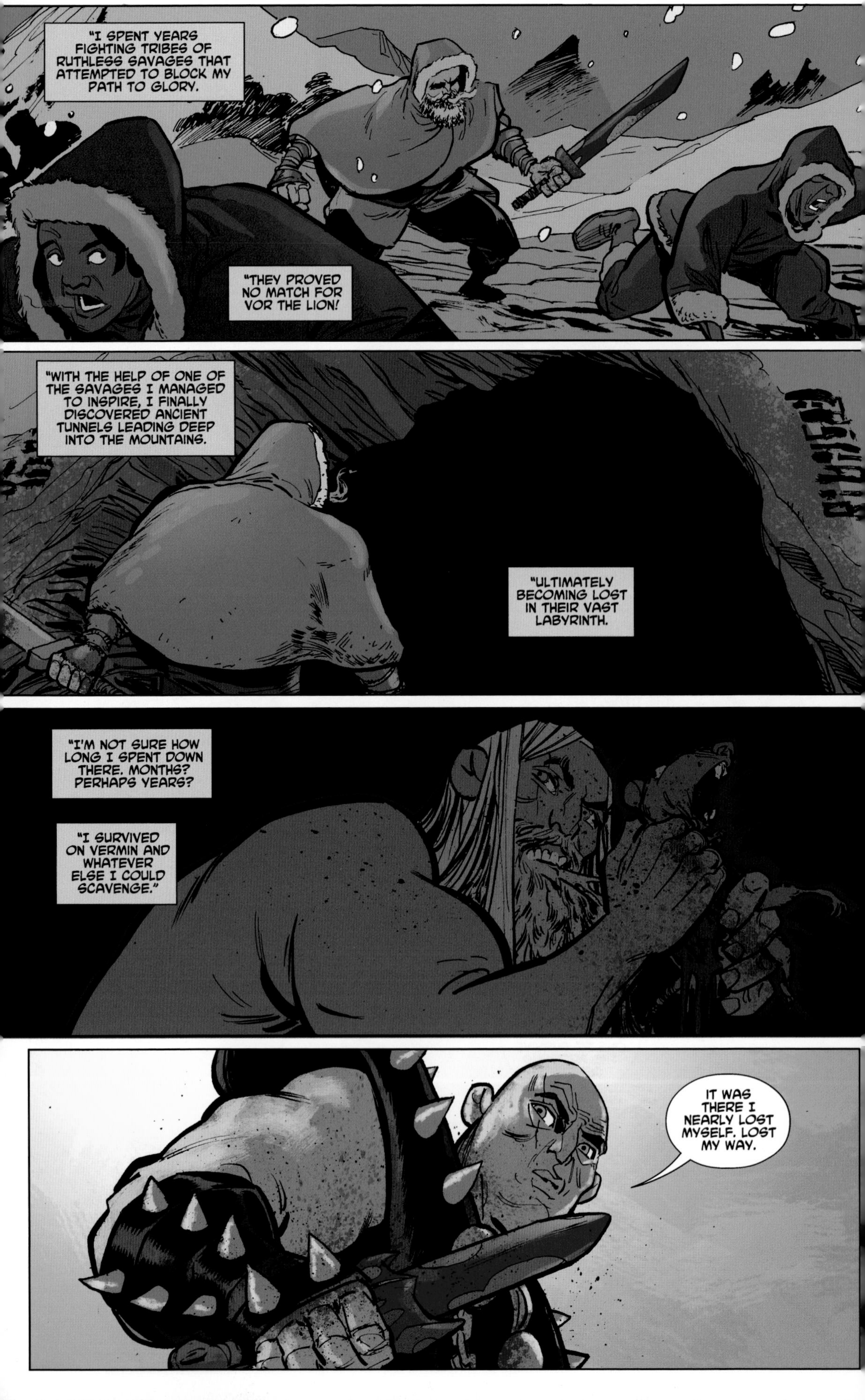
"I SPENT YEARS FIGHTING TRIBES OF RUTHLESS SAVAGES THAT ATTEMPTED TO BLOCK MY PATH TO GLORY.
"THEY PROVED NO MATCH FOR VOR THE LION!
"WITH THE HELP OF ONE OF THE SAVAGES I MANAGED TO INSPIRE, I FINALLY DISCOVERED ANCIENT TUNNELS LEADING DEEP INTO THE MOUNTAINS.
"ULTIMATELY BECOMING LOST IN THEIR VAST LABYRINTH.
"I'M NOT SURE HOW LONG I SPENT DOWN THERE. MONTHS? PERHAPS YEARS?
"I SURVIVED ON VERMIN AND WHATEVER ELSE I COULD SCAVENGE."
IT WAS THERE I NEARLY LOST MYSELF. LOST MY WAY.

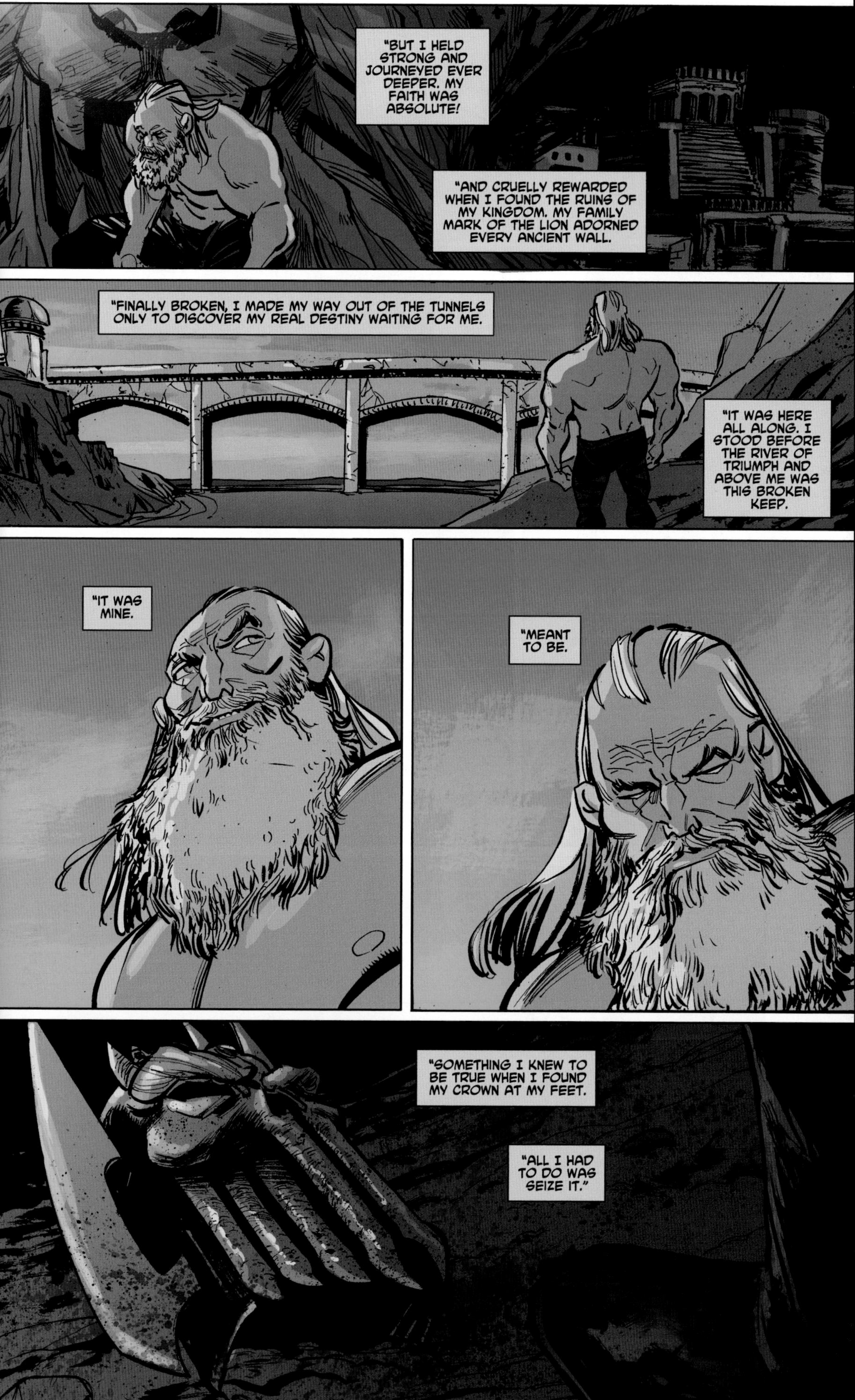
"BUT I HELD STRONG AND JOURNEYED EVER DEEPER. MY FAITH WAS ABSOLUTE!
"AND CRUELLY REWARDED WHEN I FOUND THE RUINS OF MY KINGDOM. MY FAMILY MARK OF THE LION ADORNED EVERY ANCIENT WALL.
"FINALLY BROKEN, I MADE MY WAY OUT OF THE TUNNELS ONLY TO DISCOVER MY REAL DESTINY WAITING FOR ME.
"IT WAS HERE ALL ALONG. I STOOD BEFORE THE RIVER OF TRIUMPH AND ABOVE ME WAS THIS BROKEN KEEP.
"IT WAS MINE.
"MEANT TO BE.
"SOMETHING I KNEW TO BE TRUE WHEN I FOUND MY CROWN AT MY FEET.
"ALL I HAD TO DO WAS SEIZE IT."

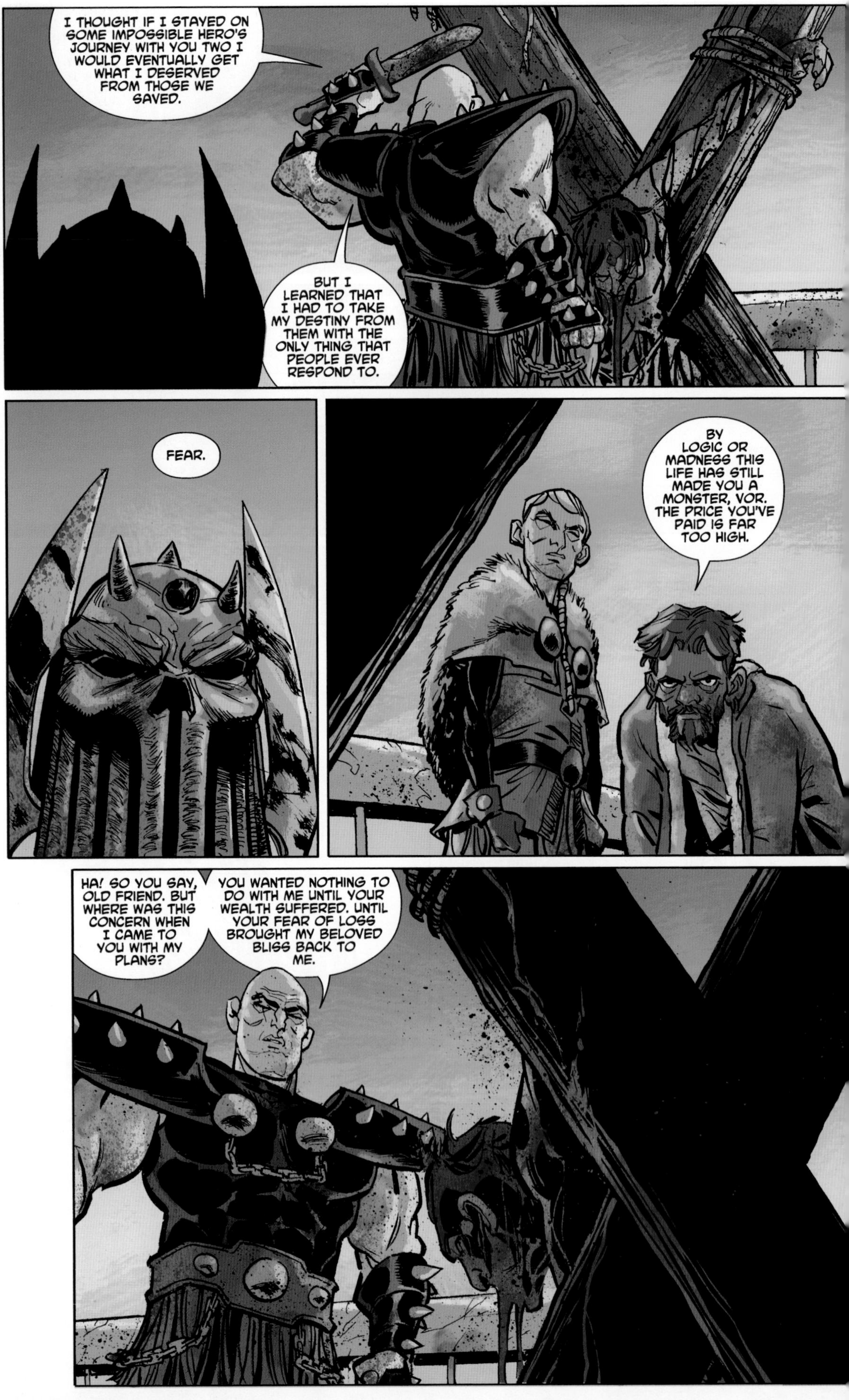
I THOUGHT IF I STAYED ON SOME IMPOSSIBLE HERO'S JOURNEY WITH YOU TWO I WOULD EVENTUALLY GET WHAT I DESERVED FROM THOSE WE SAVED.
BUT I LEARNED THAT I HAD TO TAKE MY DESTINY FROM THEM WITH THE ONLY THING THAT PEOPLE EVER RESPOND TO.
FEAR.
BY LOGIC OR MADNESS THIS LIFE HAS STILL MADE YOU A MONSTER, VOR. THE PRICE YOU'VE PAID IS FAR TOO HIGH.
HA! SO YOU SAY, OLD FRIEND. BUT WHERE WAS THIS CONCERN WHEN I CAME TO YOU WITH MY PLANS?
YOU WANTED NOTHING TO DO WITH ME UNTIL YOUR WEALTH SUFFERED. UNTIL YOUR FEAR OF LOSS BROUGHT MY BELOVED BLISS BACK TO ME.

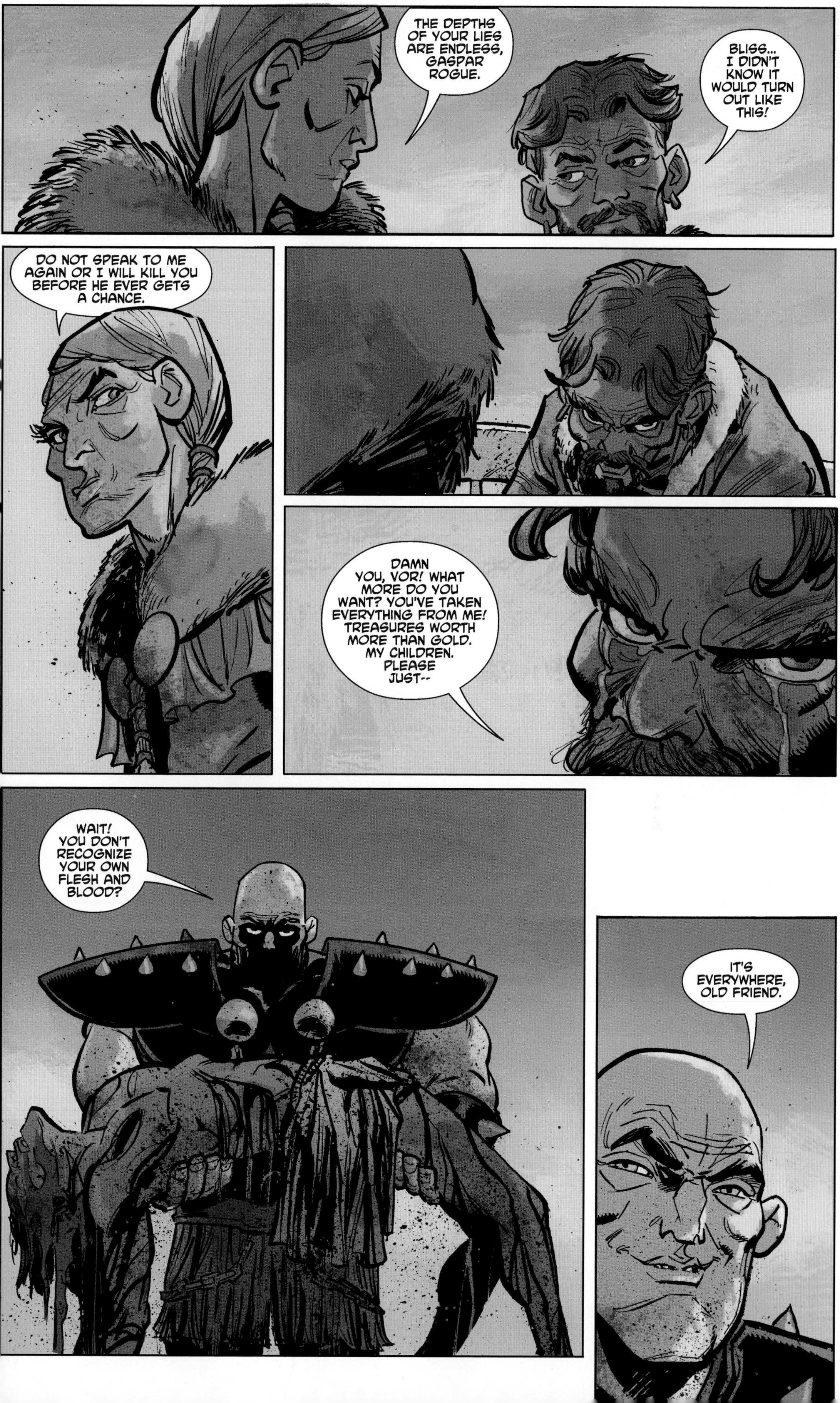
THE DEPTHS OF YOUR LIES ARE ENDLESS, GASPAR ROGUE.
BLISS... I DIDN'T KNOW IT WOULD TURN OUT LIKE THIS!
DO NOT SPEAK TO ME AGAIN OR I WILL KILL YOU BEFORE HE EVER GETS A CHANCE.
DAMN YOU, VOR! WHAT MORE DO YOU WANT? YOU'VE TAKEN EVERYTHING FROM ME! TREASURES WORTH MORE THAN GOLD. MY CHILDREN. PLEASE JUST--
WAIT! YOU DON'T RECOGNIZE YOUR OWN FLESH AND BLOOD?
IT'S EVERYWHERE, OLD FRIEND.

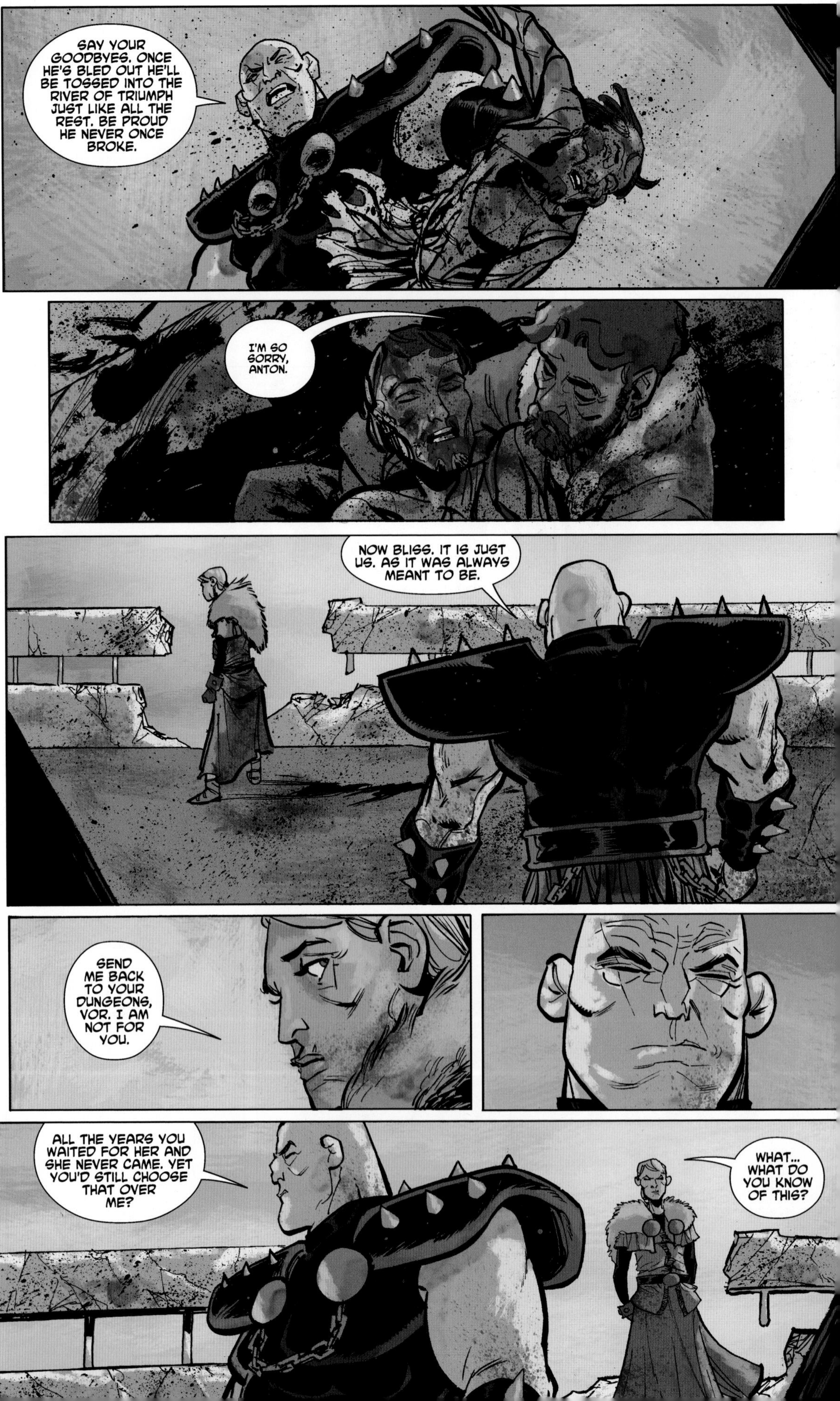
SAY YOUR GOODBYES. ONCE HE'S BLED OUT HE'LL BE TOSSED INTO THE RIVER OF TRIUMPH JUST LIKE ALL THE REST. BE PROUD HE NEVER ONCE BROKE.
I'M SO SORRY, ANTON.
NOW BLISS. IT IS JUST US. AS IT WAS ALWAYS MEANT TO BE.
SEND ME BACK TO YOUR DUNGEONS, VOR. I AM NOT FOR YOU.
ALL THE YEARS YOU WAITED FOR HER AND SHE NEVER CAME. YET YOU'D STILL CHOOSE THAT OVER ME?
WHAT... WHAT DO YOU KNOW OF THIS?

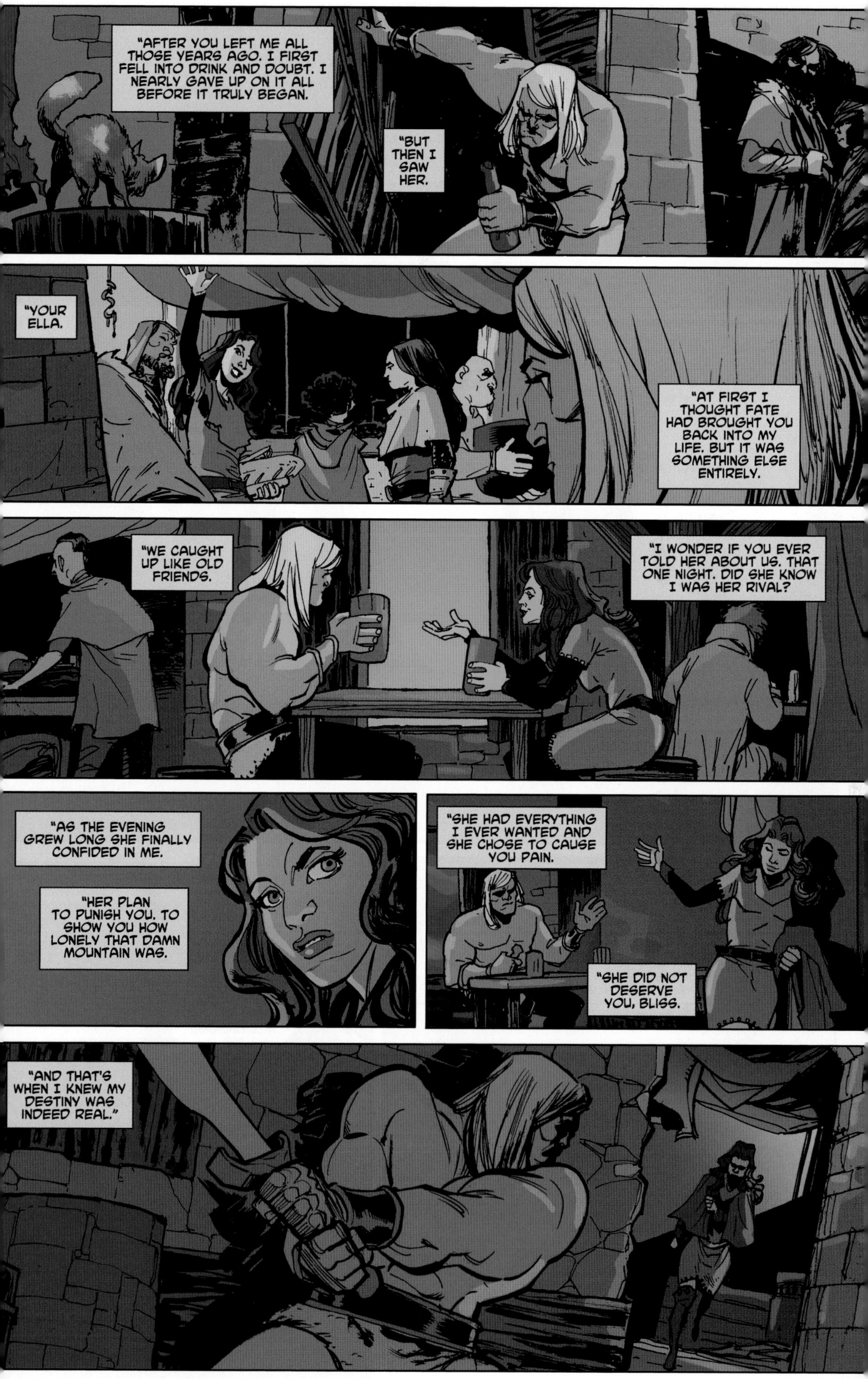
"AFTER YOU LEFT ME ALL THOSE YEARS AGO. I FIRST FELL INTO DRINK AND DOUBT. I NEARLY GAVE UP ON IT ALL BEFORE IT TRULY BEGAN.
"BUT THEN I SAW HER.
"YOUR ELLA.
"AT FIRST I THOUGHT FATE HAD BROUGHT YOU BACK INTO MY LIFE. BUT IT WAS SOMETHING ELSE ENTIRELY.
"WE CAUGHT UP LIKE OLD FRIENDS.
"I WONDER IF YOU EVER TOLD HER ABOUT US. THAT ONE NIGHT. DID SHE KNOW I WAS HER RIVAL?
"AS THE EVENING GREW LONG SHE FINALLY CONFIDED IN ME.
"HER PLAN TO PUNISH YOU. TO SHOW YOU HOW LONELY THAT DAMN MOUNTAIN WAS.
"SHE HAD EVERYTHING I EVER WANTED AND SHE CHOSE TO CAUSE YOU PAIN.
"SHE DID NOT DESERVE YOU, BLISS.
"AND THAT'S WHEN I KNEW MY DESTINY WAS INDEED REAL."

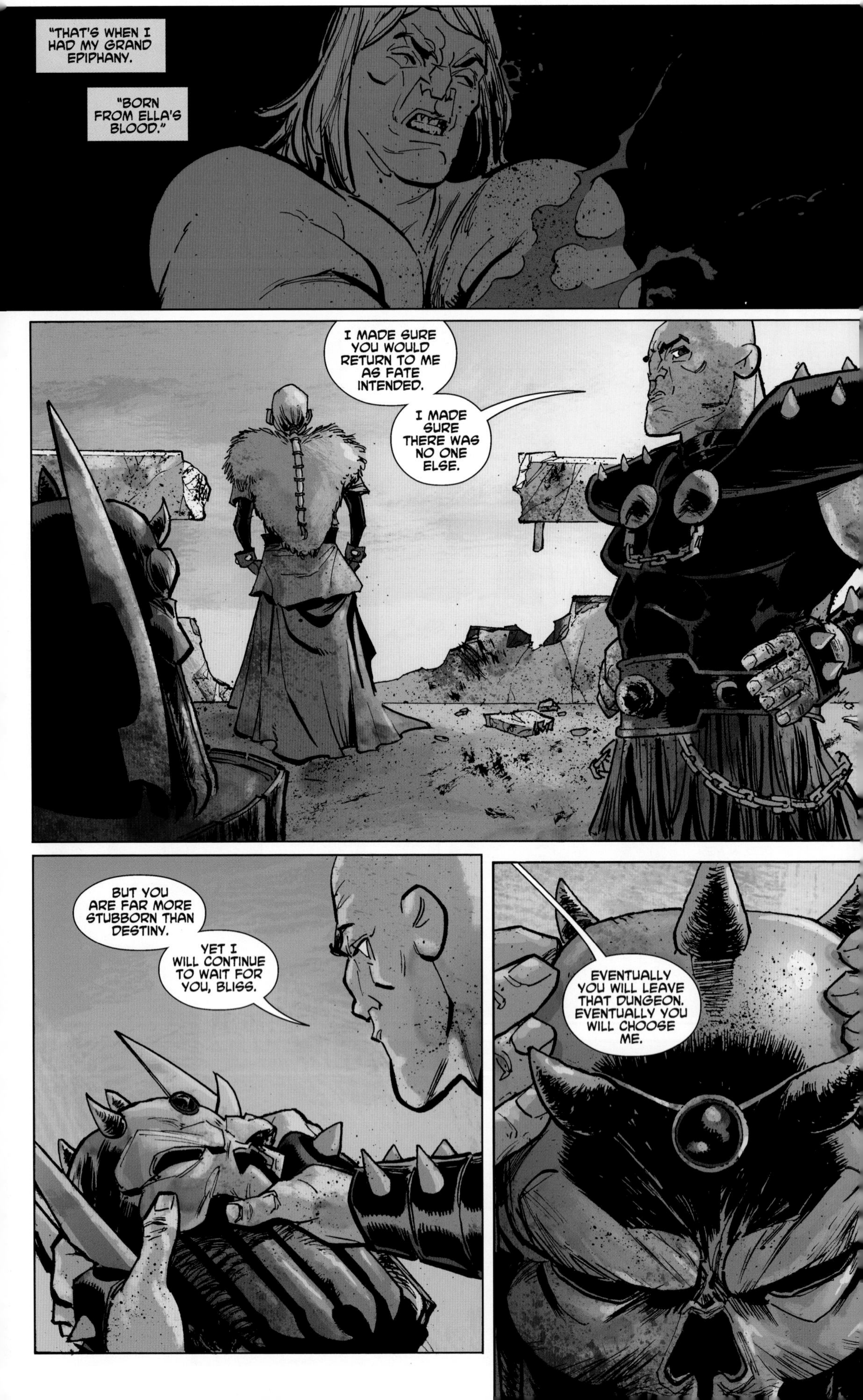
"THAT'S WHEN I HAD MY GRAND EPIPHANY.
"BORN FROM ELLA'S BLOOD."
I MADE SURE YOU WOULD RETURN TO ME AS FATE INTENDED.
I MADE SURE THERE WAS NO ONE ELSE.
BUT YOU ARE FAR MORE STUBBORN THAN DESTINY.
YET I WILL CONTINUE TO WAIT FOR YOU, BLISS.
EVENTUALLY YOU WILL LEAVE THAT DUNGEON. EVENTUALLY YOU WILL CHOOSE ME.

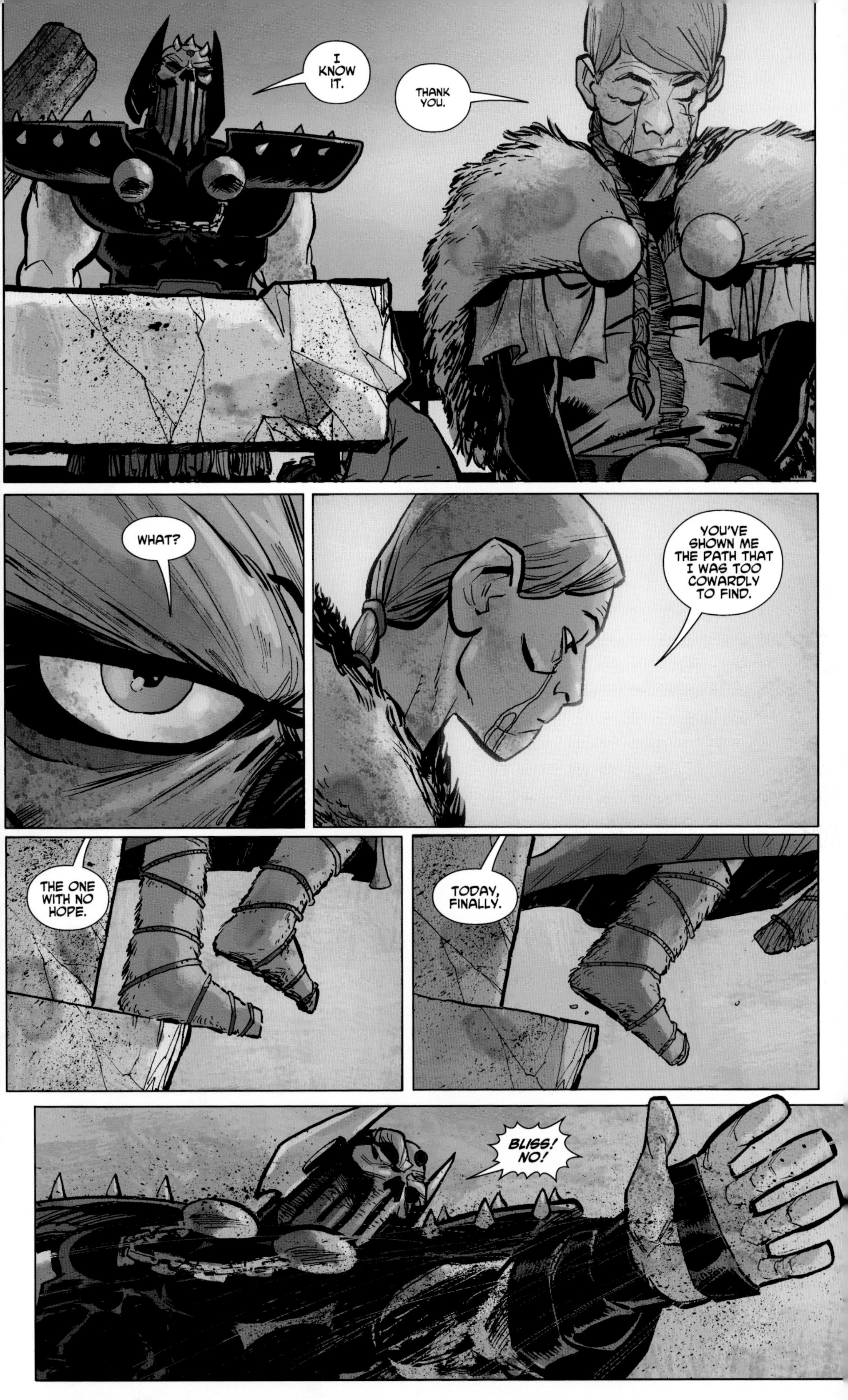

I KNOW IT.
THANK YOU.
WHAT?
YOU'VE SHOWN ME THE PATH THAT I WAS TOO COWARDLY TO FIND.
THE ONE WITH NO HOPE.
TODAY, FINALLY.
BLISS! NO!

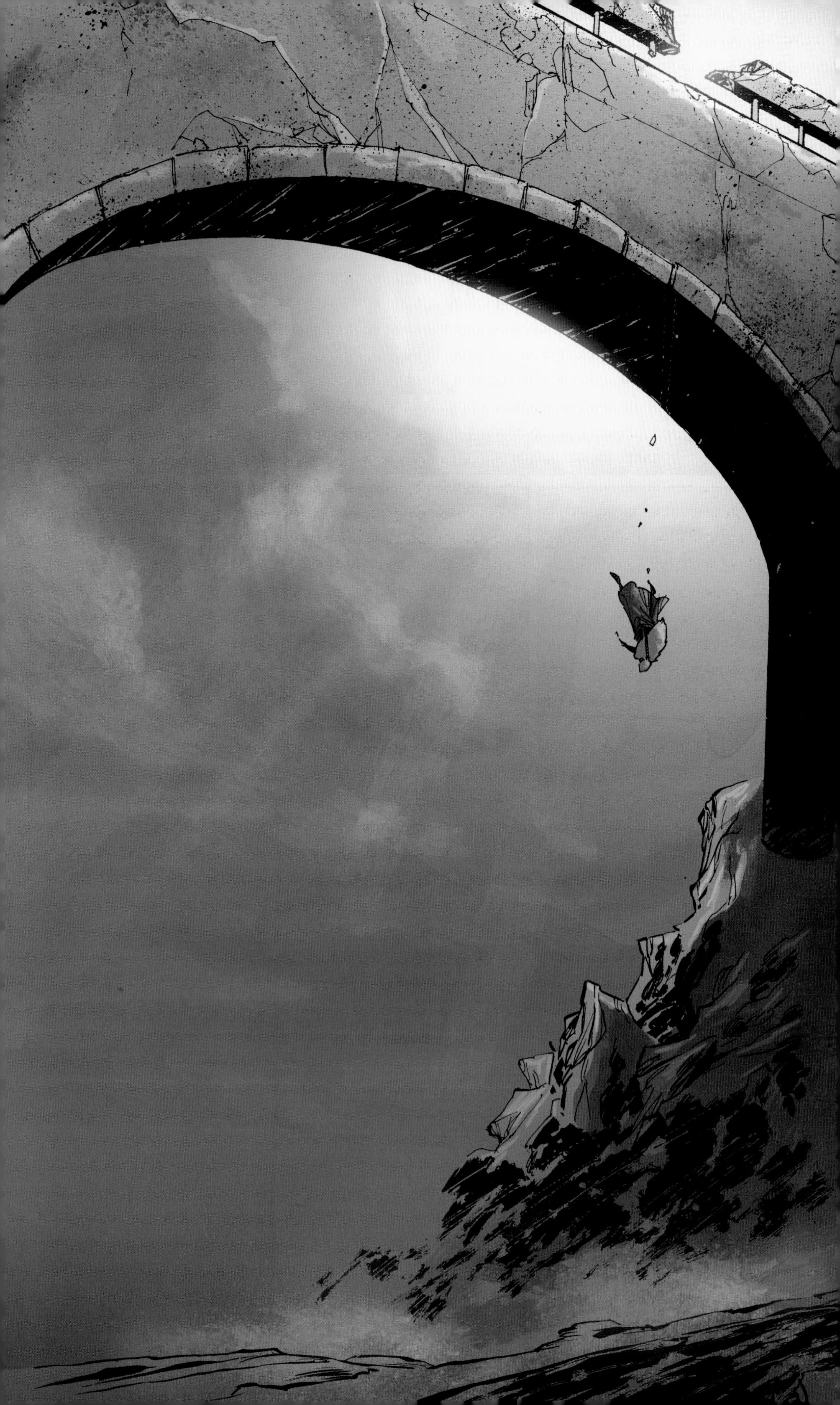

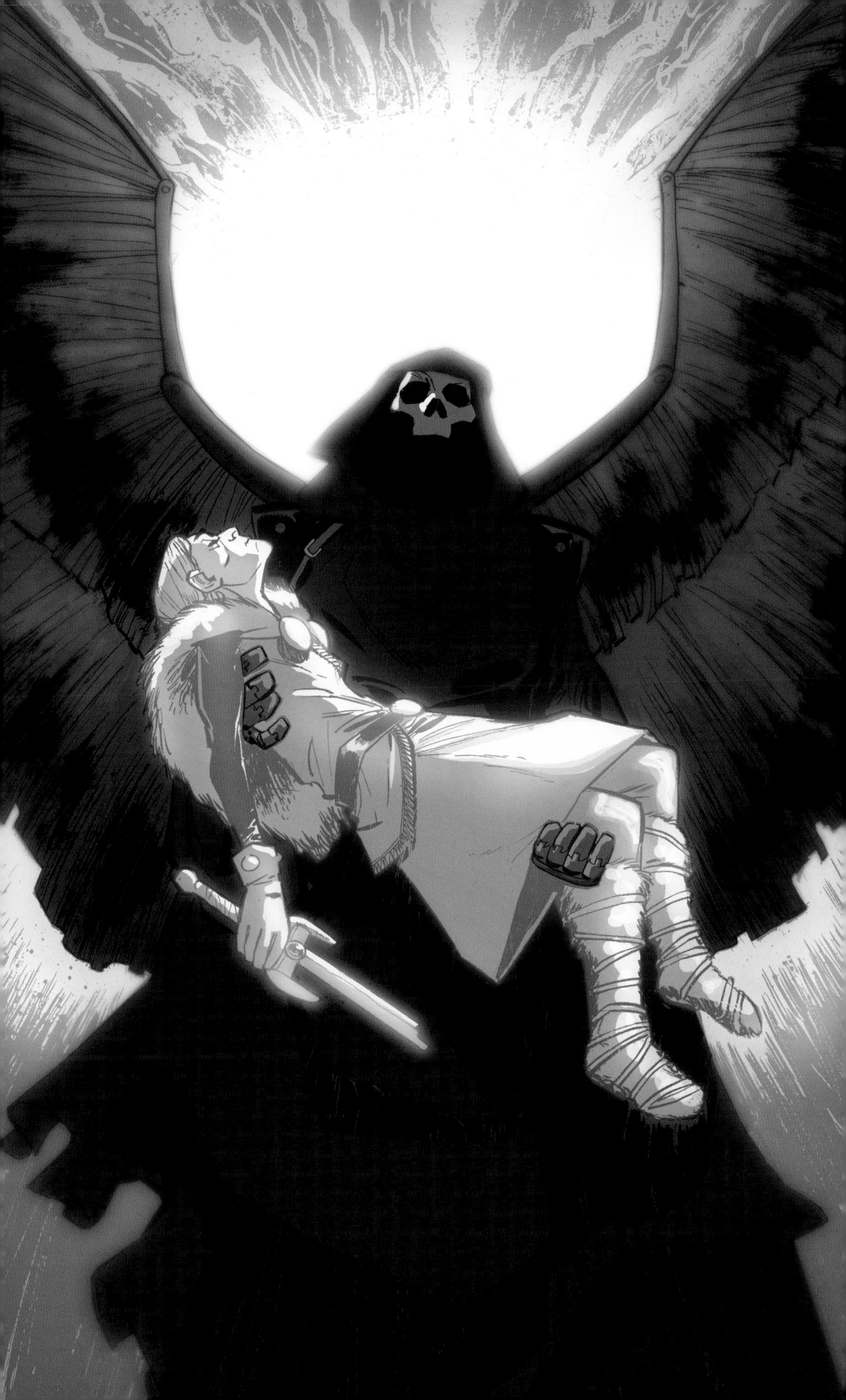

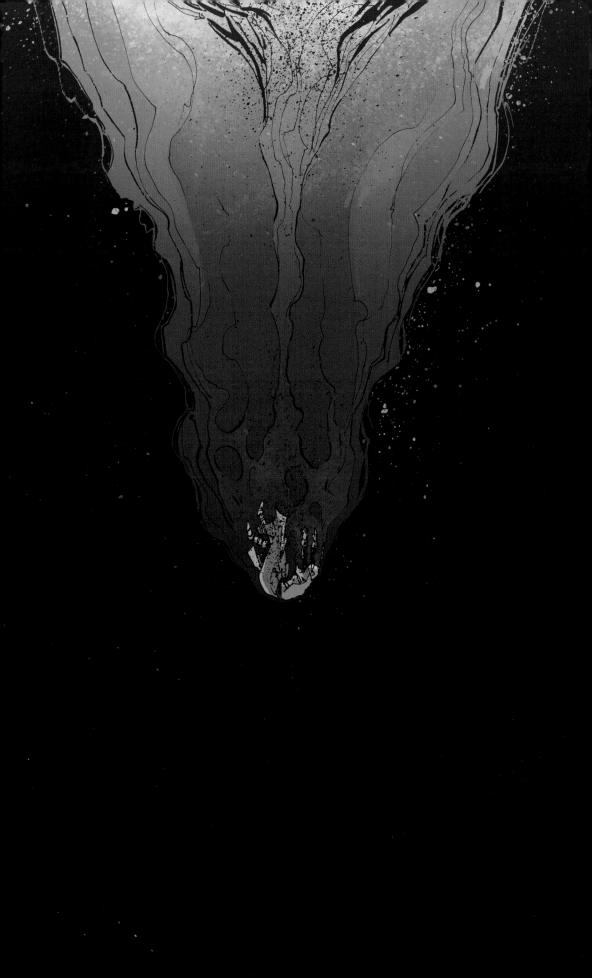

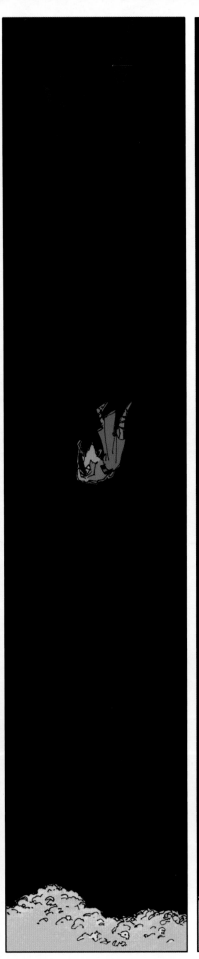

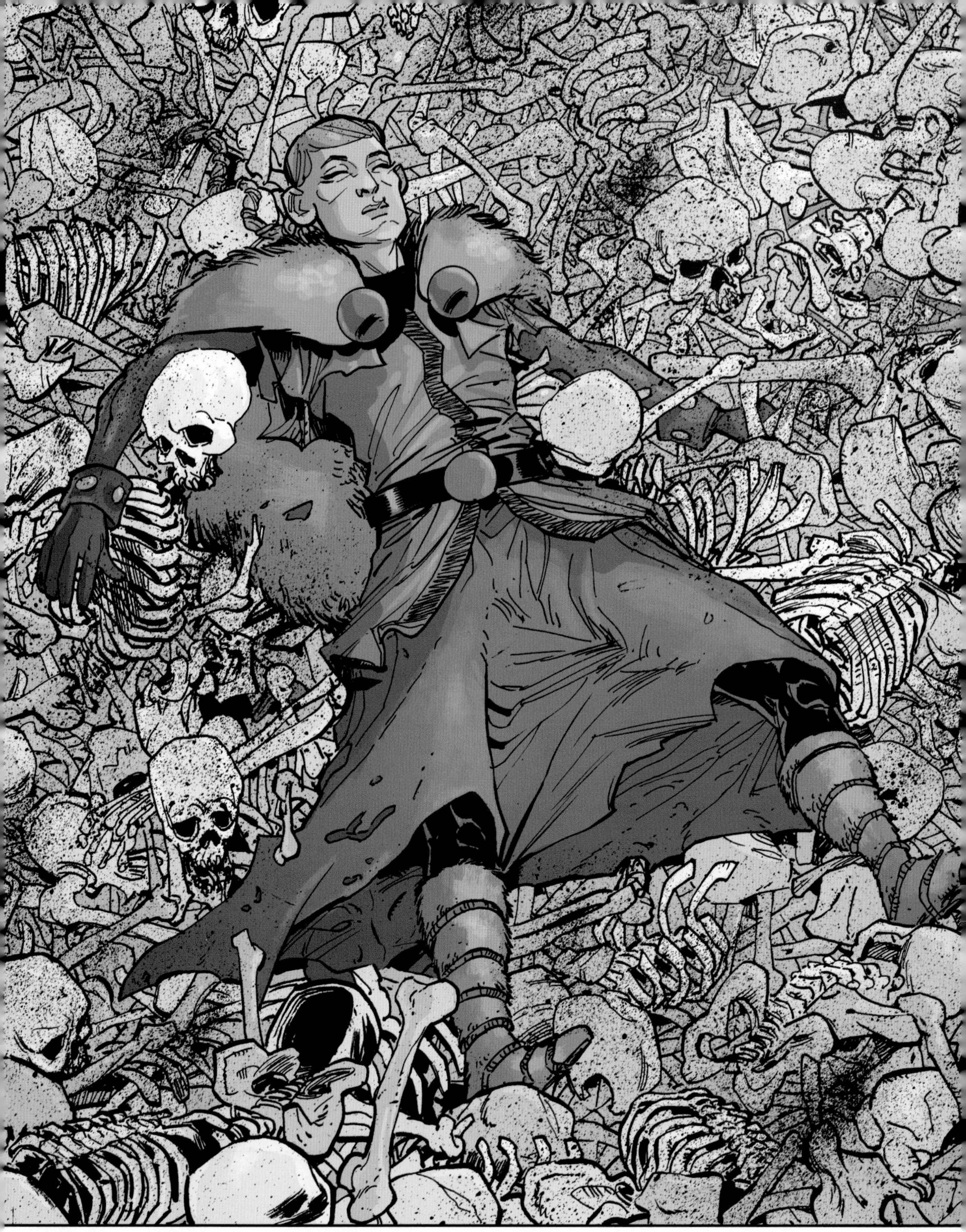

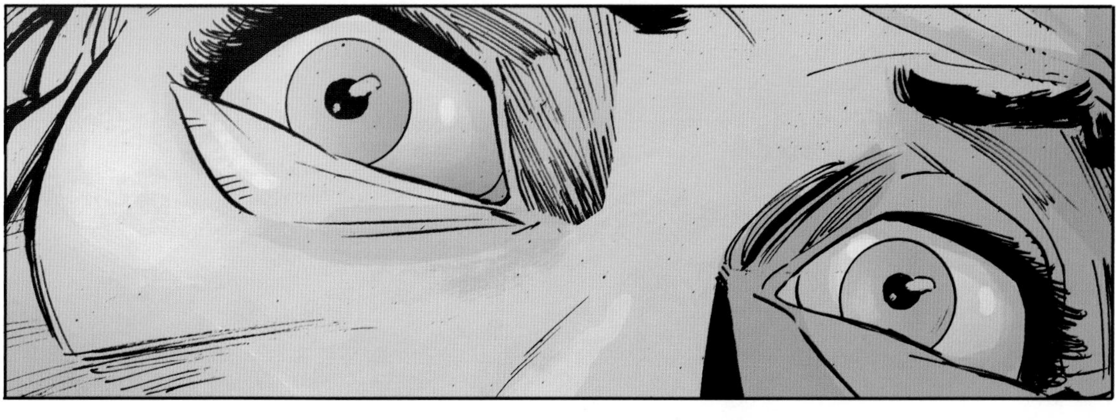

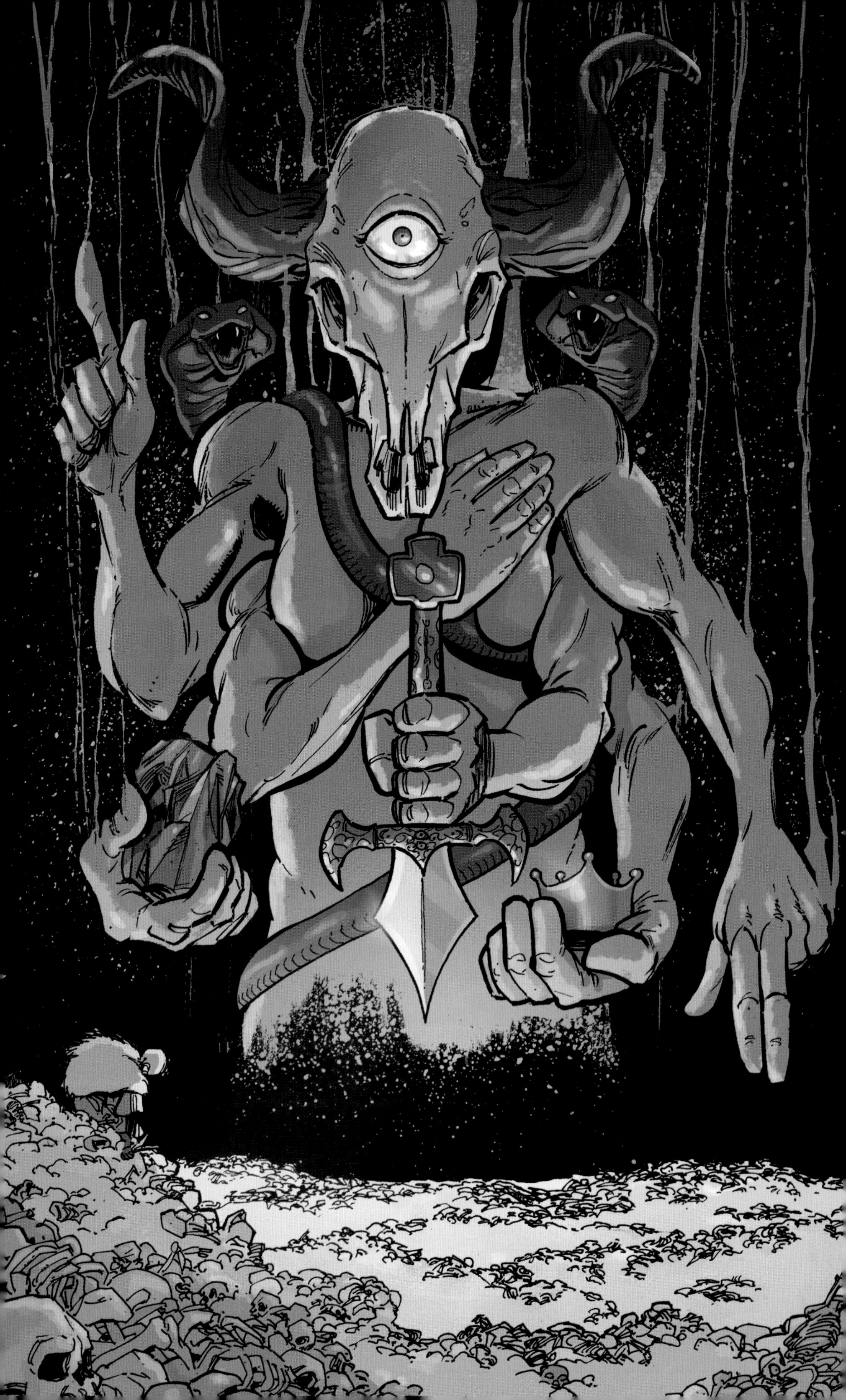

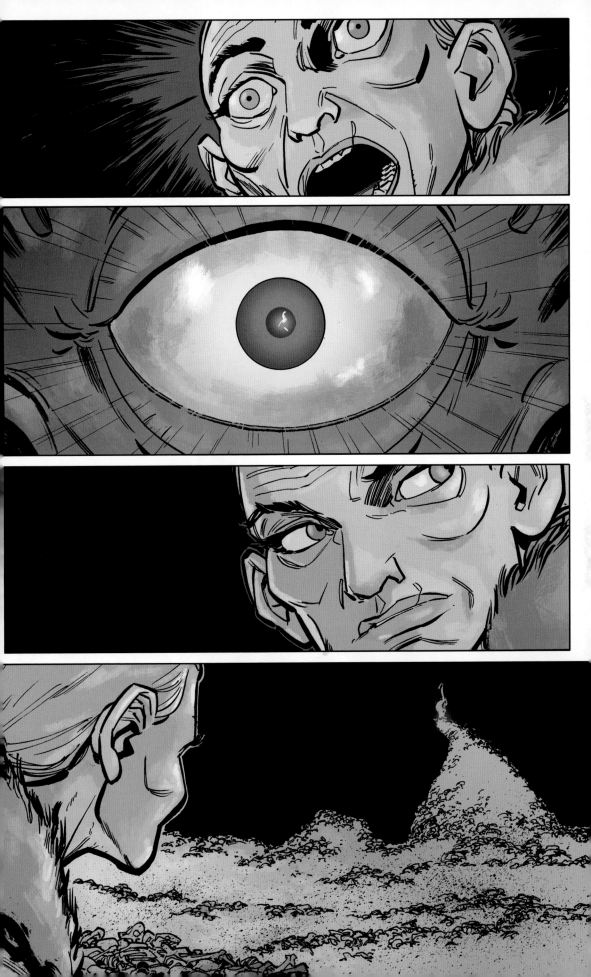

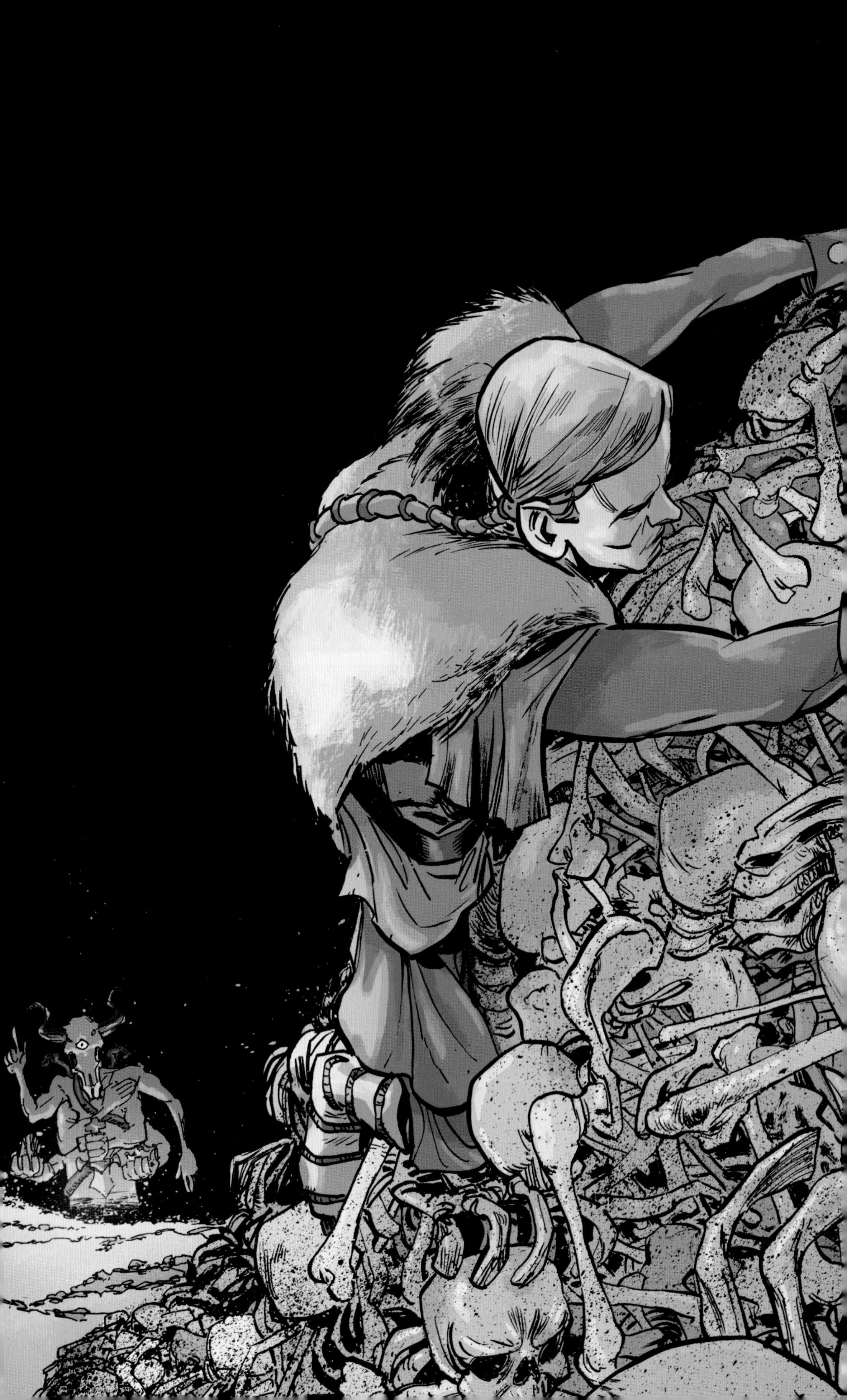

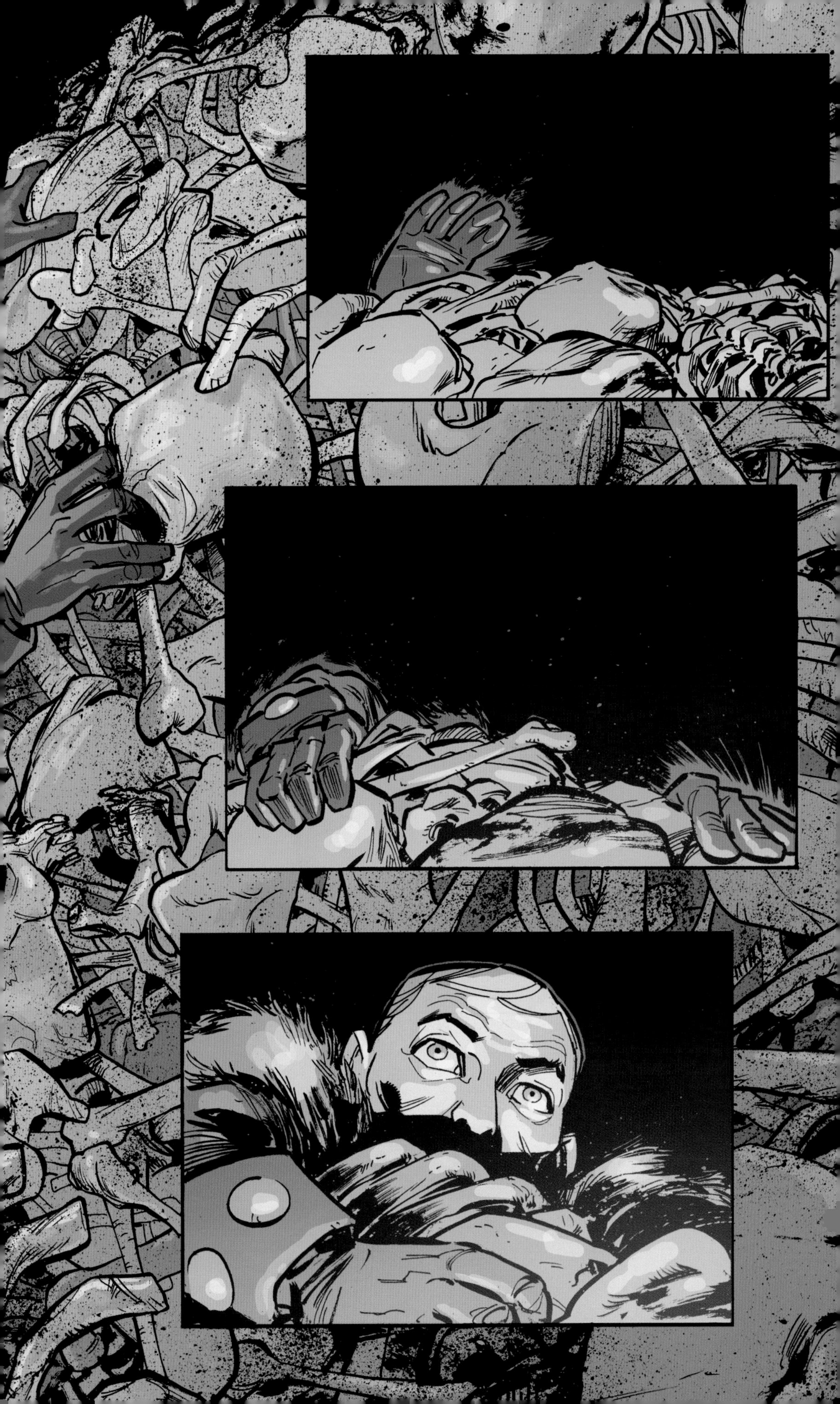

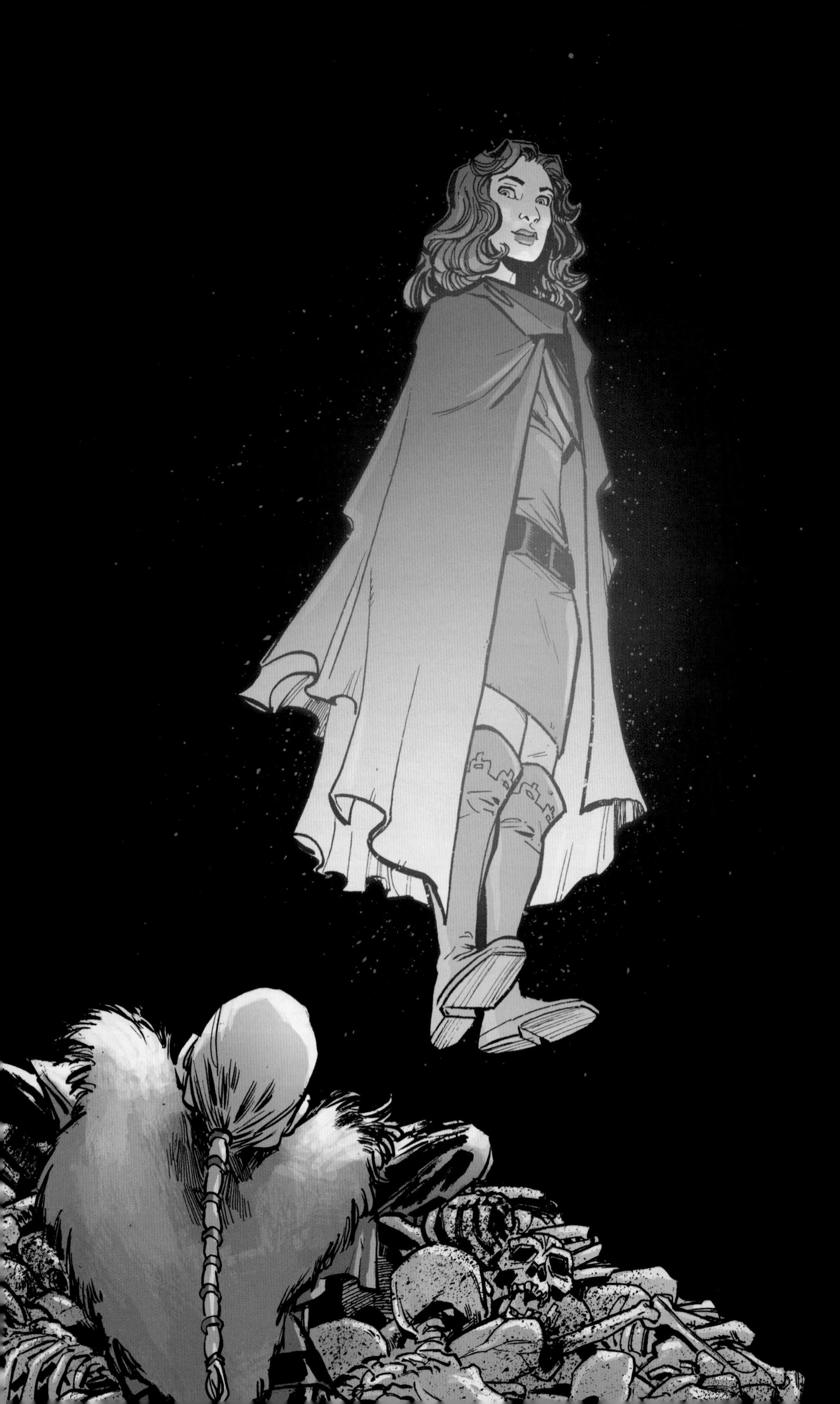

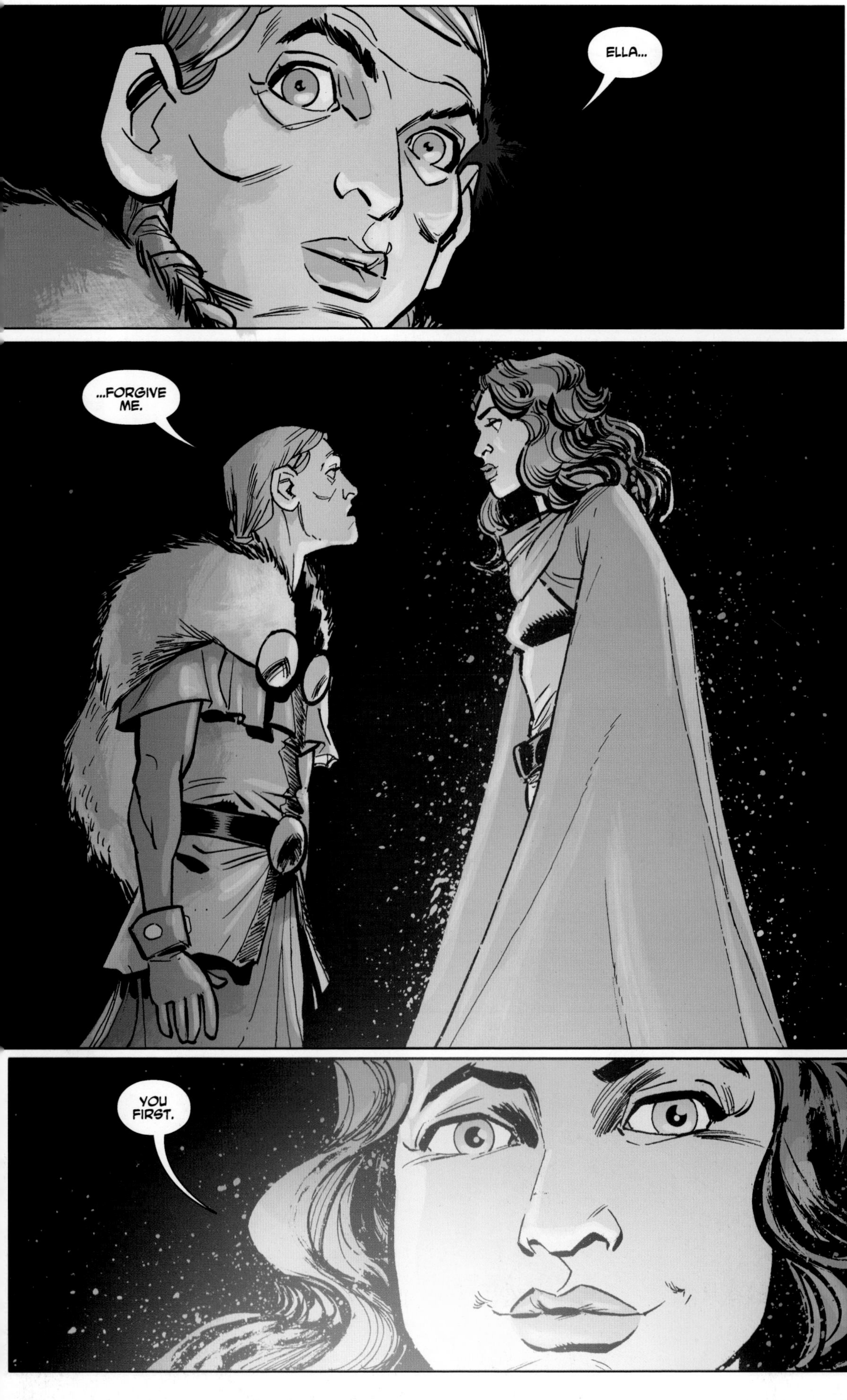
ELLA...
...FORGIVE ME.
YOU FIRST.

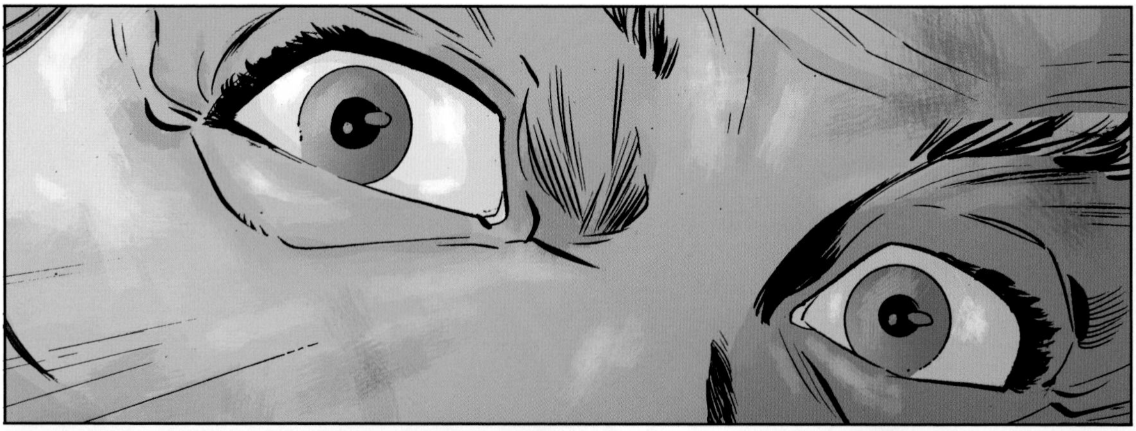

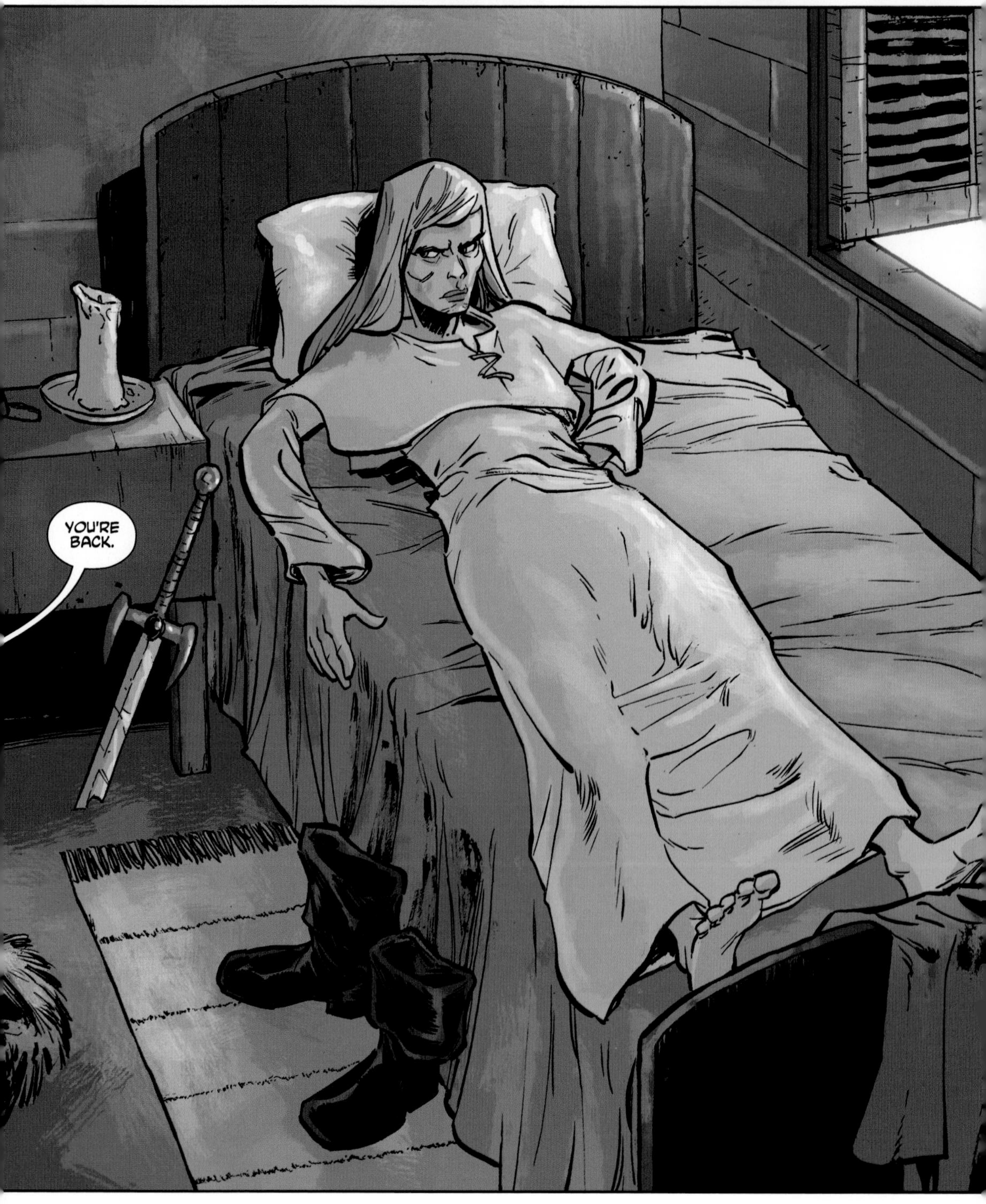
YOU'RE BACK.

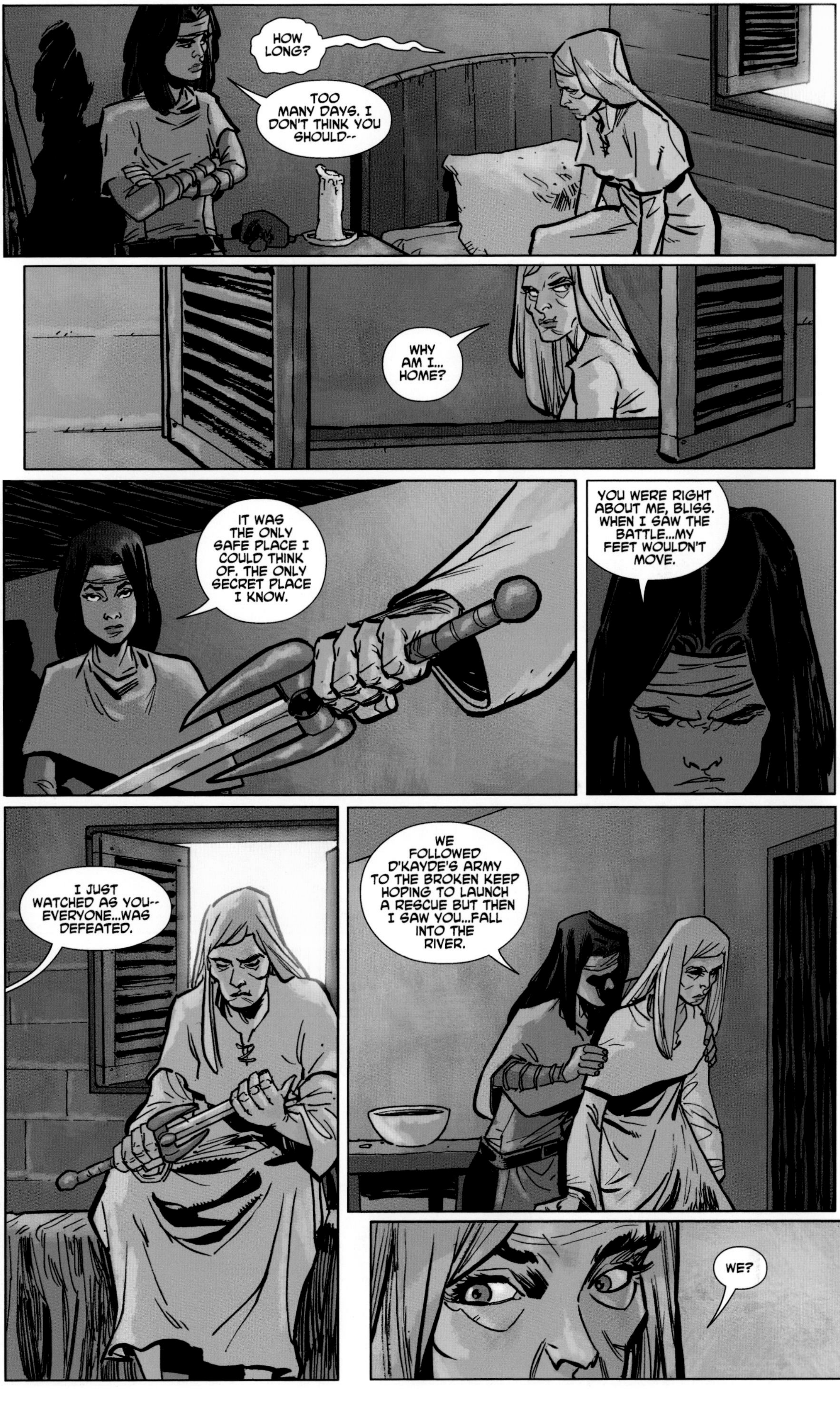
HOW LONG?
TOO MANY DAYS. I DON'T THINK YOU SHOULD--
WHY AM I... HOME?
IT WAS THE ONLY SAFE PLACE I COULD THINK OF. THE ONLY SECRET PLACE I KNOW.
YOU WERE RIGHT ABOUT ME, BLISS. WHEN I SAW THE BATTLE...MY FEET WOULDN'T MOVE.
I JUST WATCHED AS YOU-- EVERYONE...WAS DEFEATED.
WE FOLLOWED D'KAYDE'S ARMY TO THE BROKEN KEEP HOPING TO LAUNCH A RESCUE BUT THEN I SAW YOU...FALL INTO THE RIVER.
WE?

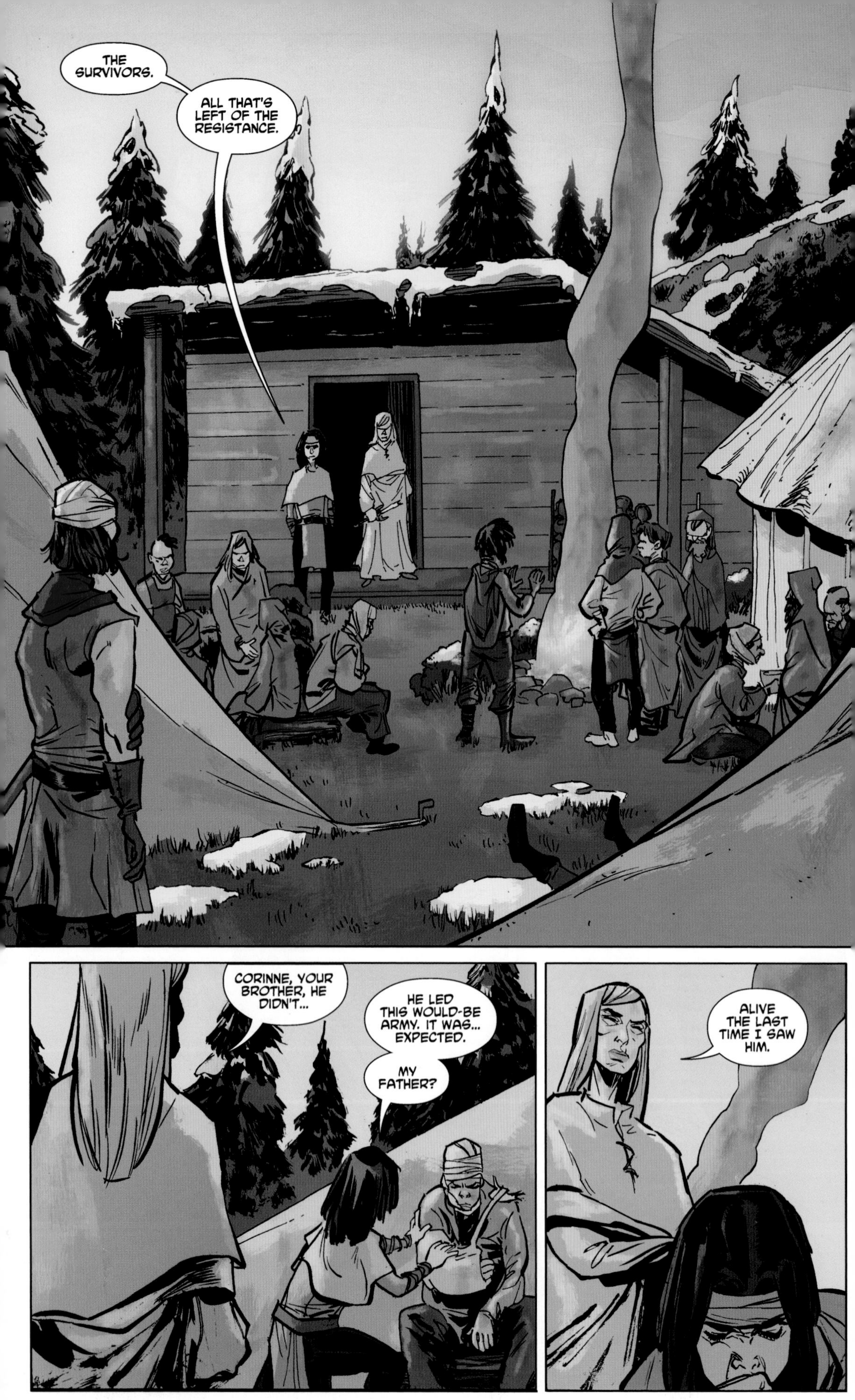
THE SURVIVORS.
ALL THAT'S LEFT OF THE RESISTANCE.
CORINNE, YOUR BROTHER, HE DIDN'T...
HE LED THIS WOULD-BE ARMY. IT WAS... EXPECTED.
MY FATHER?
ALIVE THE LAST TIME I SAW HIM.

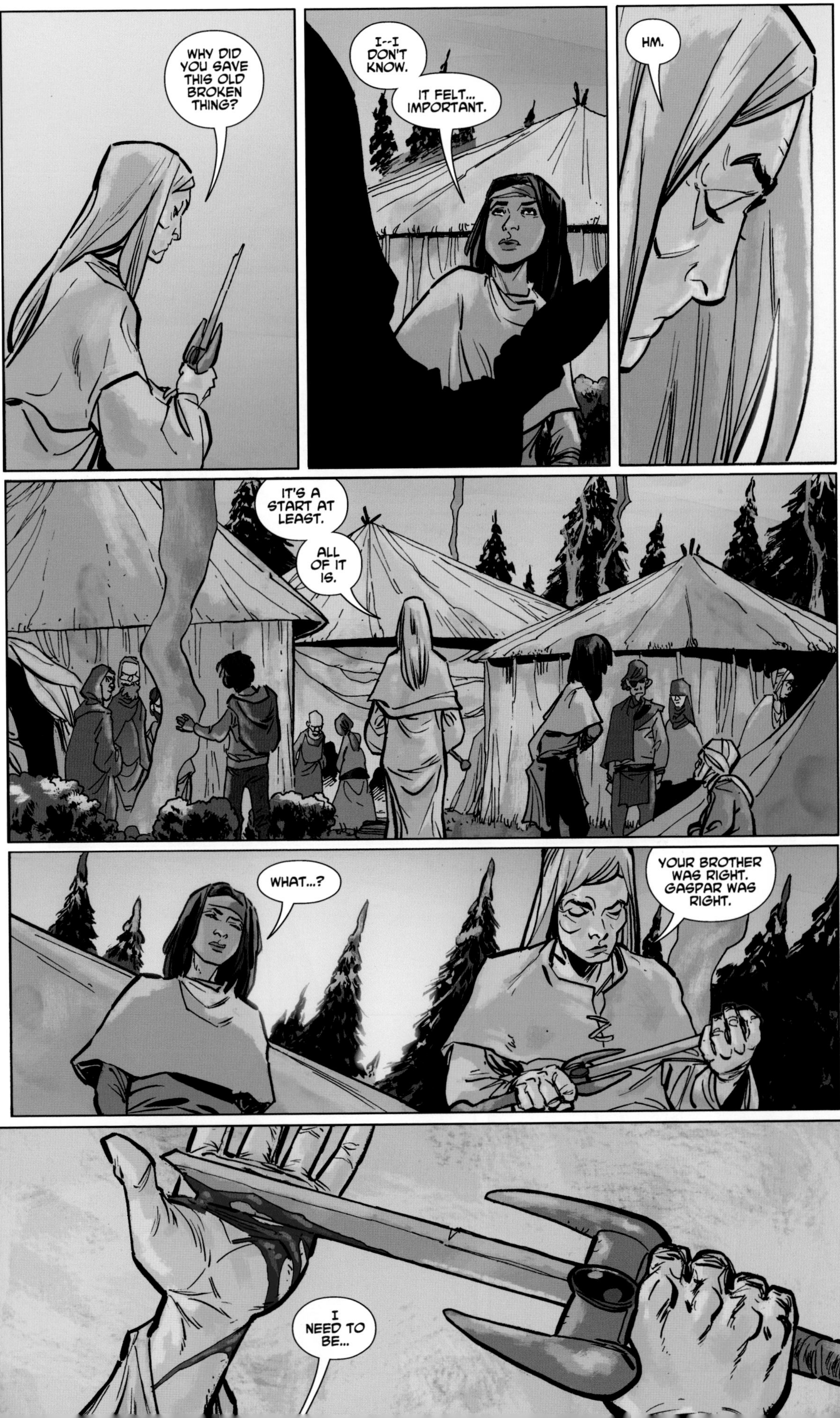
WHY DID YOU SAVE THIS OLD BROKEN THING?
I--I DON'T KNOW.
IT FELT... IMPORTANT.
HM.
IT'S A START AT LEAST.
ALL OF IT IS.
WHAT...?
YOUR BROTHER WAS RIGHT. GASPAR WAS RIGHT.
I NEED TO BE...

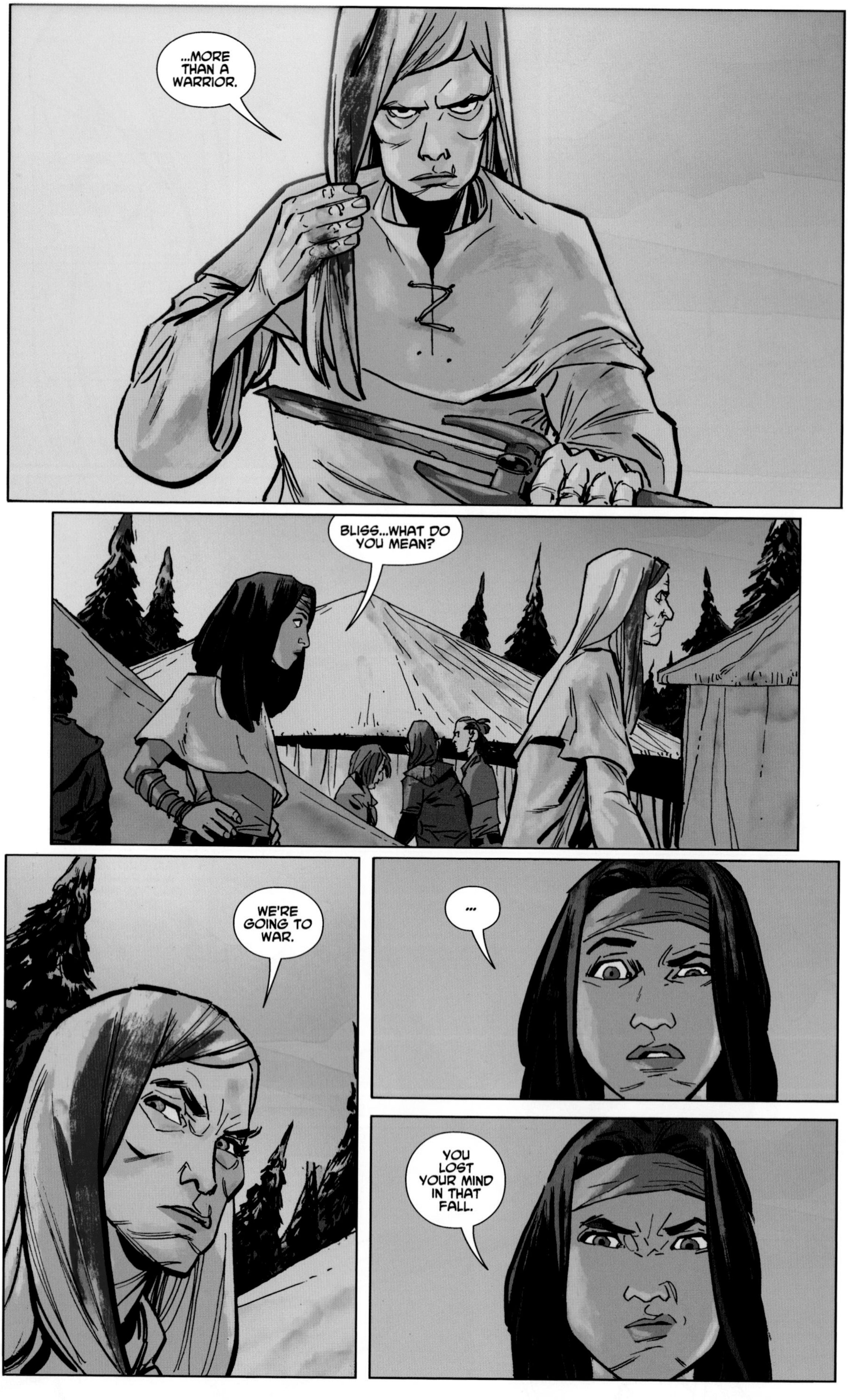
...MORE THAN A WARRIOR.
BLISS...WHAT DO YOU MEAN?
WE'RE GOING TO WAR.
...
YOU LOST YOUR MIND IN THAT FALL.

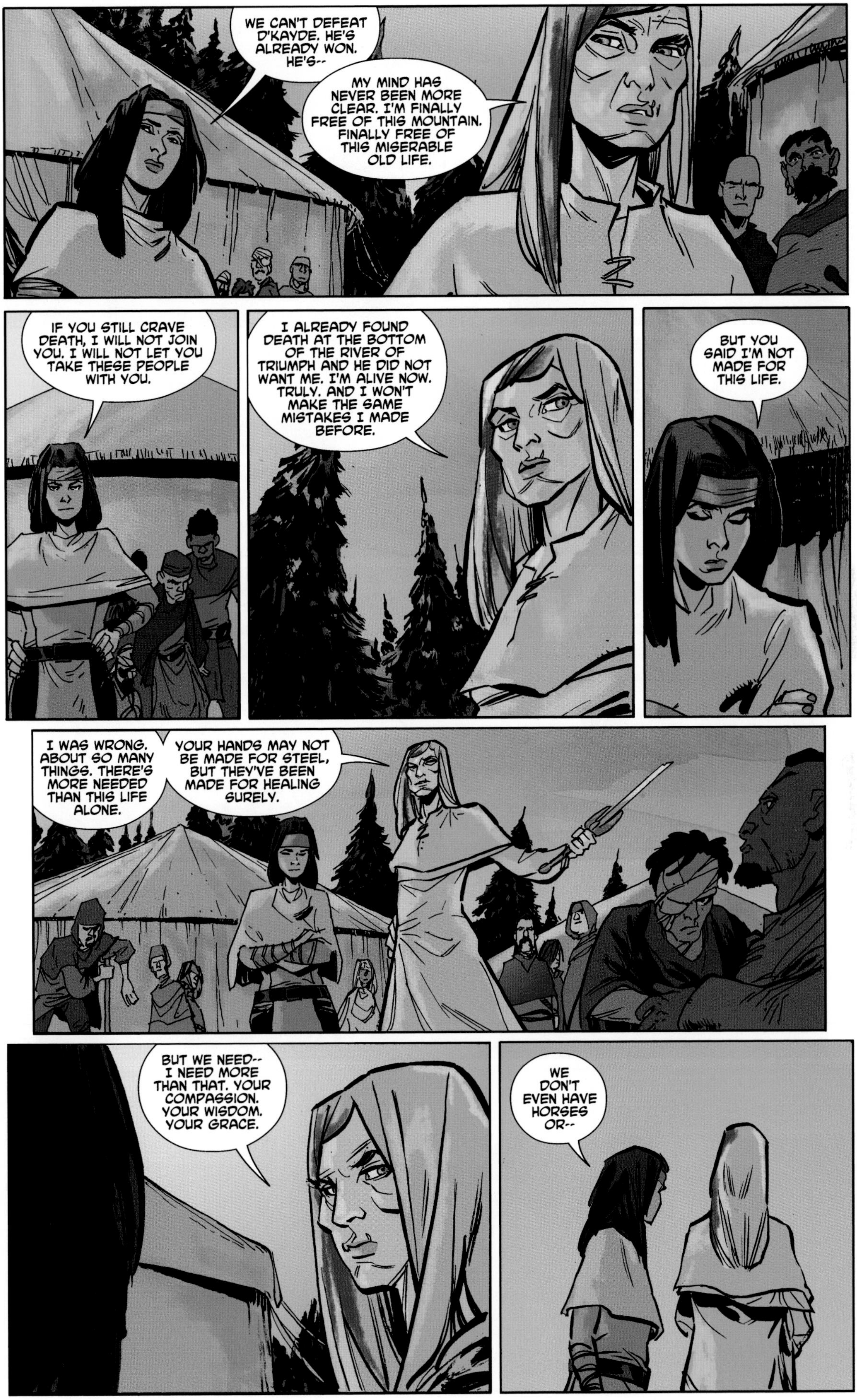
WE CAN'T DEFEAT D'KAYDE. HE'S ALREADY WON. HE'S--
MY MIND HAS NEVER BEEN MORE CLEAR. I'M FINALLY FREE OF THIS MOUNTAIN. FINALLY FREE OF THIS MISERABLE OLD LIFE.
IF YOU STILL CRAVE DEATH, I WILL NOT JOIN YOU. I WILL NOT LET YOU TAKE THESE PEOPLE WITH YOU.
I ALREADY FOUND DEATH AT THE BOTTOM OF THE RIVER OF TRIUMPH AND HE DID NOT WANT ME. I'M ALIVE NOW. TRULY. AND I WON'T MAKE THE SAME MISTAKES I MADE BEFORE.
BUT YOU SAID I'M NOT MADE FOR THIS LIFE.
I WAS WRONG. ABOUT SO MANY THINGS. THERE'S MORE NEEDED THAN THIS LIFE ALONE.
YOUR HANDS MAY NOT BE MADE FOR STEEL, BUT THEY'VE BEEN MADE FOR HEALING SURELY.
BUT WE NEED-- I NEED MORE THAN THAT. YOUR COMPASSION. YOUR WISDOM. YOUR GRACE.
WE DON'T EVEN HAVE HORSES OR--

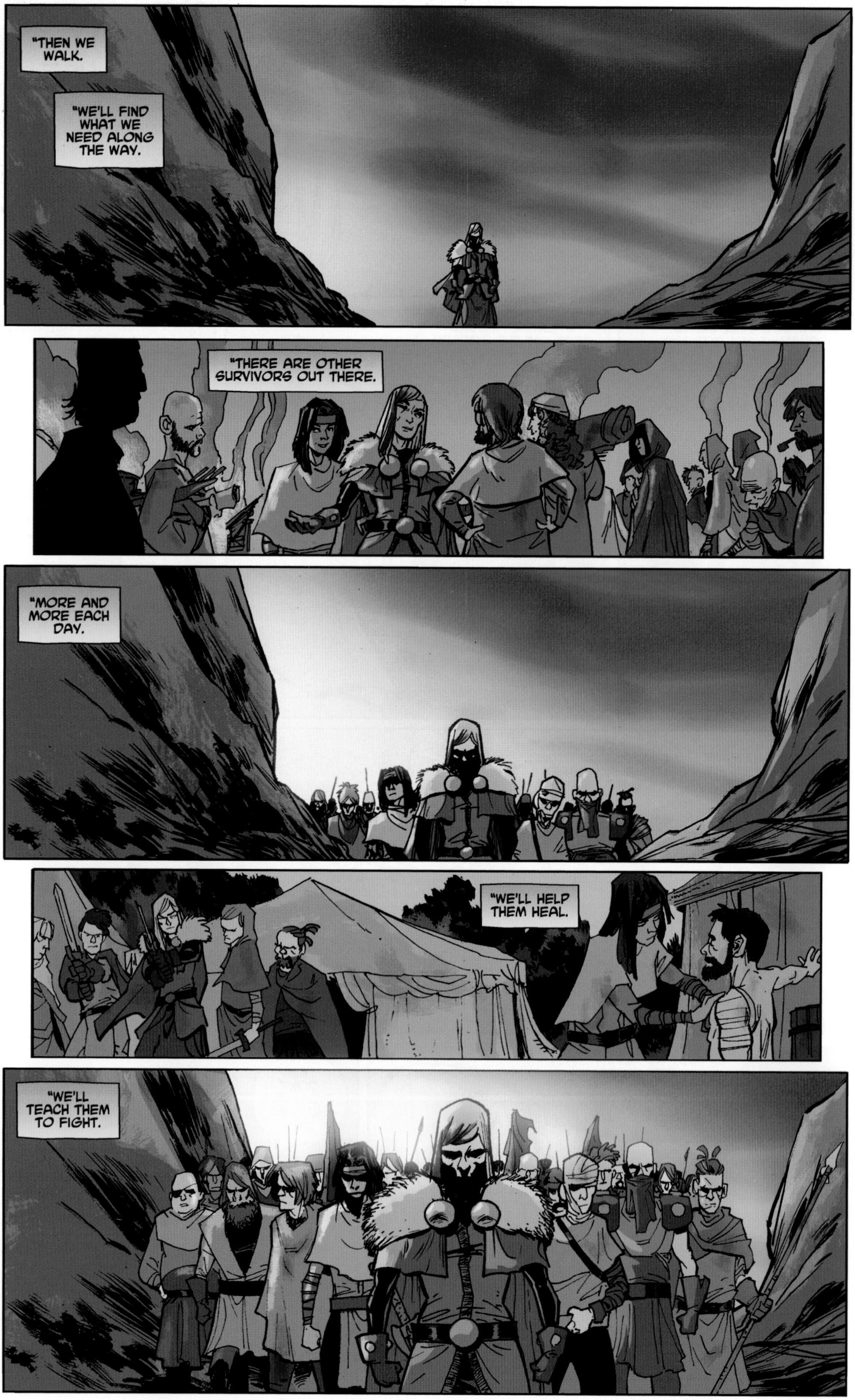
"THEN WE WALK.
"WE'LL FIND WHAT WE NEED ALONG THE WAY.
"THERE ARE OTHER SURVIVORS OUT THERE.
"MORE AND MORE EACH DAY.
"WE'LL HELP THEM HEAL.
"WE'LL TEACH THEM TO FIGHT.

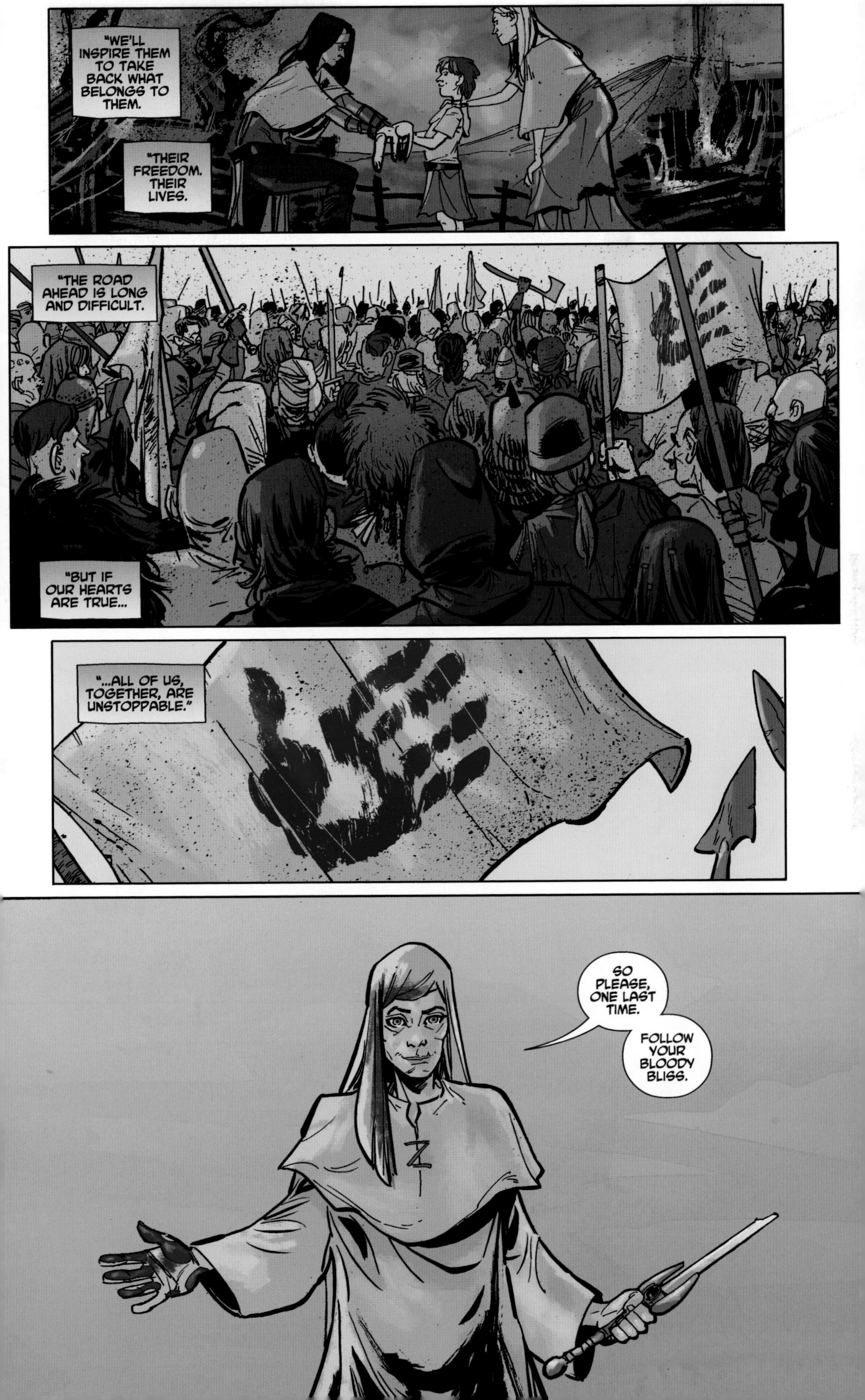
"WE'LL INSPIRE THEM TO TAKE BACK WHAT BELONGS TO THEM.
"THEIR FREEDOM. THEIR LIVES.
"THE ROAD AHEAD IS LONG AND DIFFICULT.
"BUT IF OUR HEARTS ARE TRUE...
"...ALL OF US, TOGETHER, ARE UNSTOPPABLE."
SO PLEASE, ONE LAST TIME.
FOLLOW YOUR BLOODY BLISS.

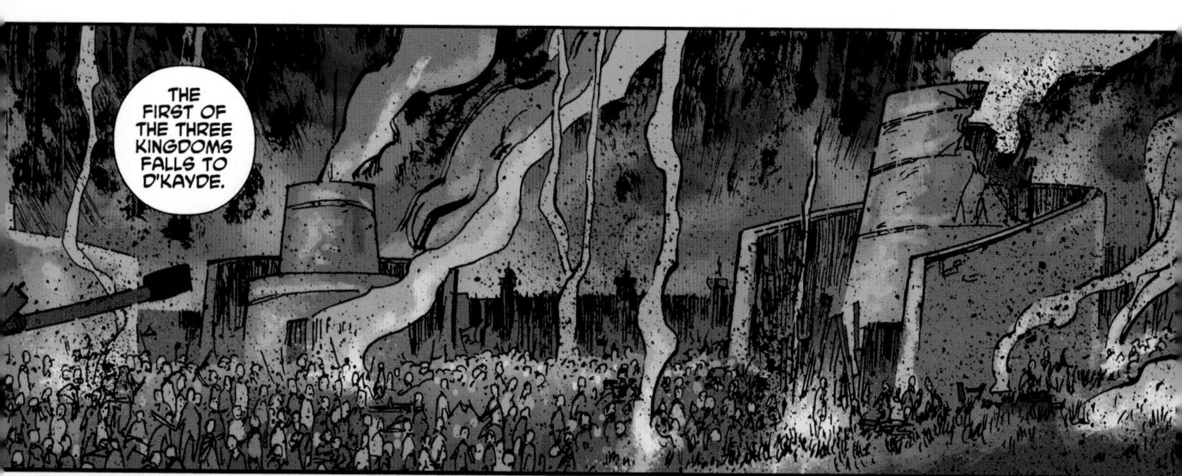
THE FIRST OF THE THREE KINGDOMS FALLS TO D'KAYDE.

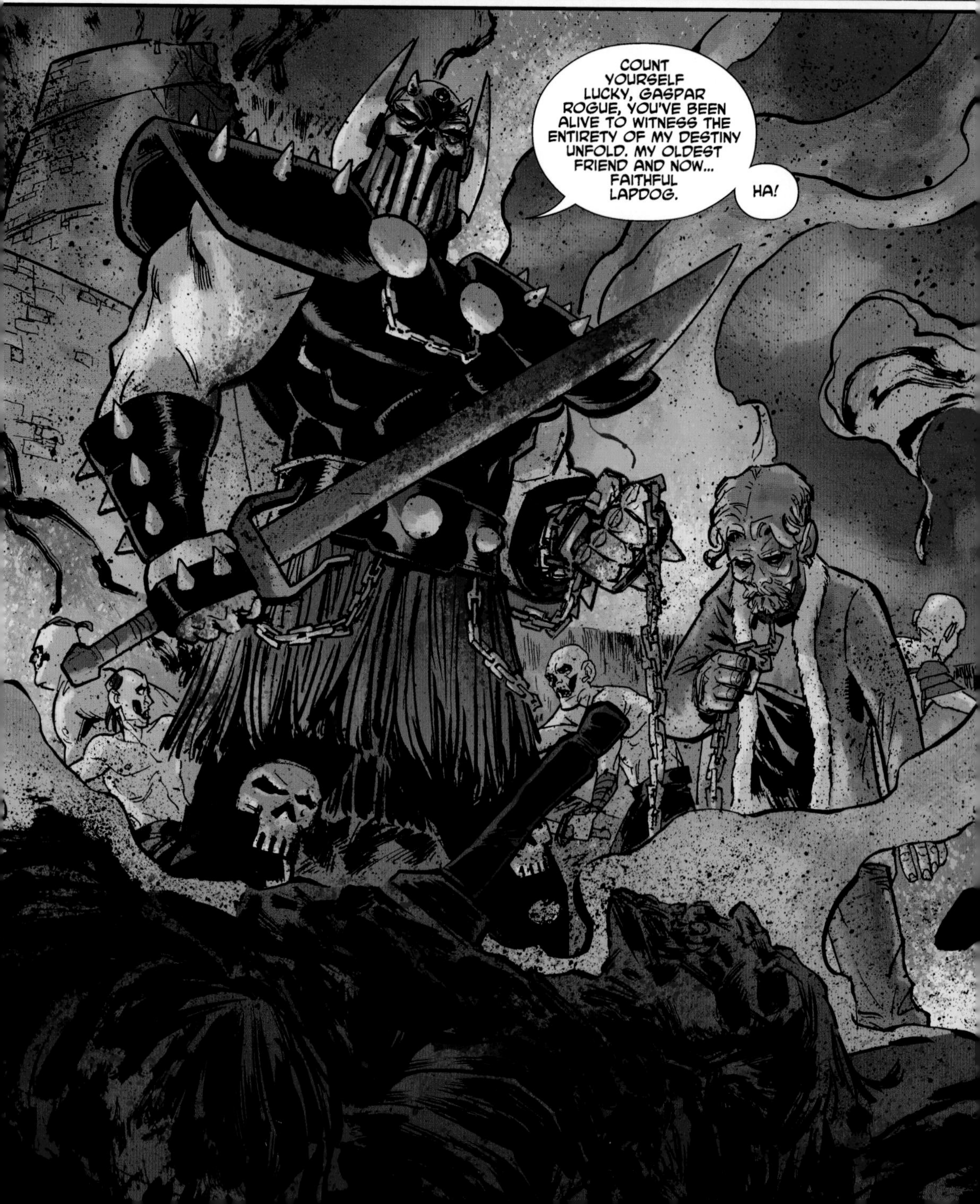
COUNT YOURSELF LUCKY, GASPAR ROGUE, YOU'VE BEEN ALIVE TO WITNESS THE ENTIRETY OF MY DESTINY UNFOLD. MY OLDEST FRIEND AND NOW... FAITHFUL LAPDOG.
HA!

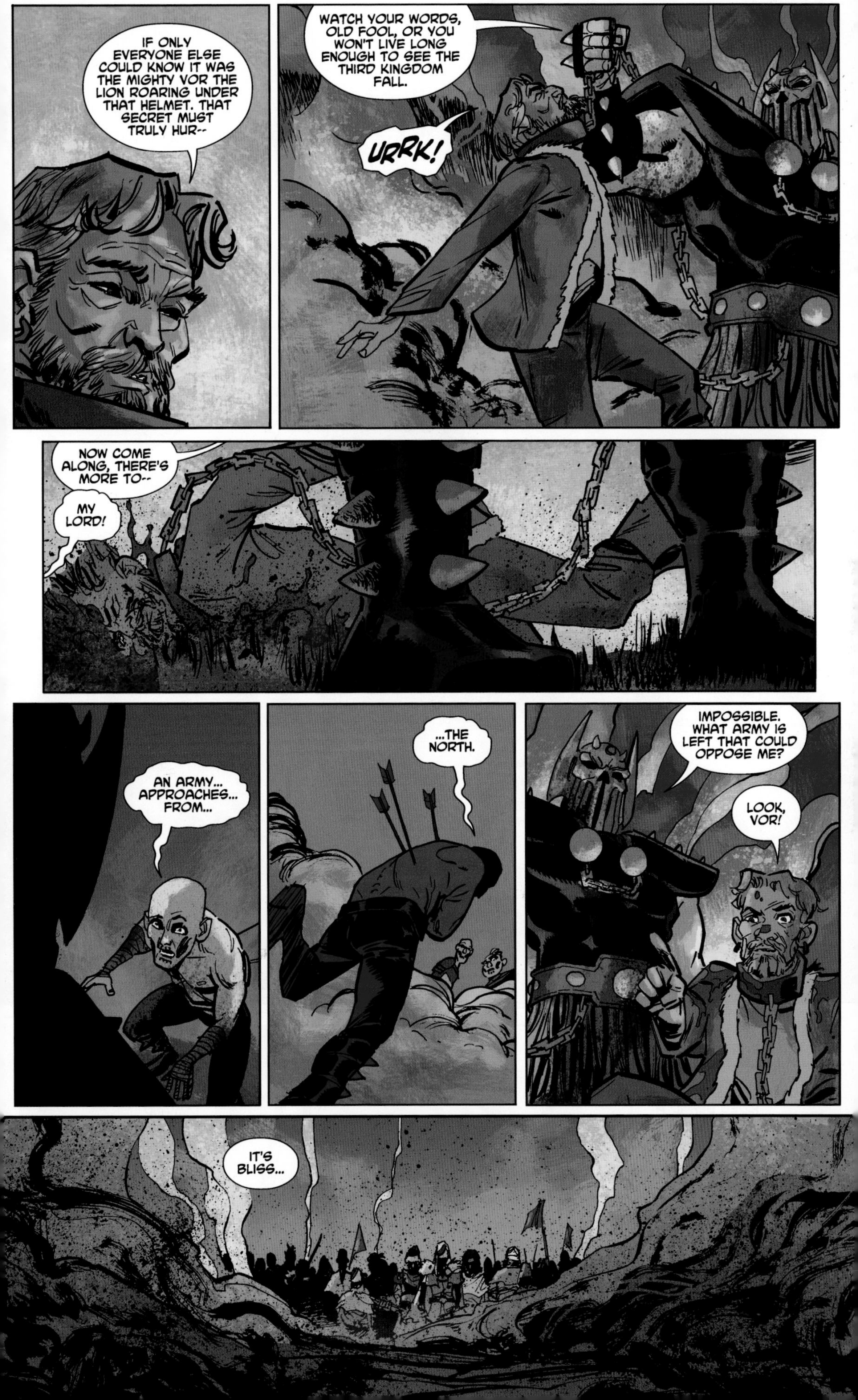
IF ONLY EVERYONE ELSE COULD KNOW IT WAS THE MIGHTY VOR THE LION ROARING UNDER THAT HELMET. THAT SECRET MUST TRULY HUR--
WATCH YOUR WORDS, OLD FOOL, OR YOU WON'T LIVE LONG ENOUGH TO SEE THE THIRD KINGDOM FALL.
URRK!
NOW COME ALONG, THERE'S MORE TO--
MY LORD!
AN ARMY... APPROACHES... FROM...
...THE NORTH.
IMPOSSIBLE. WHAT ARMY IS LEFT THAT COULD OPPOSE ME?
LOOK, VOR!
IT'S BLISS...

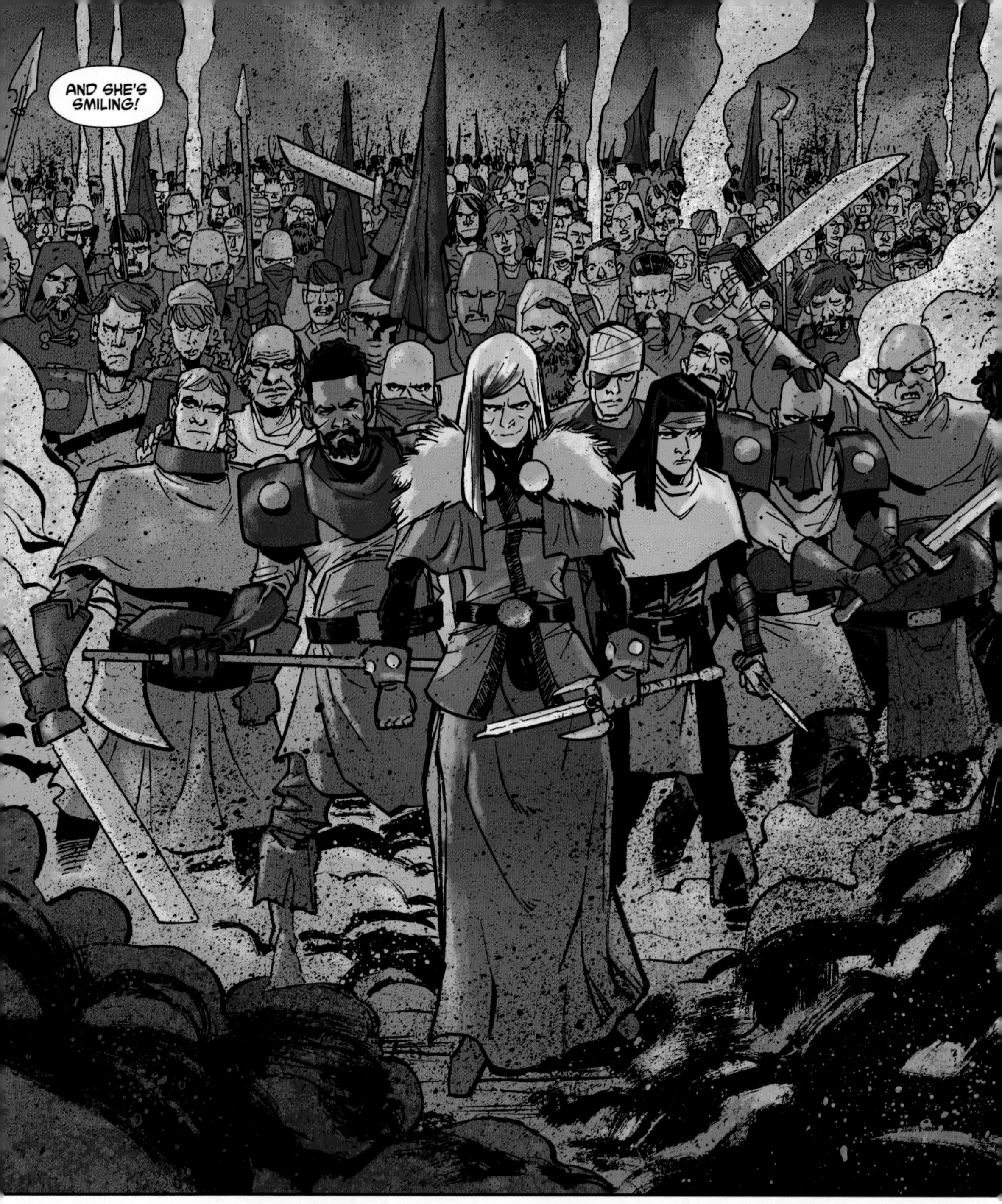
AND SHE'S SMILING!

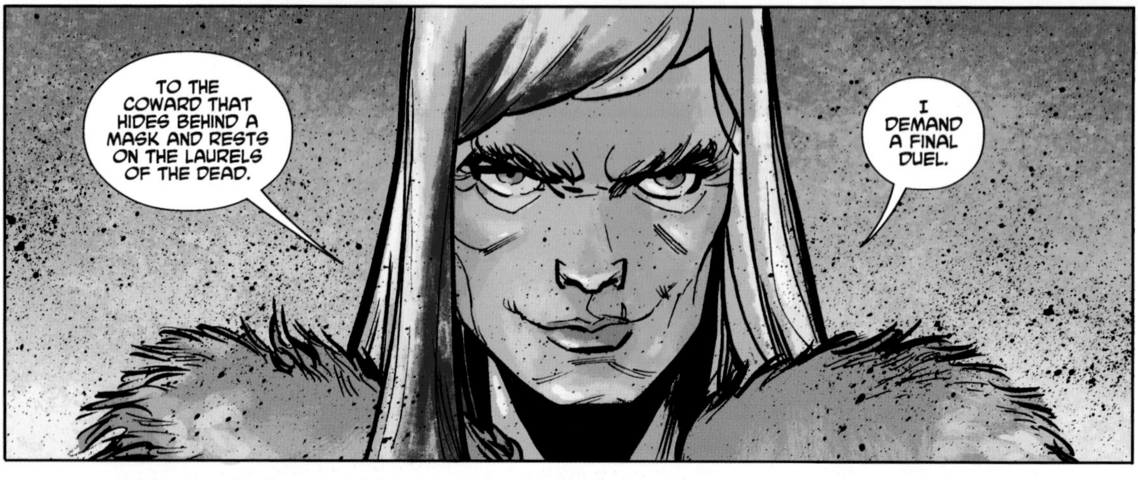
TO THE COWARD THAT HIDES BEHIND A MASK AND RESTS ON THE LAURELS OF THE DEAD.
I DEMAND A FINAL DUEL.

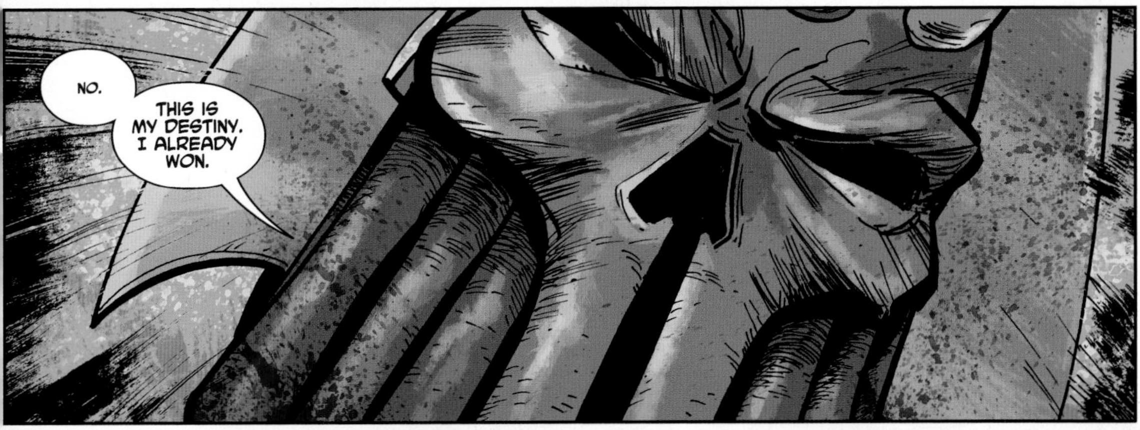
NO.
THIS IS MY DESTINY. I ALREADY WON.

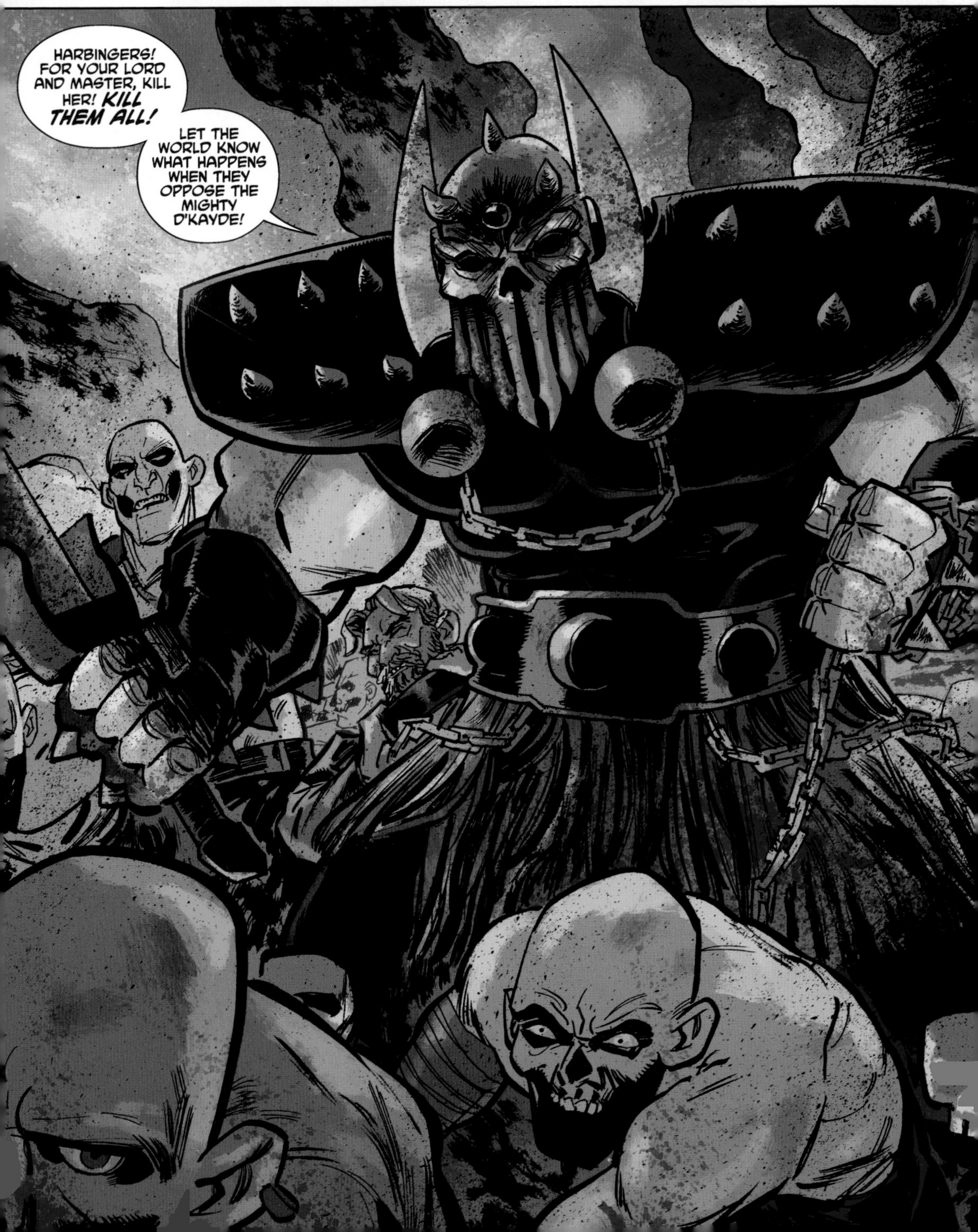
HARBINGERS! FOR YOUR LORD AND MASTER, KILL HER! ***KILL THEM ALL!***
LET THE WORLD KNOW WHAT HAPPENS WHEN THEY OPPOSE THE MIGHTY D'KAYDE!

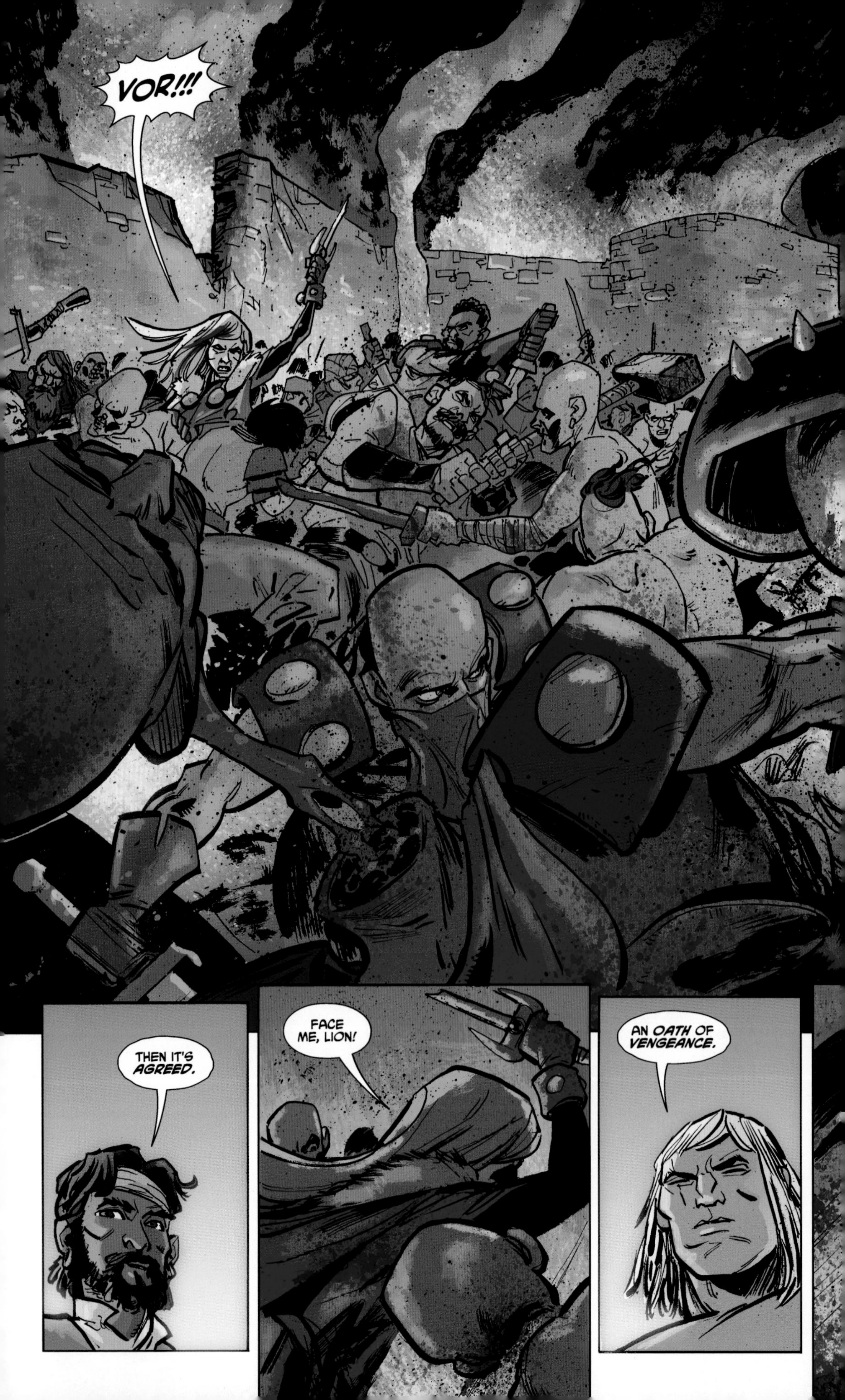
VOR!!!
THEN IT'S AGREED.
FACE ME, LION!
AN OATH OF VENGEANCE.

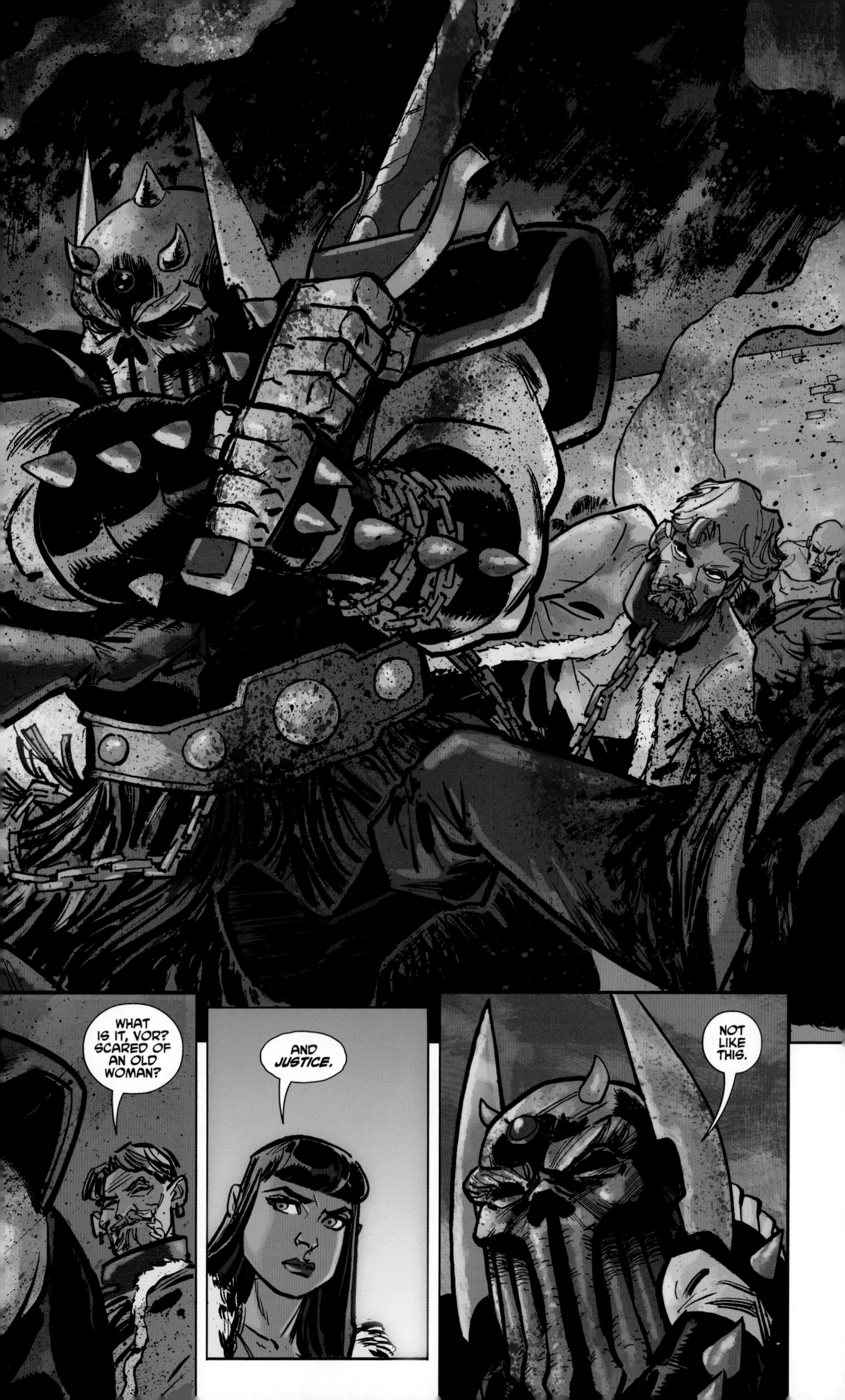
WHAT IS IT, VOR? SCARED OF AN OLD WOMAN?
AND *JUSTICE.*
NOT LIKE THIS.

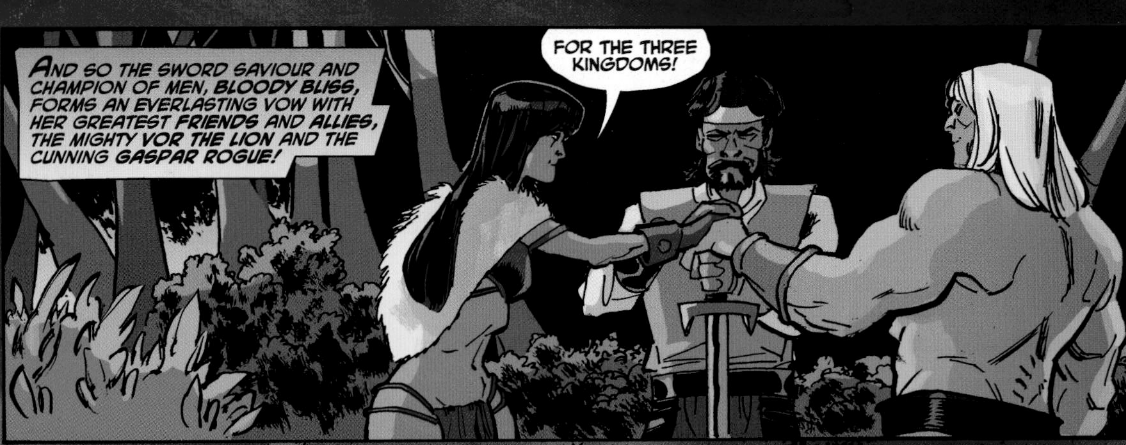
AND SO THE SWORD SAVIOUR AND CHAMPION OF MEN, BLOODY BLISS, FORMS AN EVERLASTING VOW WITH HER GREATEST FRIENDS AND ALLIES, THE MIGHTY VOR THE LION AND THE CUNNING GASPAR ROGUE!
FOR THE THREE KINGDOMS!

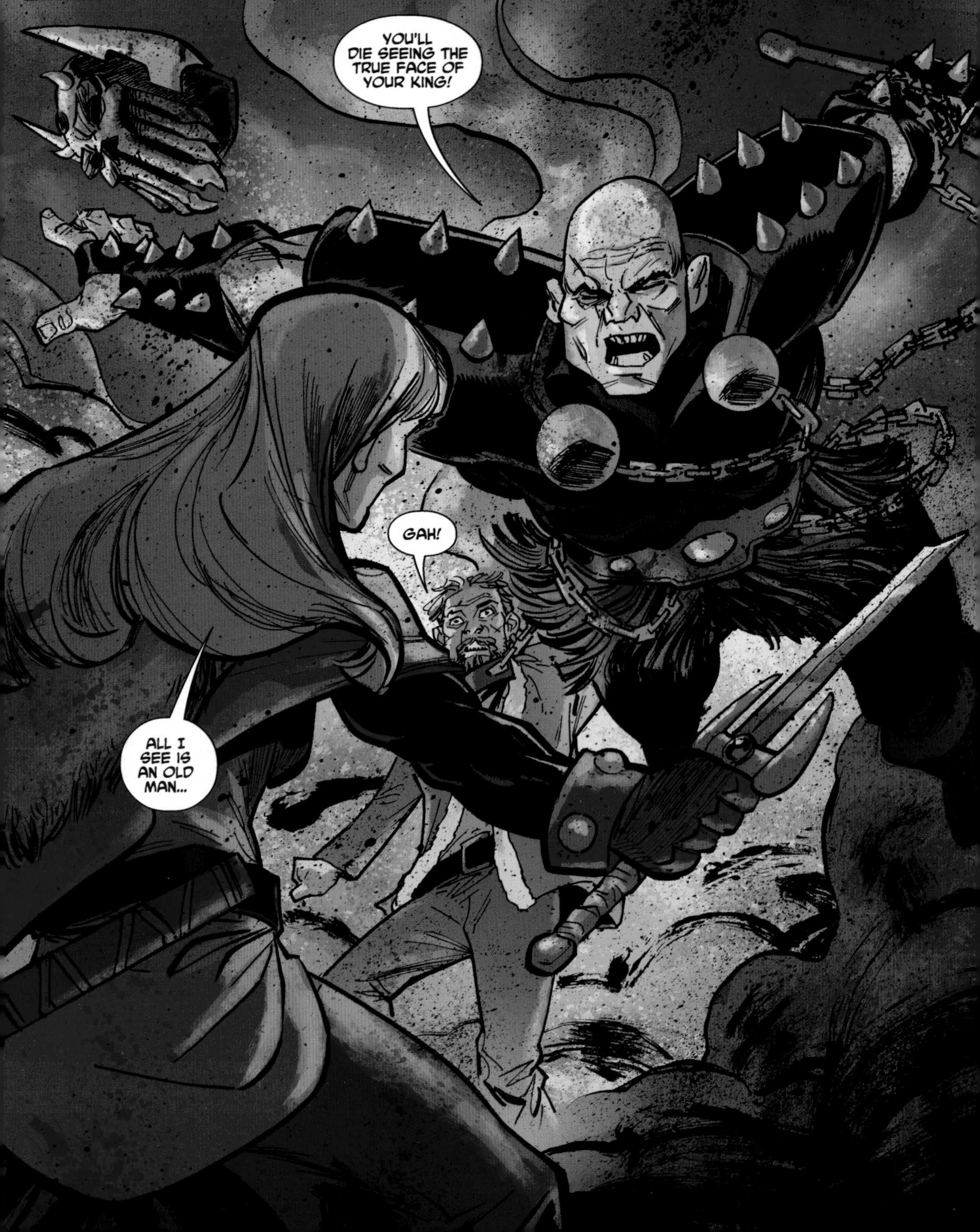
YOU'LL DIE SEEING THE TRUE FACE OF YOUR KING!
GAH!
ALL I SEE IS AN OLD MAN...

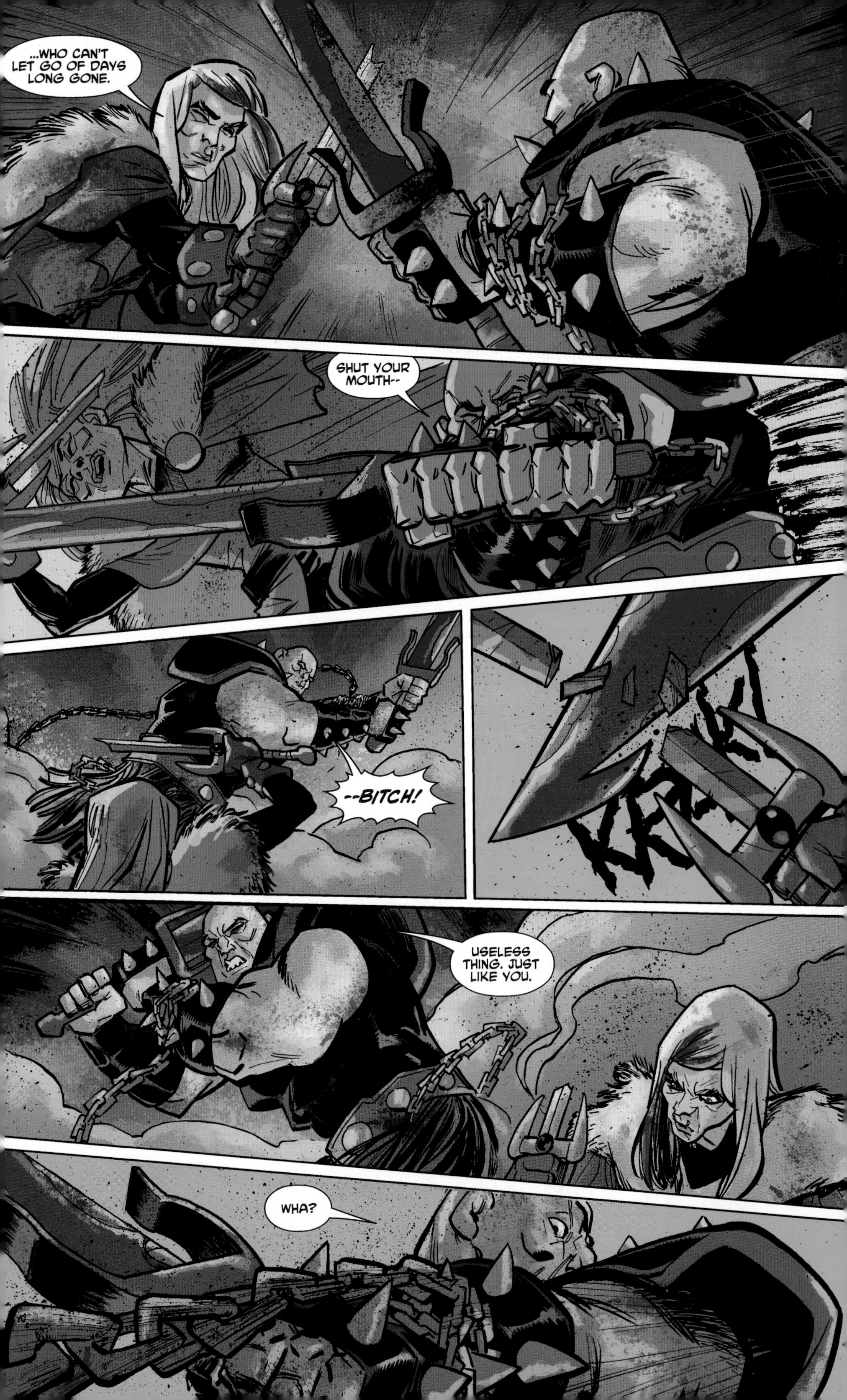
...WHO CAN'T LET GO OF DAYS LONG GONE.
SHUT YOUR MOUTH--
--BITCH!
USELESS THING. JUST LIKE YOU.
WHA?

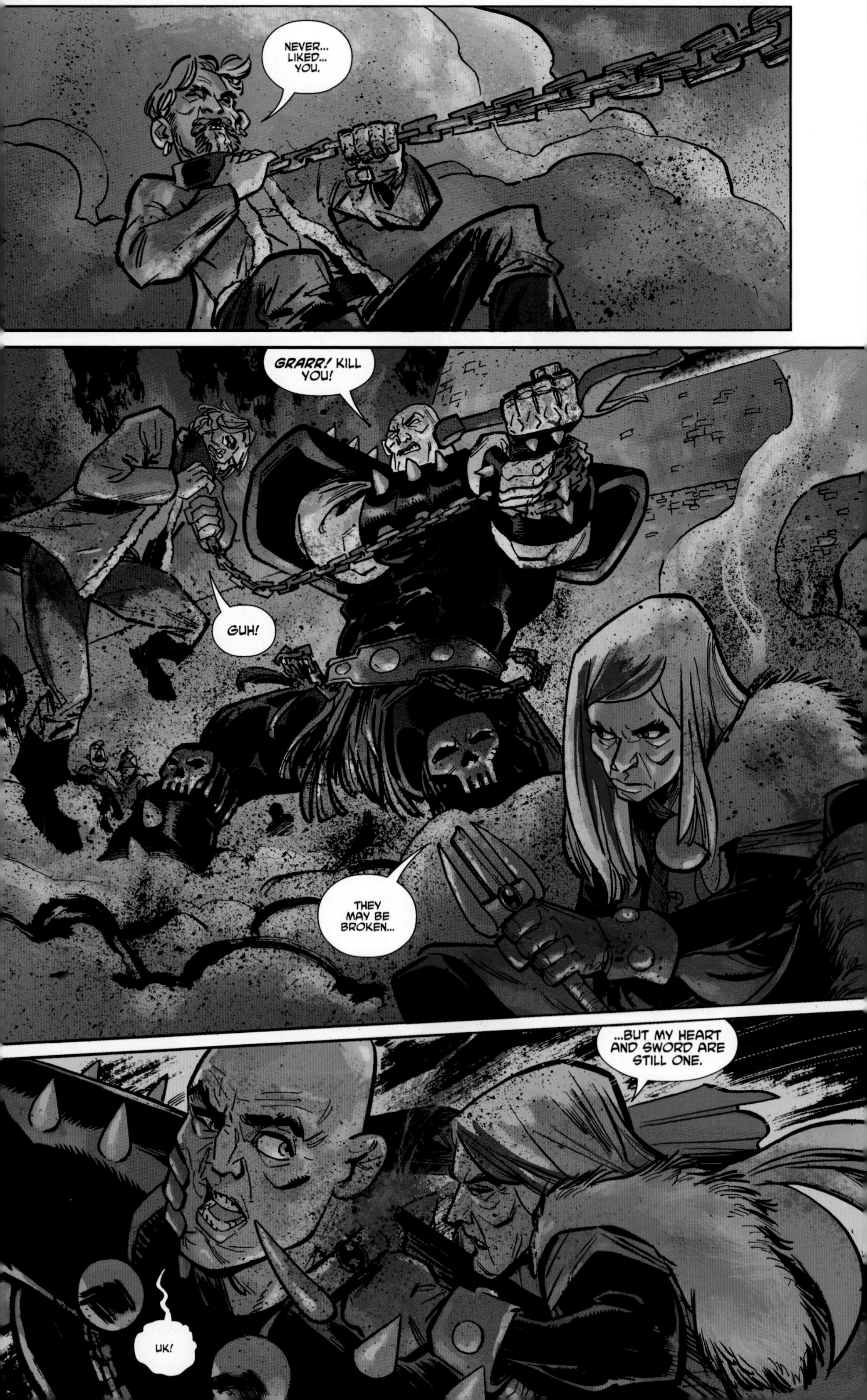
NEVER... LIKED... YOU.
GRARR! KILL YOU!
GUH!
THEY MAY BE BROKEN...
...BUT MY HEART AND SWORD ARE STILL ONE.
UK!

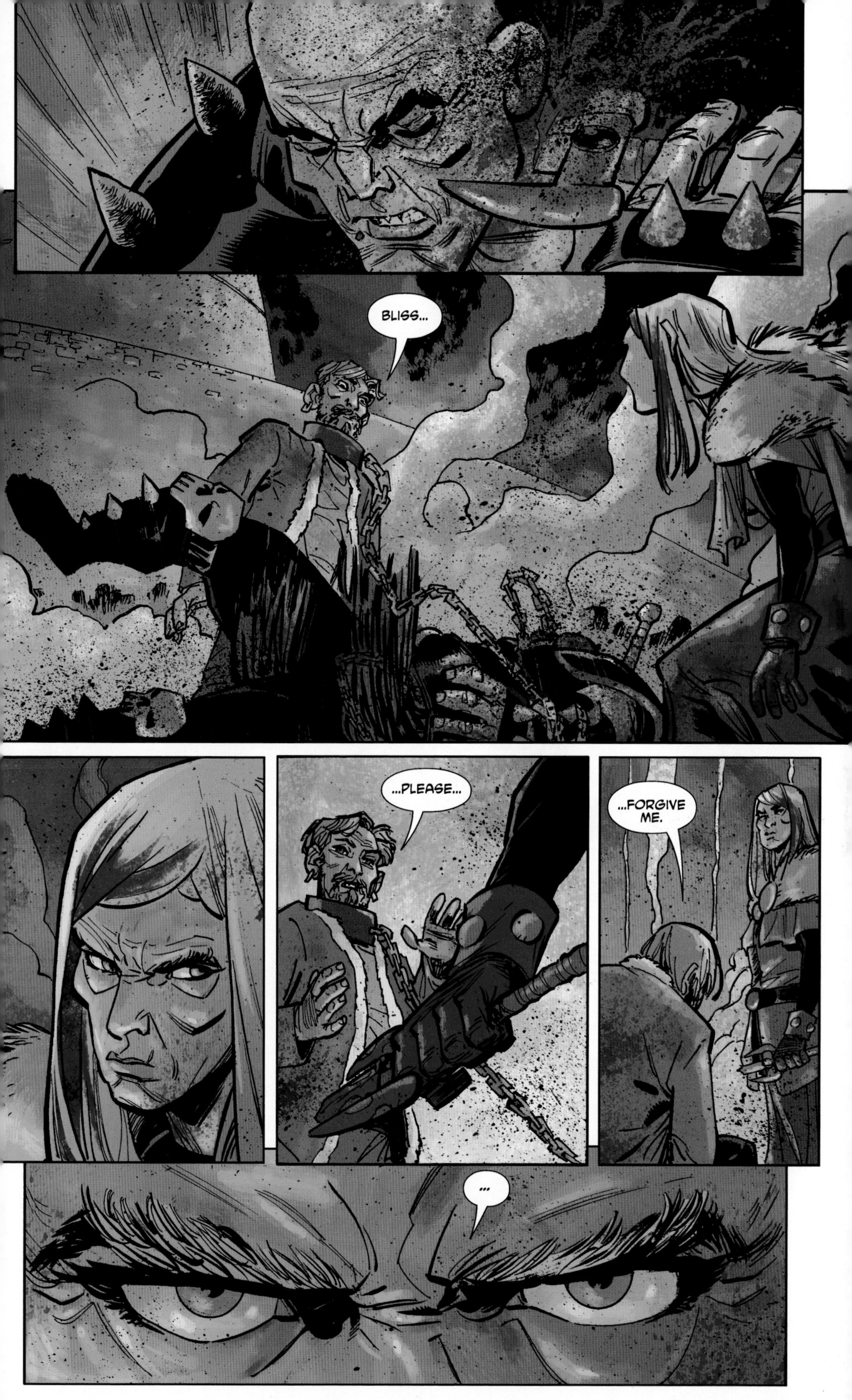
BLISS...
...PLEASE...
...FORGIVE ME.
...

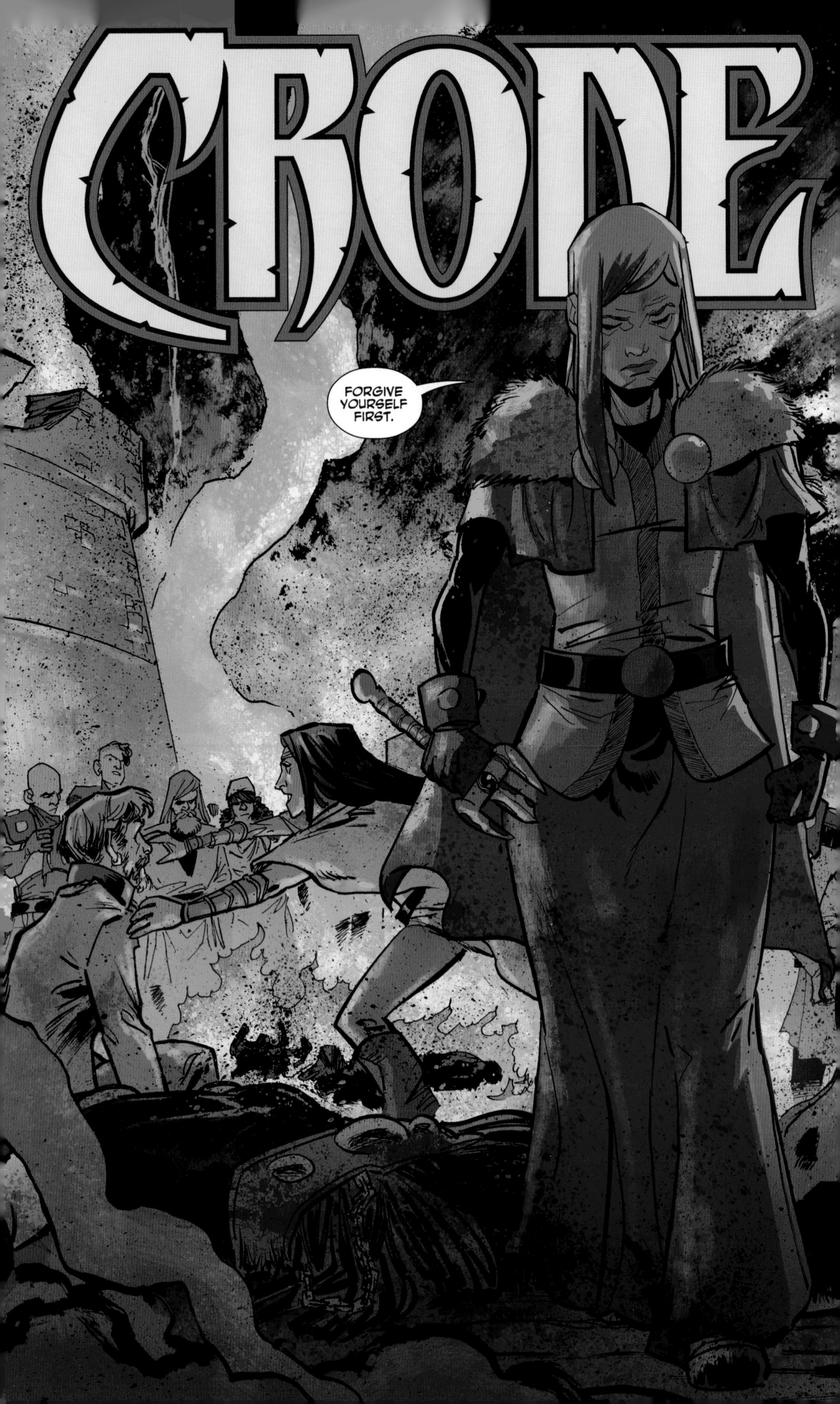
CRONE
FORGIVE YOURSELF FIRST.

CRONE

SKETCHBOOK

Commentary by Dennis Culver
and Justin Greenwood

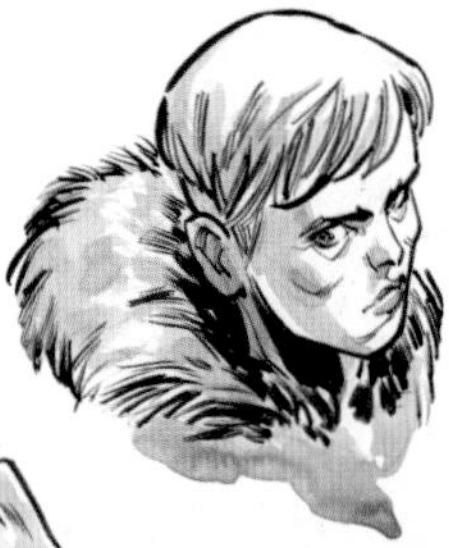

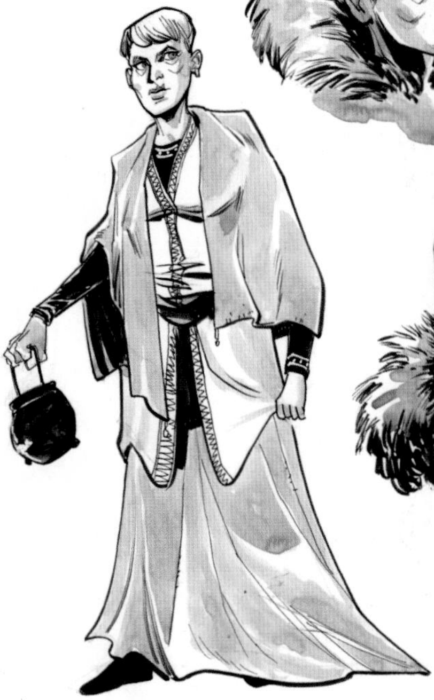

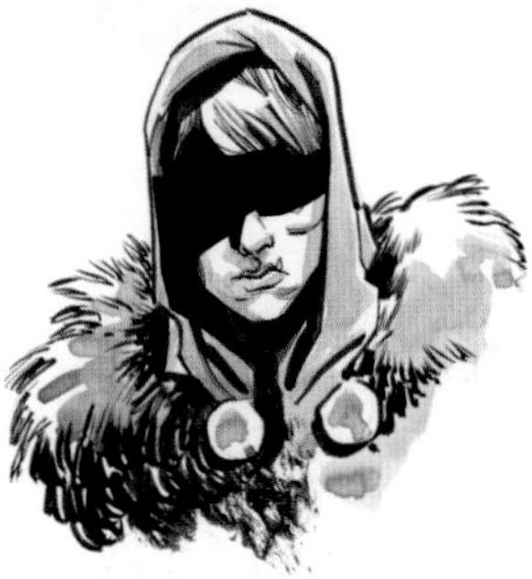

JUSTIN: The juxtaposition between Young and Old Bliss is one of my favorite parts of *Crone*. I really enjoy drawing characters who display their personalities on their faces and in their gestures, and ol' Bloody Bliss has that in spades. Her younger self is idealized and feels bigger than life, while older Bliss is on the edge of throwing it all away and easily misjudged at a glance. Bringing these elements into the drawing is really fun and adds a lot to the way the story feels.

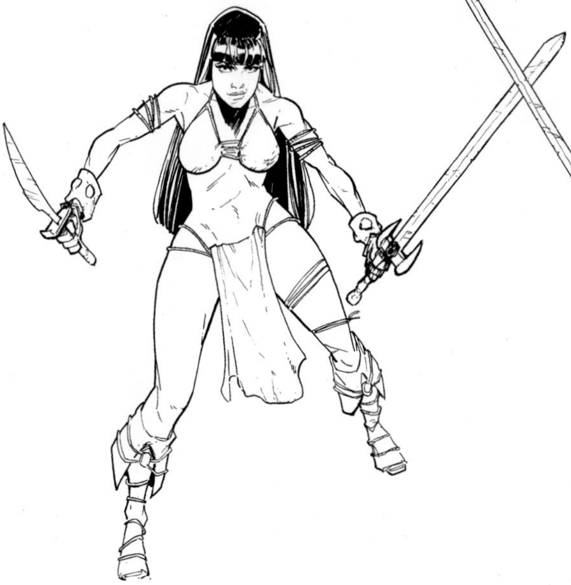

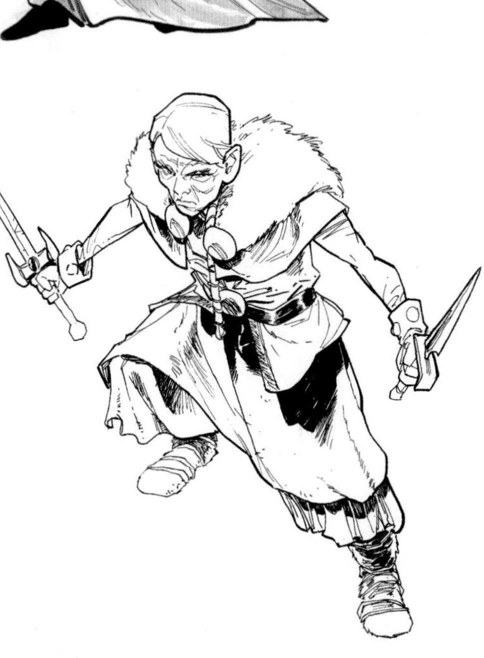

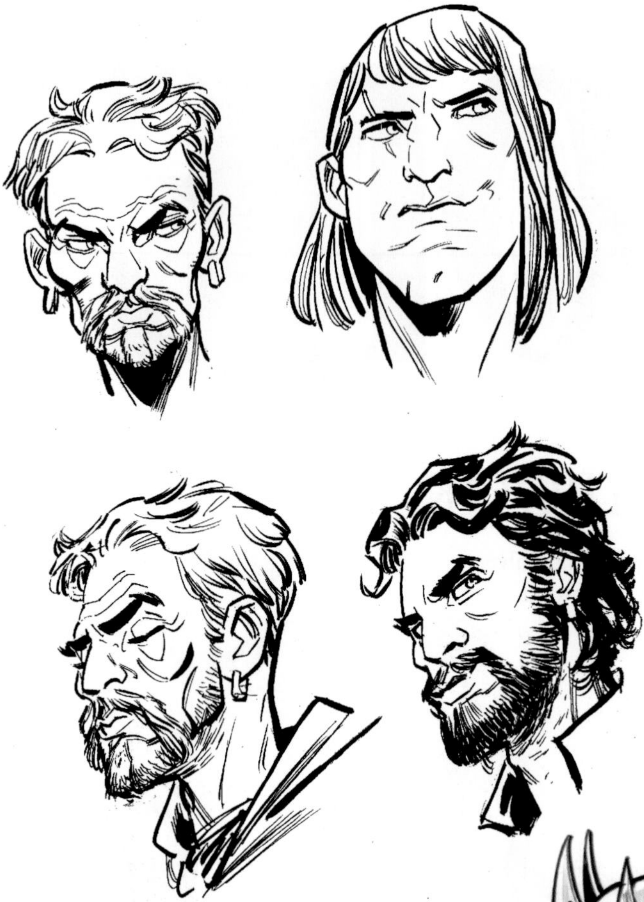

JUSTIN (RIGHT): Building this world is where our colorist Brad Simpson really shines, giving the different settings and time periods very specific and surprising palettes. He's great at taking something that could be very traditionally tied to the genre and breathing new life into it.

DENNIS (THIS PAGE): D'Kayde is a juggernaut. Not just physically but emotionally as well. Justin worked hard on all of the character designs and gave each character a distinct look and feel that sums them up perfectly. He nailed it!

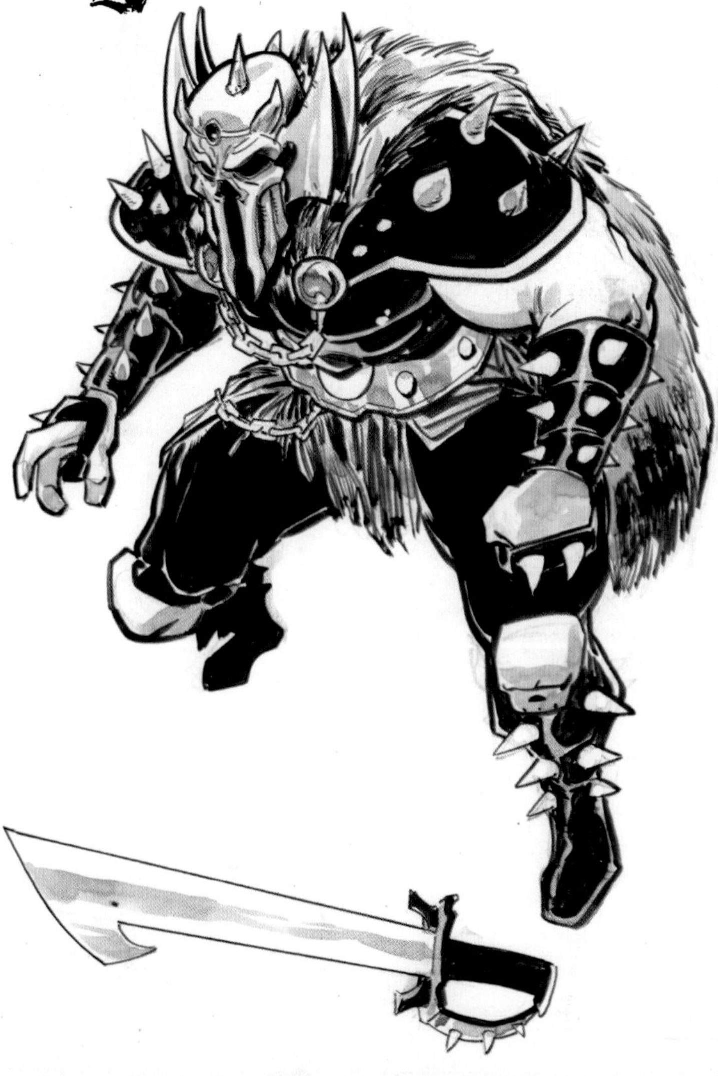

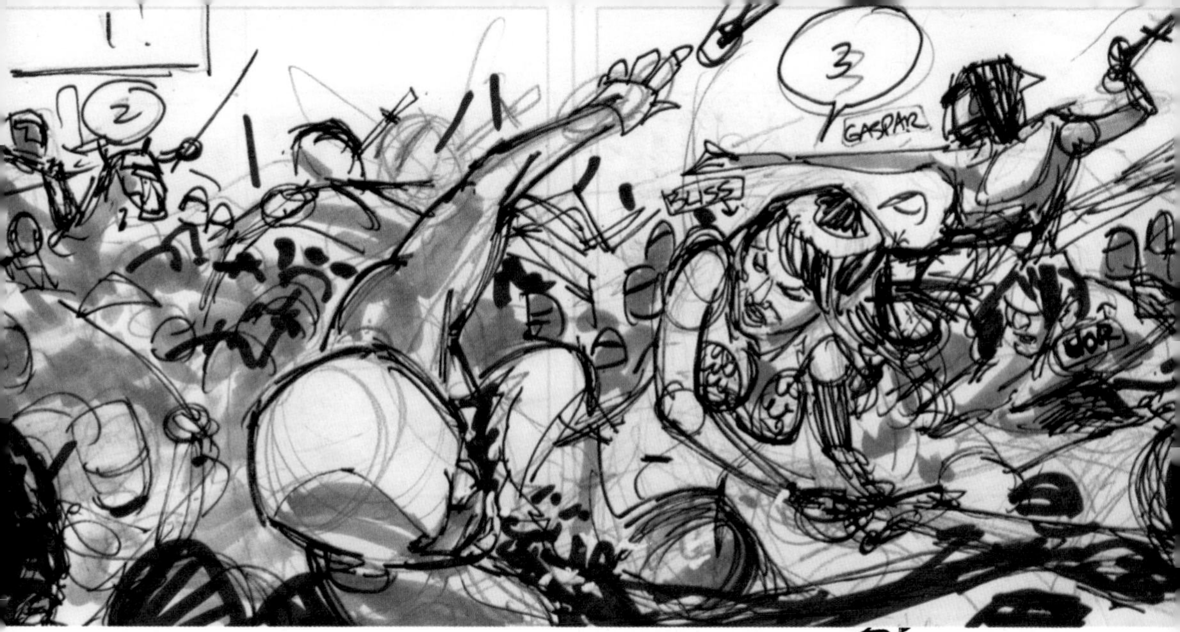
1
2
3
GASPAR
BLISS

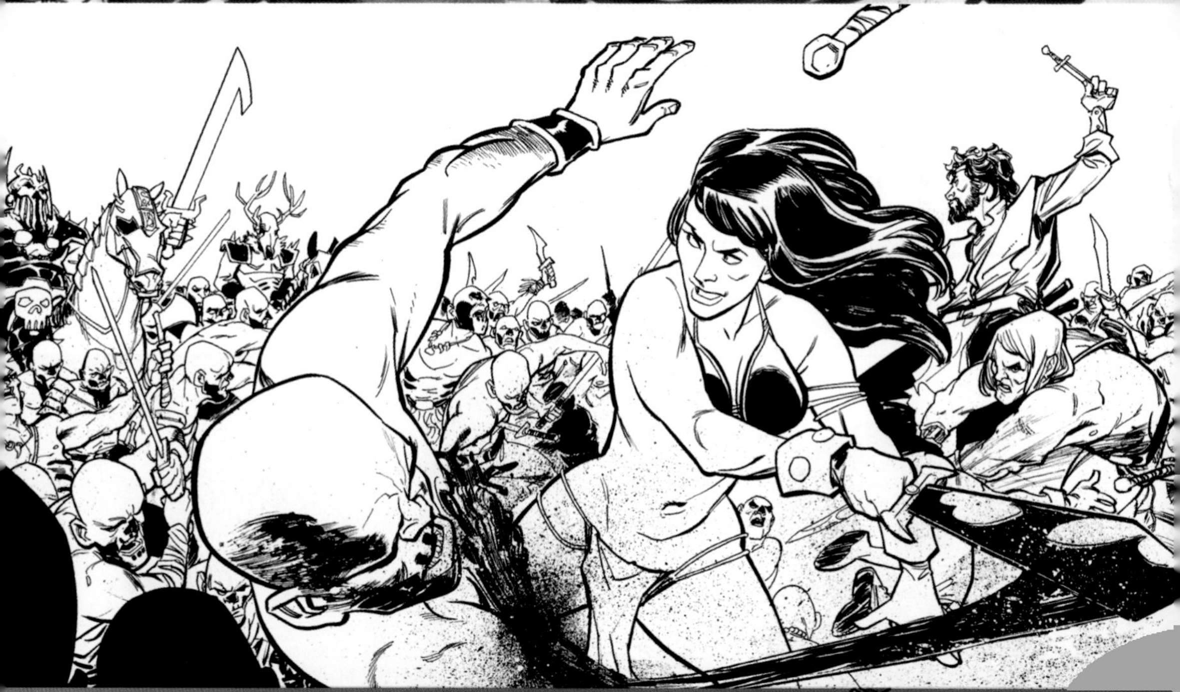

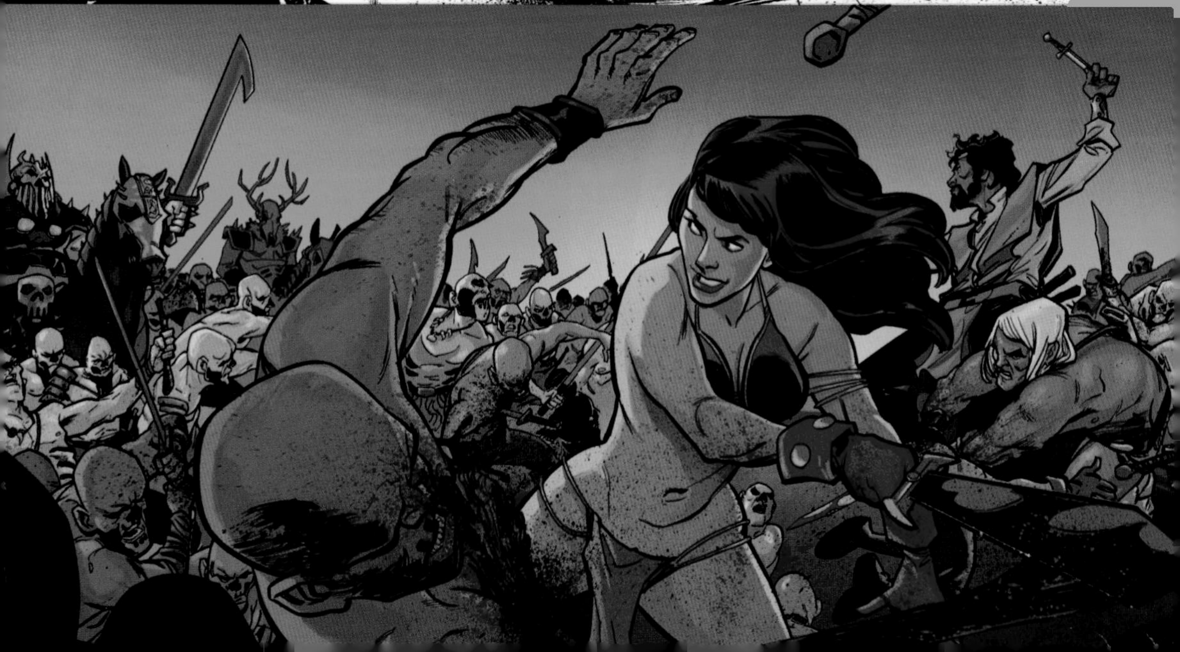

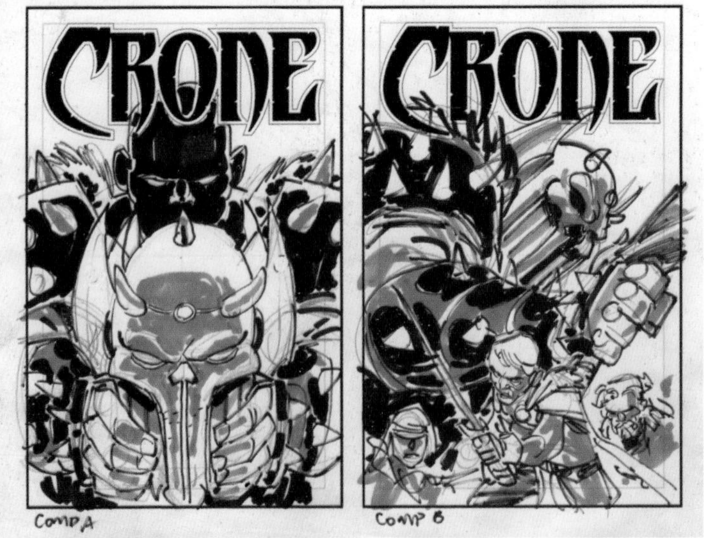
CRONE
CRONE
COMP A
COMP B

DENNIS: One of my favorite parts of the book is all the iconic covers we got to cook up together. Justin's initial layouts based on our talks are all winners and it was always a tough choice narrowing it down to the final design. Brad's colors were always unexpected and yet exactly right. Adding the incredible logo designed by Patrick made the whole thing sing.

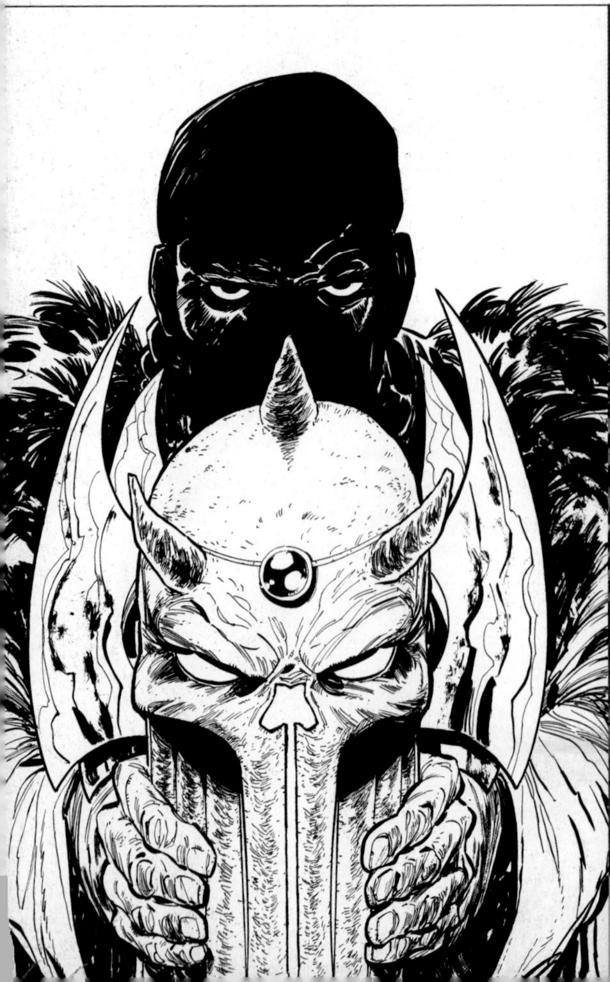

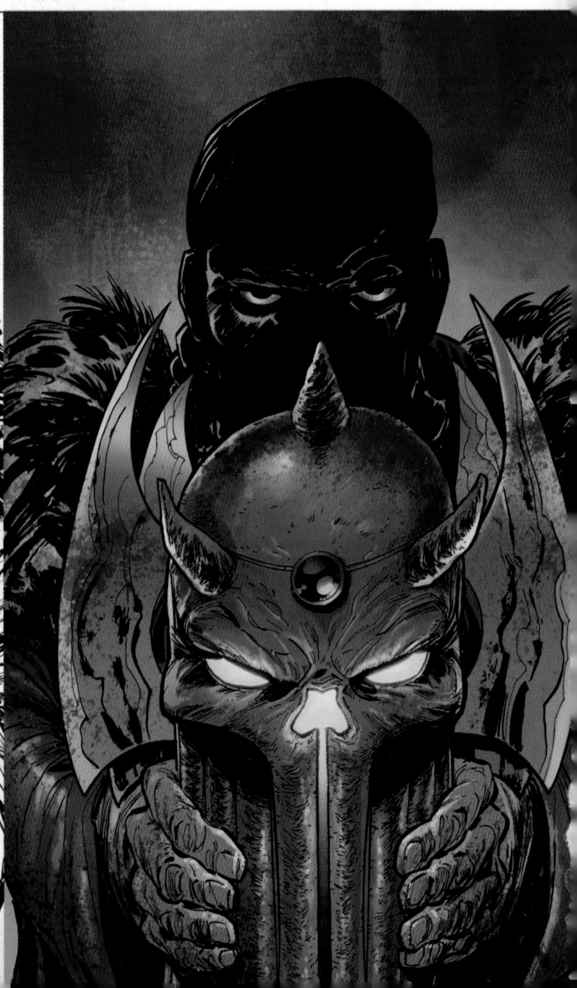